THE

INSTITUTES OF JUSTINIAN,

WITH THE

NOVEL AS TO SUCCESSIONS.

TRANSLATED BY

WILLIAM GRAPEL, ESQ., M.A.,

OF LINCOLN'S INN, BARRISTER-AT-LAW,

PROFESSOR OF ENGLISH LITERATURE, AND JUNIOR PROFESSOR OF LAW,
IN THE PRESIDENCY COLLEGE, CALCUTTA.

THE LAWBOOK EXCHANGE, LTD.
Clark, New Jersey

ISBN-13: 9781584779056 (cloth)
ISBN-13: 9781616190231 (paperback)

Lawbook Exchange edition 2008, 2010

The quality of this reprint is equivalent to the quality of the original work.

THE LAWBOOK EXCHANGE, LTD.
33 Terminal Avenue
Clark, New Jersey 07066-1321

Please see our website for a selection of our other publications and fine facsimile reprints of classic works of legal history:
www.lawbookexchange.com

Library of Congress Cataloging-in-Publication Data

Institutiones. English
  The Institutes of Justinian : with the novel as to successions / translated by William Grapel.
     p. cm.
  Originally published: Cambridge : Macmillan & Co., 1855.
  Includes index.
  ISBN-13: 978-1-58477-905-6 (cloth : alk. paper)
  ISBN-10: 1-58477-905-5 (cloth : alk. paper)
  1. Roman law--Sources. I. Grapel, William, b. 1822. II. Title.
  KJA1086 2008
  340.5'4--dc22
                              2008014006

Printed in the United States of America on acid-free paper

THE

INSTITUTES OF JUSTINIAN,

WITH THE

NOVEL AS TO SUCCESSIONS.

TRANSLATED BY

WILLIAM GRAPEL, ESQ., M.A.,

OF LINCOLN'S INN, BARRISTER-AT-LAW,
PROFESSOR OF ENGLISH LITERATURE, AND JUNIOR PROFESSOR OF LAW,
IN THE PRESIDENCY COLLEGE, CALCUTTA.

CAMBRIDGE:

MACMILLAN & CO.,

LONDON:

BELL AND DALDY, 186, FLEET STREET.

1855.

CALCUTTA:
F. CARBERY, MILITARY ORPHAN PRESS.

PREFACE.

Of those three legal compilations, the Code, the Pandects, and the Institutes, whereto Justinian gave the sanction of his name, the last alone admitted of anything approaching to harmony or systematic arrangement. The Code, with its supplement of Novels, was but a gathering together of Imperial Constitutions, from the day of Hadrian. The Pandects, or Digest, but an attempt to compress and place in manageable order, the best of the rulings of the ancient Jurists.

The Code, or Collection of Imperial Constitutions, was begun A. D. 528, and received the Imperial confirmation on the 7th of April, A. D. 533. This first Code proving, however, to be most imperfect, a second one was called for; and in November, A. D. 534, appeared that other compilation, which took the name of Code, with all authority of law, to the absolute suppression of the first. The Novels — "*Novellæ Constitutiones*,"—were New Constitutions put forth from time to time by Justinian in order to meet discovered failings in the settled Code. They were remedial measures, the

Acts "to amend an Act," whereof, even now-a-days, collective wisdom wotteth something. The first bears date November, A. D. 535, just twelve months after the solemn promulgation of the amended Code; the last belongs to November, A. D. 565, the very year and month when the law-loving Emperor died.

The Digest, like the Code, was published with unlooked-for speed; the Emperor gave ten years for the work, the compilers finished it in three. The Imperial Commission for its execution bore date December 15th, A. D. 530; the work received Imperial Sanction on the 30th of December, A. D. 533. The rapidity of execution may in some sort explain, if not excuse, the very easily discovered blots which mar it. In some nine thousand extracts, it gives the pith of what before, in more than twenty thousand volumes, was spread through three millions of lines.

That Constitution which in December, A. D. 530, gave commission to Tribonian and his fellows to arrange the Pandects, spake also of the Emperor's will that another work should be prepared; a work, wherein the whole body of the Roman Civil Law, as settled then, should be arranged and set forth for the uses of all students in the law. The work was entrusted to three learned men; to Tribonian, "most magnificent, the master and ex-quæstor of Our Sacred Palace"; to Theophylus, law-professor at Constantinople; and to Dorotheus, law-professor at Beyrout. In the work several ancient treatises, now lost, were used; but the chief guide whom the compilers followed was that Gaius, whose Book, called also "Institutes," was, in 1816, found so strangely by Niebuhr, as a palimpsest in the Cathedral book-stores at Verona. Justinian's Institutes—for by his name they go,—were sanctioned on the 21st November, A. D. 533; and received their final ratification as law, on the 30th December, A. D. 533, the same day from which the Digest was to take effect.

The several parts of which mention has been made, to wit, the Code, the Novels, the Pandects, and the Institutes, form together that *Corpus Juris Civilis*—"Body of Civil Law"—which supplies us with almost all we know of the legal system of the Romans. Of the worth of that system, after all abatement made, it were not meet to argue here. To say nothing of the great Jurists who on the Continent have been so hearty in its praise, it is enough for an Englishman to think of the Roman Civil Law as that which moulded the Judgments of Stowell; which was the ground-work of Holt's Rulings; which gave their scientific clearness to the Decrees of Hardwicke; and which is the life-giving principle in that Commercial Law of England, wherewith the name of Mansfield is for ever linked. Few who have studied the Law Books of Justinian will look upon them with other than strange interest; not alone that general interest which every thing of the nature of law possesses, as, to use Arnold's words, "the expression of the deliberate mind of the Supreme Government of society"; but an interest quite special and peculiar, as the legal voice of that great State, with which, as Niebuhr says, the stories of all ancient peoples end, the stories of all modern ones begin.

Of the translation here given of the Institutes, needs to say little; written mainly for students unversed in the language which Tribonian used, its first great aim is clearness. Each Latin word, if technical, has been carefully given in a plain English equivalent; and where it has been deemed advisable to give the original term, a literal rendering has been always added. The Novel 118, printed in the Appendix, is given, because of its very great importance; not only does it wholly set aside the several rules of succession in intestacy, as laid down in the Institutes; but it has from the date of publication (A. D. 533) been, and still is, the law in all countries where the Roman law obtains; in England, also, in cases where other rules are silent, its principles are even now upheld.

PRESIDENCY COLLEGE,
July 1855.

CONTENTS.

BOOK I.

		Page.
Title	1.—OF LAW AND JUSTICE,	1
,,	2.—OF THE LAW OF NATURE; THE LAW OF NATIONS; AND THE CIVIL LAW,	2
,,	3.—OF THE RIGHTS OF PERSONS,	6
,,	4.—OF THE FREE-BORN,	7
,,	5.—OF FREEDMEN,	8
,,	6.—OF DISABILITIES TO MANUMIT,	10
,,	7.—OF THE REPEAL OF THE LEX FUSIA CANINIA,	13
,,	8.—OF PERSONS INDEPENDENT, AND OF THOSE SUBJECT TO OTHERS,	14
,,	9.—OF PARENTAL AUTHORITY,	15
,,	10.—OF MARRIAGE,	16
,,	11.—OF ADOPTION,	20
,,	12.—OF THE DISSOLUTION OF THE PATERNAL AUTHORITY,	23
,,	13.—OF WARDSHIPS,	27
,,	14.—OF TUTORS APPOINTED BY TESTAMENT,	28
,,	15.—OF GUARDIANSHIP BY AFFINITY OF BLOOD,	30
,,	16.—OF SOCIAL DIMINUTION,	31
,,	17.—OF THE LEGAL GUARDIANSHIP OF PATRONS,	32
,,	18.—OF THE LEGAL GUARDIANSHIP OF PARENTS,	33
,,	19.—OF FIDUCIARY GUARDIANSHIP,	34
,,	20.—OF GUARDIANSHIP BY MAGISTERIAL APPOINTMENT,	35

viii   CONTENTS.

		Page.
Title 21.—Of the Authority of Guardians, ...		37
,, 22.—Of the Expiration of Guardianship, ...		38
,, 23.—Of Curators, ...		39
,, 24.—Of the Security required of Guardians and Curators, ...		41
,, 25.—Of the Exemptions of Guardians and Curators.		43
,, 26.—Of Tutors and Curators under Suspicion of Fraud, ...		47

BOOK II.

Title 1.—Of the Classification of Things; and the Acquisition of Property, ...	50
,, 2.—Of Things Corporeal and Incorporeal, ...	65
,, 3.—Of Servitudes, ...	66
,, 4.—Of Usufruct, ...	67
,, 5.—Of Use and Habitation, ...	69
,, 6.—Of Title by Prescription, ...	71
,, 7.—Of Donations, ...	75
,, 8.—Of the Power to Alienate, ...	79
,, 9.—Of the Persons by whom Property may be acquired, ...	81
,, 10.—Of Testaments, ...	85
,, 11.—Of the Testaments of Soldiers, ...	89
,, 12.—Of those who may not make Testaments,	92
,, 13.—Of the Disinherison of Descendants, ...	95
,, 14.—Of the Institution of Heirs, ...	99
,, 15.—Of Vulgar Substitution, ...	104
,, 16.—Of Pupillary Substitution, ...	105
,, 17.—Of the Avoidance of Testaments, ...	108
,, 18.—Of Unnatural Testaments, ...	111
,, 19.—Of the several kinds of Heirs, ...	114
,, 20.—Of Legacies, ...	118
,, 21.—Of the Revocation and Transfer of Legacies, ...	131
,, 22.—Of the Falcidian Law, ...	ib.
,, 23.—Of Bequests in Trust, ...	134

CONTENTS.   ix
                                                Page.

TITLE 24.—OF INDIVIDUAL THINGS BEQUEATHED IN
            TRUST, ... 141
  ,, 25.—OF CODICILS, ... 143

BOOK III.

TITLE 1.—OF INHERITANCES IN CASES OF INTESTACY,.. 145
  ,,   2.—OF THE SUCCESSION, BY LAW, OF AGNATES, ... 154
  ,,   3.—OF THE TERTULLIAN DECREE, ... 159
  ,,   4.—OF THE ORPHITIAN DECREE, ... 162
  ,,   5.—OF THE SUCCESSION OF COGNATES,... 163
  ,,   6.—OF THE DEGREES OF RELATIONSHIP, ... 165
  ,,   7.—OF THE SUCCESSION OF FREEDMEN, ... 169
  ,,   8.—OF THE ASSIGNMENT OF FREEDMEN, ... 173
  ,,   9.—OF SUCCESSION BY THE PRÆTOR'S GRANT, ... 174
  ,, 10.—OF THE ACQUISITION OF PROPERTY BY ARRO-
            GATION,... 179
  ,, 11.—OF THE ASSIGNMENT FOR SUSTAINING EN-
            FRANCHISEMENTS, ... 180
  ,, 12.—OF ACQUISITIONS BY SALE OF GOODS TAKEN
            IN EXECUTION, ... 183
  ,, 13.—OF OBLIGATIONS, ... 184
  ,, 14.—OF OBLIGATIONS CONTRACTED BY THE THING, 185
  ,, 15.—OF OBLIGATIONS CONTRACTED BY WORDS, ... 188
  ,, 16.—OF JOINT VERBAL CONTRACTS,... 191
  ,, 17.—OF STIPULATIONS WITH SLAVES, ... 192
  ,, 18.—OF THE SEVERAL KINDS OF STIPULATIONS,... 193
  ,, 19.—OF VOID STIPULATIONS, ... 194
  ,, 20.—OF SURETIES, ... 201
  ,, 21.—OF OBLIGATIONS CONTRACTED BY WRITING,... 203
  ,, 22.—OF OBLIGATIONS CONTRACTED BY CONSENT,... 204
  ,, 23.—OF BARGAINS AND SALES, ... ib.
  ,, 24.—OF LETTING AND HIRING, ... 208
  ,, 25.—OF PARTNERSHIP, ... 211
  ,, 26.—OF MANDATE OR PROCURATION, ... 214
  ,, 27.—OF OBLIGATIONS FROM IMPROPER CONTRACTS, 217
  ,, 28.—OF PERSONS THROUGH WHOM OBLIGATIONS
            ARISE, ... 220
  ,, 29.—OF THE EXTINCTION OF OBLIGATIONS, ... 222

BOOK IV.

		Page.
TITLE	1.—OF OBLIGATIONS WHICH ARISE FROM WRONG,	225
,,	2.—OF ROBBERY,	232
,,	3.—OF INJURY TO PROPERTY,	234
,,	4.—OF INJURY TO PERSONS,	239
,,	5.—OF OBLIGATIONS WHICH ARISE FROM QUASI-WRONG,	243
,,	6.—OF ACTIONS,	245
,,	7.—OF ACTIONS ON CONTRACTS ENTERED INTO WITH PERSONS UNDER POWER,	260
,,	8.—OF NOXAL ACTIONS,	265
,,	9.—OF NOXAL ACTIONS IN THE CASE OF BEASTS,	268
,,	10.—OF REPRESENTATIVES IN ACTIONS,	269
,,	11.—OF SECURITIES,	270
,,	12.—OF ACTIONS PERPETUAL AND TEMPORARY,	273
,,	13.—OF EXCEPTIONS,	274
,,	14.—OF REPLICATIONS,	278
,,	15.—OF INTERDICTS,	280
,,	16.—OF PENALTIES IMPOSED UPON RASH LITIGANTS,	285
,,	17.—OF THE DUTY OF A JUDGE,	287
,,	18.—OF PUBLIC PROSECUTIONS,	290

THE INSTITUTES OF JUSTINIAN.

BOOK I.

TITLE 1.

OF LAW AND JUSTICE.

JUSTICE is the constant and perpetual wish to give to every one his right.

Section I.—Jurisprudence is the knowledge of things, human and divine; the exact discernment of what is just and unjust.

Section II.—These general terms being then explained, and being now about to enter on our exposition of the Law of the Roman People, it seems that this will be most advantageously delivered if we pursue, at first, a plain and easy method, and then go on to explain particular details with the utmost care and exactness. Otherwise, if at the very outset we overload the mind of the student, while yet unpractised and not able to bear much, with a great number or variety of subjects, we shall cause one of two evils;—either, namely, we shall make him abandon his studies,—or bring him, after great toil, and often after much lack of confidence (a fault which frequently leads youths astray), in the end to that point to which he might by an easier method have been sooner led with no great toil, and without any lack of confidence.

Section III.—The maxims of law are these;—to live honorably, not to hurt any man, and to give every one his due.

Section IV.—This science has two distinct branches; to wit, Public and Private. Public Law regards the constitution of the Commonwealth; Private Law looks to the interests of individuals. Private Law, of which we have now to treat, consists of three elements; being composed of maxims from the Law of Nature, the Law of Nations, and the Civil Law.

TITLE 2.

OF THE LAW OF NATURE; THE LAW OF NATIONS; AND THE CIVIL LAW.

The Law of Nature is that which Nature hath implanted in all living things. For this Law belongs not to man's race alone, but to every living thing, whether produced on earth, in air, or water. Hence comes that union of male and female which, in our species, we call Matrimony; hence, too, the begetting of children, and the bringing of them up. We see, indeed, that the rest of the animal creation are considered to possess a knowledge of this Law.

Section I.—Civil Law, again, is thus distinguished from the Law of Nations. All nations, which are under the governance of laws and usages, avail themselves partly of their own particular laws, and partly of those which are common to all mankind. Now that Law which a people enacts for its own governance, is the special property of that State, and is called the Civil Law, as being the Law exclusively of that particular State. But that Law which natural reason hath laid down for all mankind, is guarded with equal jealous care by all peoples, and is called the Law of Nations, because all Nations avail themselves of it. And so the people of Rome are governed partly by their own peculiar laws, and partly by those which are common to all men. But of each of these Laws, and the distinctions between them, we will treat in their proper places.

Section II.—Now Civil Law takes its name from the particular State where it holds, as, for example, from Athens; for a man would not go wrong in speaking of the laws of Solon, or of Draco, as the Civil Law of Athens. So too we speak of that law which the Roman people uses, as the Civil Law of the Romans; or of the Quirites, as being used by Quirites; for the Romans are called Quirites, after Quirinus. But whenever we speak of " Civil Law" and do not add the name of any particular State, then we allude peculiarly to our own law; just as when " THE *poet*" is spoken of and no particular name is given, the great Homer is understood by the Greeks; and by us Romans, Virgil. The Law of Nations, on the other hand, is common to all mankind; for nations have established certain laws, as occasion and the emergencies of human life required. For wars arose, and in their train came captivity and slavery, both of which are contrary to the law of nature; for by that law all men are originally born free. Besides, by this same Law of Nations almost all contracts were first introduced as, for example, purchases, sales leases, hirings, partnerships, bailments, loans, and others out of number.

Section III.—Our Law is composed of the written, and the unwritten; just as among the Greeks some laws were in writing, others not. Now the Written Law comprehends; 1, Laws;—2, Plebiscites;—3, Decrees of the Senate;—4, Acts of the Emperors;—5, Edicts of the Magistrates;—and, 6, Answers of the Jurists.

Section IV.—A LAW is what the Roman People enacted at the recommendation of a Magistrate of senatorial rank; as, for example, of a Consul. A PLEBISCITE is what the Roman Commons enacted at the recommendation of a Magistrate of the plebeian order; as, for example, of a Tribune. Now the *Commons* differs from the *People*, of Rome, as does the species from its genus; for under the term " people" are comprehended all the citizens, inclusive of patricians and senators. By the term " commons", however, are understood all citizens exclusive of patricians and senators. The Plebiscites, however, after the passing of the Hortensian Law, began to have the same influence as the Laws themselves.

Section V.—A DECREE OF THE SENATE is that which the Senate commands and ordains; for when the Roman people was increased in such measure as to make it difficult to assemble them together for the enacting of laws, it seemed but fair that the Senate should be consulted in the place of the whole people.

Section VI.—The ACT OF THE EMPEROR has also the force of law; for the people, by the *Lex Regia* which was enacted to confer on him his power, made over and granted to him their whole authority and power. Whatever, therefore, the Emperor has enacted by Rescript, decreed on inquiry made before him, or ordained by edict, is unquestionably Law; and these Acts are what are called Constitutions.

Now of these some are evidently personal, and are not to be considered as precedents, since such was not the intention of the Emperor. For if he granted some indulgence to one man by reason of his deserts; or if he inflicted some punishment on another; or to another granted some relief contrary to the common course of law, these acts do not extend beyond the particular individual. But other Constitutions, being general, are beyond all doubt binding on every one.

Section VII.—The EDICTS OF THE PRÆTORS also have no small authority. These Edicts we are wont to call *Honorary Law*, because they who bear honours in the state, namely, the Magistrates, have given them their sanction. The *curule ædiles* also used, on certain occasions, to publish their Edicts; and these, too, become part of the *Honorary Law*.

Section VIII.—The ANSWERS OF THE JURISTS are the decisions and opinions of those who were authorized to settle the law. For in former days it was provided that there should be persons to give public interpretations of the laws; and these were, by the Emperor, authorized to decide questions of law, upon consultations. They were called Jurisconsults; and their decisions and opinions, when they were all unanimous, were of such authority, that the judge could not, according to the Constitution, decide contrary to them.

Section IX.—What long usage sanctioned became Law without being written; for long prevailing customs, being sanctioned by the consent of those who use them, assume the Nature of Laws.

Section X.—The Civil Law seems to be not improperly divided into two kinds; for its origin seems to have been in the customs of the two States, to wit of Athens and Lacedæmon. For in these States it used to be so managed that the

Lacedæmonians rather committed to memory what they observed as laws; while the Athenians observed those things which, being in writing, were included in the number of their laws.

Section XI.—The Laws of Nature which are observed equally by all Nations, being established by a Divine Providence, remain for ever firm and immutable. But those Laws which each State has enacted for its own Government, are wont to be often changed, either by the tacit consent of the people, or by some new Law which repeals the former.

TITLE 3.

OF THE RIGHTS OF PERSONS.

ALL Law which prevails among us has reference to persons, to things, or to actions. And first let us treat of persons; for it is of little purpose to know the Law if we do not know the persons for whose sake the Law was made. The first chief division of persons, with reference to their rights, is this: that all men are either free or slaves.

Section I.—Freedom (whence men are said to be free) is the natural power of doing what each man pleases, unless he be restrained by force or law.

Section II.—Slavery is an institution of the Law of Nations by which one man is made the property of another, in opposition to natural right.

Section III.—Slaves are called *servi* (from the verb *servare*, to preserve), because generals are wont to sell their captives, and so *to preserve*, and not destroy them. Slaves are also called *mancipia* (from *a manu capere*, to take with the hand) because they are taken from the enemy with the strong hand.

Section IV.—Slaves are either born such, or become so. They are born such when their mother is a slave; they become so either by the Law of Nations, that is, by captivity; or by the Civil law, as when a free person, above twenty years of age, permits himself to be sold, in order that he may share in the price given for him.

Section V.—In the condition of slaves there is no distinction; but among those who are free there are many; for they are either free-born, or have been set free.

TITLE 4.

OF THE FREE-BORN.

THE term *ingenuus* denotes one who at the moment of birth is free, by being born in lawful wedlock, of parents who have been either both born free, or both set free; or of whom one has been born, and the other set free. And when the mother is free and the father a slave, the child is nevertheless free-born; just as when the mother is free, and it be uncertain who the father is, for then he had no legal father. And it is enough if the mother be free at the moment of birth, albeit she were a slave when she conceived. Contrariwise if, when she conceived, she were a freewoman, and afterwards, when reduced to slavery, have borne her child, still such child is held to be free-born; for the misfortune of the mother ought not to prejudice her child unborn. Hence this question has been mooted;—if a female slave with child be set free, but afterwards, and before the child is born, become once more a slave, is the child when born, free or bond? Marcellus holds that it is born free; for, says he, it is enough for the child unborn that the mother have been free at any time between conception and delivery: and this opinion is the true one.

Section I.—When a man has been free-born, it will not injure him to have been in slavery, and subsequently enfranchised; for it has over and above again been settled that enfranchisement does not prejudice the rights of birth.

TITLE 5.

OF FREEDMEN.

FREEDMEN are they who have been manumitted from just slavery. Manumission is the process of freeing from the " hand" *(a manu)*; for so long as any one is in slavery he is subject to the " hand" and power of another; but when manumitted he is free from this power. This manumission had its rise in the Law of Nations; for by the Law of Nature all men were born free; and manumission was not heard of, since slavery was unknown. But when slavery, under sanction of the Law of Nations, encroached on liberty, the boon of manumission followed. And whereas at first all were known by the common name of " men," there began, by the Law of Nations, to be three kinds of men, to wit,—freemen,—in opposition to these, slaves,—and thirdly, freedmen, who had ceased to be slaves.

Section I.—Manumission is effected in various ways; either (1) in the face of the church, according to the Imperial Constitutions; or (2) by the *vindicta;* or (3) in the presence of friends; or (4) by deed; or (5) by testament, or any other expression of a man's last will. Besides a slave may gain his freedom in many other ways; some of which were introduced by the Constitutions of former Emperors, and others by our own.

Section II.—Slaves may, further, be manumitted by their masters at any time; even the Magistrate in passing along; as when a Prætor, a Governor of a province, or a Proconsul is on his way to the baths, or to the theatre.

Section III.—The social standing of freedmen was formerly of three kinds. For those who were manumitted obtained sometimes a perfect and complete liberty, and became Roman Citizens: sometimes a liberty less perfect, and became Latins, according to the *Lex Julia Norbana;* and sometimes a liberty still more incomplete, and were called *Dedititii (i. e.* " surrendered at discretion"*)* under the *Lex Ælia Sentia.* But this lowest class, of the Dedititii, has already for a very long time disappeared, and the name of Latins become less frequent. And, therefore, our benevolence urging us to complete every thing and bring it to a better condition, has prompted us by two Constitutions to reform this, and to re-establish the ancient usage: for in the very earliest infancy of the State, there was but one simple liberty; that, namely, which he who conferred manumission on his slave was in possession of; save only that he who was manumitted became only a freedman, while his manumittor was free-born, or *ingenuus*. The class, then, of Dedititii we have abolished by a Constitution published among our decisions; by which, at the instance of Tribonian, that eminent man, our Quæstor, we have settled all disputes arising out of the ancient law. We have further, at the suggestion of the same Quæstor, altered the condition of the *Latini Juniani*, and corrected all matters with reference to them, by another Constitution, which shines forth among our other imperial ordinances. We, by our free gift, have made all freedmen Citizens of Rome; and this without regard to the age of the slave set free, to the interest of him who enfranchises him, or to any special form of manumission, as was anciently observed. We have also introduced many new methods by which slaves may gain their liberty, and with it the rights of Roman Citizens; the only kind of liberty which can be now conferred.

TITLE 6.

OF DISABILITIES TO MANUMIT.

It is not, however, in the power of every master who wishes it to grant a manumission. He who seeks to do so, with intent to defraud his creditors, effects nothing; for the *Lex Sentia* restrains the liberty so granted.

Section I.—A master, however, who is insolvent may, by his testament, institute a slave as his heir, and at the same time give him his liberty; so that the slave becoming free may be his sole and necessary heir. Provided always there is no other heir under the same testament; a thing which may occur, either because no person was instituted heir, or because he who was instituted does, from some cause or other, not become heir. Now this privilege was established by the same *Lex Ælia Sentia,* and on good grounds: for it was very essential to see to it, that men in needy circumstances, who could get no other heir, might get a slave as necessary heir, to satisfy creditors; or if he were unable to do so, that the creditors might sell the hereditary effects of the master, in the name of the slave; so that no disgrace might attach to the deceased.

Section II.—The Law is similar when a slave is instituted heir, although no mention of his freedom is made in the testament; for our Constitution with reference not only to masters who are insolvent, but generally by a fresh act of our humanity, decides that the mere institution of a slave as heir implies the grant of liberty. Since it is not very probable that a testator, although he has omitted the express gift of freedom in his testament, should have wished that the person whom he has chosen as his heir, should remain a slave, and that he himself should be without an heir.

Section III.—A person may be said to manumit in fraud of creditors, who is either insolvent, at the time when he grants the manumission; or who becomes so by the act of manumission itself. The prevailing opinion, however, seems to be, that unless the manumittor had an intent to defraud, the gift of liberty may not be impeached, even though his goods be insufficient for the payment of his creditors: for men frequently hope that they are in better circumstances than they really are. So then, we understand the gift of liberty to be then only invalidated when creditors are doubly defrauded; that is to say, both by the intention of the manumittor, and in reality; namely, by his goods being of insufficient value to answer their demands.

Section IV.—By the before-mentioned *Lex Ælia Sentia,* a master under twenty years of age, cannot manumit save by the *vindicta,* and on some just ground assigned, which has been approved by a council appointed for the purpose.

Section V.—Now the following are valid reasons for manumission—when the minor alleges that the person to be manumitted is his father or mother, his son or daughter, his brother or sister, his teacher, his nurse, his preceptor, his foster-child or his foster-brother; or when he says, that he wishes to manumit his slave in order to make him his proctor; or his bondwoman, with intent to marry her; provided always he do marry her within six months, unless some good reason hinder him. And provided also that he who is manumitted for the purpose of being made a proctor, be not so manumitted at less than seventeen years of age.

Section VI.—A ground of manumission, however, being once sanctioned, cannot afterwards be disallowed; whether the reasons on which it is based be true or false.

Section VII.—Since, therefore, by the *Lex Ælia Sentia,* certain limits were assigned to all under the age of twenty with reference to manumission, the result was that any person who had completed his fourteenth year might make a testament, institute an heir, and bequeath legacies; and yet if less than twenty he could not enfranchise a slave. This, now, was unbearable; that the man to whom was given the power of disposing of all his effects by will, should still not be allowed to give his freedom to a single slave. Why should we not give him the like power of disposing of his slaves as of all his other effects, by testament, precisely as he likes; and also of giving them their liberty? But since liberty is beyond all price, and since the ancient laws forbade any person under twenty to give it to a slave; we, therefore, making choice of a middle course, permit a person under twenty years of age to enfranchise his slaves by testament, only if he have completed his seventeenth, and entered upon his eighteenth year. For since by ancient usage, persons at eighteen were permitted to plead for others, why should not the soundness of their judgment be considered sufficient to enable them to bestow the gift of liberty on their own slaves?

TITLE 7.

OF THE REPEAL OF THE LEX FUSIA CANINIA.

By the *Lex Fusia Caninia* a certain limit was assigned to the number of slaves who might be enfranchised by testament; this law we have deemed it right to repeal, as being odious, and throwing obstacles in the way of liberty. It seemed, indeed, unreasonable enough to permit men in their lifetime, if no special hindrance existed, to enfranchise a whole household of slaves; and to deprive the dying of the privilege of doing the same thing by testament.

TITLE 8.

OF PERSONS INDEPENDENT, AND OF THOSE SUBJECT TO OTHERS.

WE come now to another division, relative to the rights of persons; for some are independent and some are subject to the power of others. Of those, again, who are subject to the power of others, some are in the power of parents, others in that of masters. Let us, then, first inquire as to those who are subject to others: for when we have ascertained who these are, we shall, at the same time, discover who are independent. And first let us inquire as to those who are in the power of masters.

Section I.—Slaves are in the power of their masters. This power is derived from the Law of Nations; for among all nations alike it is observable that masters have had the power of life and death over their slaves; and that whatsoever is acquired by the slave is acquired for the master.

Section II.—But at the present time, no subjects of the Empire are permitted, save for some reason recognized by the laws, to inflict any extraordinary punishment upon their slaves. For according to a Constitution of the Emperor Antoninus, he who, without due reason, slays his own slave, is to be punished with no less rigour than if he had slain the slave of another. Excessive severity on the part of masters is also restrained by another Constitution of the same Emperor. For, when consulted by certain Governors of provinces concerning those slaves who take sanctuary either in temples, or at the statues of the Emperors, he ordained that if the severity of the masters should appear excessive, they

should be compelled to make sale of their slaves on equitable terms, so that the masters might receive the full value of such slaves. And this decision is a just one; for it greatly concerns the public weal, that no one be permitted to misuse even his own property. The exact words of this Rescript so sent by Antoninus to Ælius Marcianus are as follows:——
"The power of masters over their slaves ought by no means to be wrongfully diminished. But it is for the interest of masters themselves that relief against cruelty, denial of sustenance, or any other insufferable wrong, should not be refused to those who crave it on just grounds. Take cognizance, therefore, of the complaints of those slaves, belonging to the family of Julius Sabinus, who have fled for sanctuary to the statue of the Emperor; and if you are assured that they have been over-harshly treated, or wantonly disgraced, order them to be sold, so that they may not again fall into the power of their former master; and, if Sabinus seek to evade this, my Constitution, let him know that I shall severely visit his contumacy."

TITLE 9.

OF PARENTAL AUTHORITY.

Our children, begotten in lawful wedlock, are in our power.

Section I.—Marriage, or Matrimony, is a binding together of a man and woman, obliging to an indivisible union during life.

Section II.—The right of power, however, which we have over our childen is peculiar to citizens of Rome; for there are no other nations which have the same power over their children, as we have over ours.

Section III.—The issue of yourself and your lawful wife, is in your power. So also is the issue of your son and his wife, to wit, your grand-son, or grand-daughter; the like may be said of your great-grand-children; and so of all your other descendants. But the issue of your daughter is not in your power, but in that of its own father.

TITLE 10.

OF MARRIAGE.

CITIZENS of Rome contract lawful matrimony when they unite according to the precepts of the law; the males having attained the age of puberty, and the females a marriageable age. And this whether the males are fathers or sons of a family; but, if the latter, they must first have the consent of the parents under whose power they are. For both natural reason and the law convinces us that this consent of parents should precede marriage. Hence the question has been mooted as to whether the son of a madman could marry, or his daughter be given in marriage. And as opinions were divided as to the son, we gave it as our decision, that as the daughter of a madman might marry, so also might the son, without the intervention of the father; provided always such marriage were in accordance with the rules set forth in our Constitution.

Section I.—Men may not marry every woman without

distinction; for there are some, with whom marriage is forbidden. Marriage, for example, cannot be contracted between persons standing to one another in the relation of either ascendant or descendant; as between a father and daughter, a grand-father and his grand-daughter, a mother and her son, a grand-mother and her grand-son; and so on continually. And if such persons unite together, they are said to have contracted an infamous and incestuous marriage. And so much is this the case, that even though they hold the place of ascendants and descendants in virtue of adoption only, still they cannot marry; nay more, even when the adoption is dissolved, the same prohibition remains in force. Her, therefore, whom adoption has made your daughter or grand-daughter, cannot become your wife; even though you may have emancipated her, and loosed the tie of adoption.

Section II.—Between collateral relations, somewhat similar prohibitions exist with reference to matrimony; but the restrictions are not so extensive. A brother and sister are, naturally, forbidden to marry; and this whether they are the children of the same father and mother, or of one of the two only. And if a woman become your sister by adoption, so long as such adoption subsists, a marriage between you and her is certainly invalid; but when the adoption is put an end to, by emancipation, you may take her to wife; and so also if you are yourself emancipated, there will be no bar to your marriage. Hence it is manifest, that if a man would adopt his son-in-law, he ought first to emancipate his daughter: and if he would adopt his daughter-in-law he ought first to emancipate his son.

Section III.—A man may not marry a brother's or a sister's daughter; nor their grand-daughter, although she is in the fourth degree. For when it is illegal to marry the daughter of a person, it is illegal also to marry the grand-daughter. But it seems not that there is any impediment to marrying the daughter of a woman, whom your father has adopted: for she is of kin to you by no law, whether civil or natural.

Section IV.—The children of two brothers, or of two sisters, or of a brother and sister may intermarry.

Section V.—So, further, a man may not marry his aunt on the father's side, even though she be so only by adoption: nor his aunt on the mother's side; for they both are looked on in the light of ascendants. For the like reason, a man cannot contract marriage with his great-aunt either on the father's side, or the mother's.

Section VI.—There are certain other marriages from which we must abstain from regard to " affinity," or the ties created by marriage: for example, a man may not marry a wife's daughter, or a son's wife, for they are both in the place of daughters to him. And this rule must be understood to refer to those who have ever been our step-daughters, or daughters-in-law; for if a woman be still your daughter-in-law, that is, if she be still wedded to your son, you cannot marry her for another reason, namely, that she cannot be the wife of two persons at the same time. So also if your step-daughter be still your step-daughter, that is, if her mother be still wedded to you, you cannot marry her, because a man may not have two wives at the same time.

Section VII.—Again, a man is forbidden to marry his wife's mother, and his father's wife, because they are in the place of mothers to him. And this prohibition operates when the affinity is dissolved; for if the step-mother be still your step-mother, that is if she be still married to your father, she is forbidden by the common rule of law to marry you, for the same woman cannot have two husbands at the same time. So also if your wife's mother be still your wife's mother; that is, if her daughter be actually your wife, your marriage with her is forbidden, because you cannot have two wives at the same time.

Section VIII.—The son of a husband by a former wife, and the daughter of a wife by a former husband; and the daughter of a husband by a former wife, and son of a wife by a former husband, may lawfully contract marriage; even though they have a brother or sister born of the second marriage.

Section IX.—If your wife, after divorce, have a daughter by a second husband, such daughter is not your step-daughter: Julian, however, says that we ought to abstain from such nuptials: for your son's betrothed wife is not your daughter-in-law; nor your betrothed wife, your son's mother-in-law; still they who hold themselves aloof from such unions act with greater propriety, and more in accordance with law.

Section X.—It is certain that the relationship of slaves is an impediment to their marriage, even if a father and daughter, or a brother and sister have been enfranchised.

Section XI.—There are other persons too, who are forbidden, for diverse causes, to contract marriage; all which we have caused to be set out at length in the books of the Digests, or Pandects, collected from the ancient law.

Section XII.—If, in contempt of the rules which we have here laid down, any persons venture to unite themselves, there is then, in reality, no husband, no wife, no nuptials, no jointure. They, also, who are the offspring of such union, shall not be under the power of the father; but, so far as regards the father's power, are in the position of children whom a prostitute has borne, who are looked upon as having no father, because it is uncertain who he is; they are therefore called *spurious* (Latin, *spurii*), either from a Greek word σποράδην —" at hazard",—or as being *sine patre*—" without a father". Hence it follows, that after the dissolution of any such connection, there can be no legal claim for the restitution of either jointure, or gift in consideration of marriage. They, also, who contract such prohibited nuptials are liable to other penalties, which are fully set forth in our Imperial Constitutions.

Section XIII.—At times it happens, that children who at the time of birth were not under the parents' power, are afterwards brought under it. So, the natural son who is admitted into the order of the Curiales, and may be chosen Decurion, becomes subject to his father's power. The son, also, of a freewoman, with whom marriage is prohibited by no law, but with whom the father had connection only, will become subject to the father's power, so soon as marriage instruments are drawn up, in accordance with the provisions of our Constitution. The which Constitution confers the same benefits on those children who may afterwards spring from the same marriage.

TITLE 11.

OF ADOPTION.

NOT only, however, are our legitimate natural children in our power, as we have said; but so also are those whom we adopt.

Section I.—Adoption takes place in two ways: either by Imperial Rescript, or by the authority of the Magistrate. The Imperial Rescript empowers us to adopt persons whether male or female, who are independent (*sui juris,*) and this species of adoption is called "arrogation." The authority of the Magistrate empowers us to adopt persons, whether male or female, who are actually under the power of parents—whether in the first degree, as sons and daughters; or in an inferior degree, as grand-children, and great-grand-children.

Section II.—But at present, by our Constitution, when the

son of a family is, by his natural father, given in adoption to a stranger, the right of paternal authority in the natural father is by no means dissolved, nor does any right pass to the adoptive father, nor is the adopted son in his power, although such son is by us allowed the right of succession to his adoptive father, should he die intestate. But if a natural father should give his son in adoption, not to a stranger, but to the son's maternal grand-father, or if the natural father have been himself emancipated, and give the son in adoption to the son's paternal or natural grand-father, or great-grand-father, in this case, as the natural and adoptive rights concur in the same person, the power of the adoptive father, knit by natural and strengthened by adoptive ties, continues firm and unshaken; so that the adopted son is not only in the family, but in the power also of such adoptive father.

Section III.—When any one, not arrived at puberty, receives by the Imperial Rescript, that species of adoption called arrogation, such arrogation is granted only after the case has been inquired into : it is asked whether the motive be honorable and expedient for the pupil, and also on what conditions the arrogation is to be made. The arrogator enters into recognizances before a public officer, that is to say, a notary, to restore all the property of the pupil, if he should die before the age of puberty, to those who would have succeeded him if no arrogation had taken place. Nor, again, can the arrogator emancipate the person arrogated, unless, on examination held, it should appear that the latter merits emancipation; and, even then, he is bound to restore all his property to him. Also, if a father on his death-bed have disinherited an arrogated son; or, during his lifetime, have without just cause emancipated him, the law bids him leave the fourth part of his goods to the arrogated son; and this over and above what the son brought to his father at the time of arrogation, and what he acquired for him afterwards.

Section IV.—A younger cannot adopt an elder; for adoption imitates nature, and it is utterly contrary to nature for a son to be older than his father. Whoso, therefore, wishes to adopt, or arrogate a son, should be his senior by the time of puberty complete, that is, by eighteen years.

Section V.—A person may adopt a grand-son or grand-daughter, great-grandson or great-grand-daughter, or any in more distant degree; and this even though he have no son.

Section VI.—A person also may adopt the son of another as his grand-son; and the grand-son of another as his son.

Section VII.—If a person adopt a grand-son, and wish to make him son either of a son whom he has himself before adopted, or of a natural son, who is yet under his power, the consent of such son ought first to be obtained, to the end that a next heir (*suus hæres*) be not forced upon him against his will. But if, on the other hand, the grand-father give away [in adoption] the son of his son by adoption, the consent of the son is not necessary.

Section VIII.—He who is either adopted or arrogated is assimilated, in very many points, to a son born in lawful wedlock. Therefore, if any one adopts another, whether by Imperial Rescript, or before a Prætor, or before the Governor of a Province, that other, provided he be not a stranger, may be given in adoption to another.

Section IX.—It is also observed as a rule common to both kinds of adoption, that persons incapable of procreating, as for instance impotent persons, may adopt; but eunuchs may not.

Section X.—Women also cannot adopt; for they have not even their natural children in their own power. But by the indulgence of the Emperor, they are permitted, as a solace for the loss of their own children, to adopt others.

Section XI.—It is peculiar to adoption by Imperial Rescript that, if a person who has children in his own power, should give himself in arrogation, not only does he submit himself to the power of the arrogator, but his children also are in the arrogator's power; just as though they were his grand-children. Wherefore it was that Augustus did not adopt Tiberius, till Tiberius had first adopted Germanicus: so that, so soon as the adoption was made, Germanicus became the grand-son of Augustus.

Section XII.—The lawyers of old approved of Cato's written opinion, that slaves, when adopted by their masters, are, in virtue of such adoption, enfranchised. So also we, in one of our Constitutions, have enacted, that such slave as shall by his master, with due solemnities before the Magistrate, be named his son, shall thereby be free; although this does not suffice to give him the rights of a son.

TITLE 12.

OF THE DISSOLUTION OF THE PATERNAL AUTHORITY.

Let us now inquire by what methods persons who are in the power of others, can be freed from that power. And, first, how slaves are freed from the power of their masters may be fully understood from what we have before said with reference to their manumission. Next, as for those who are in the power of a parent, they become independent at his death; but this rule admits of a distinction. For when a father dies, his sons and daughters do clearly become independent; but when a grand-father dies, his grand-children do not of necessity become independent, but only if on the grand-father's death they do not fall under the power of their own father. If, therefore, when the grand-father dies, their father be still alive, and was himself in the power of the grand-father, the grand-children become subject to the power of their father. But if, when the grand-father dies, the father be already dead, or have been emancipated from the power of the grand-father, the children, in such case, as they cannot fall under the power of their father, become independent.

Section I.—If a person, convicted of some crime, be sentenced to transportation (or deportation) to some prescribed spot, he loses the rights of citizenship; it follows, that the children of a person thus deprived of the rights of Roman citizenship cease to be under his power, precisely as if he were naturally dead. For like reasons, if a son suffer transportation, he ceases to be under the power of his father. But if, thanks to the Emperor's clemency, transported criminals are restored to all their former rights, they at once resume their former social standing.

Section II.—A father, however, who is merely banished by relegation, (*i. e.* confined to some certain spot,) still retains his children in his power. Sons, also, who are relegated, still remain in the power of their father.

Section III.—When a man is by judicial decree pronounced " a Slave of punishment," he ceases to have his sons in his power. " Slaves of punishment" are those who are condemned to work in the mines, or to be exposed to wild beasts.

Section IV.—A son, though he become a soldier, a senator, or a consul, still remains in the power of his father; for from this neither military service, nor consular dignity can free him. But according to our Constitution, that special and supreme dignity of the Patriciate, conferred by the Imperial Diploma, does, immediately upon the grant, free the son from the power of his father. For it were absurd to allow that a father should, by means of emancipation, be able to release his son from the tie of his authority, and that the Imperial Majesty should be unable to free from the power of another, him whom hath chosen to be a father of the State.

Section V.—If a parent be taken prisoner by the enemy, although he becomes their slave, yet his paternal authority is only in suspense, by reason of the privilege called *jus postliminii*—or "right of return"; for captives of war, on their return, resume all their former rights. Therefore, on his return, the father will have his children in his power; for that legal fiction, the *postliminium*—or "right of return"—presumes the captive never to have been absent from the State. But, if a prisoner die in captivity the son is held to have become independent from the time when his father was taken prisoner. If a son, also, or grand-son be taken prisoner by the enemy, by reason of the aforesaid "right of return," the power of the parent is said to be held in suspense. The expression *postliminium*, is derived from *post*—"back," and *limen*—a "threshold." Whence we say of him, who, having been taken prisoner by the enemy, has returned into our territory, that he has come back thanks to the *postliminium*. For as the threshold forms, as it were, the boundary of a house, so the ancients called the boundary of an Empire, threshold—"*limen*." From this, also, comes the word *limes*, meaning boundary, limit. Thence comes, also, the word *postliminium*, because the prisoner has returned to the same boundaries, or limits, from which he had been lost. The prisoner of war, also, who is re-taken on the defeat of the enemy, is said to return by virtue of this same *postliminium*.

Section VI.—Furthermore, children cease, by emancipation, to be under the power of their parents. Now emancipation was formerly effected either in accordance with the ancient law by fictitious sales and accompanying manumissions, or by the Imperial Rescript. But our great care has, by a special Constitution, reformed this matter; so that, the ancient fiction being put an end to, parents may go at once before the proper judge, or Magistrate, and free from their authority their sons and daughters, their grand-children, or any other of their descendants. And when this is done, the parent has, according to the Prætorian edict, the same right over the goods of those descendants whom he emancipates, as has the patron over the goods of his freedman. Besides, if the descendants so emancipated be within the age of puberty, the parent obtains, by reason of the emancipation, the right of wardship over them.

Section VII.—We must also notice, that it is at the free option of a man who has in his power a son, and by that son, a grand-son or grand-daughter, to emancipate the son, and retain the grand-son or grand-daughter in his power. Or, on the other hand, to emancipate the grand-son or grand-daughter, and retain the son in his power; or, if he will, to make all independent. The like may be understood as alleged of a great-grand-son, or a great-grand-daughter.

Section VIII.—Also, if a father have a son in his power, and if he, in accordance with our Constitutions, to this end enacted, give such son in adoption to the son's own grand-father, or great-grand-father; that is if, in a formal act, he declare his intention before a competent judge, in the presence, and without contradiction on the part of the person adopted, and in the presence also of him who adopts, in such case the power of natural father is at an end; but it, by this method, passes over to the adoptive father; in whose person, as we have before observed, adoption has its fullest extent.

Section IX.—It is, also, important to know that if your son's wife become pregnant, and if during such pregnancy you either emancipate your son, or give him in adoption, the child whom she bears, will, notwithstanding, be born in your power: but if conception take place after the emancipation or adoption, he will, when born, be subject either to his emancipated father or adoptive grand-father.

Section X.—Children, whether natural or adoptive, have scarcely any means of compelling parents to free them from their power.

TITLE 13.

OF WARDSHIPS.

LET us now proceed to another division of persons. Of those who are not in the power of their parents, some are under a tutor, some under a curator, and some are not subject to either. Let us inquire, then, as to those who are under a tutor, or a curator; for so shall we clearly make out those who are subject to neither. And first, let us treat of those who are under a tutor.

Section I.—Tutelage, as Servius has defined it, is an authority and power, given and permitted by the Civil Law, exercised over a free person who, by reason of his tender age, is unable to protect himself.

Section II.—Tutors are they who possess this authority and power, and they take their name from their office: for they are called tutors, as being protectors (*tuitores*) and defenders, just as they who look after the sacred edifices are called *œditui*.

Section III.—Parents are permitted to assign tutors by testament to such of their children as have not attained the age of puberty and are under their power: and this privilege extends alike to sons and daughters. But grand-fathers can only give tutors to their grand-children when these cannot fall under the power of their father, on the death of the grandfather. So then, if at the time of your death your son be in your power, your grand-children by that son cannot have a tutor appointed by your testament, although they were in your power; and this because, when you are dead, they will be subject to the power of their own father.

Section IV.—As in many other respects, so also in this, posthumous children are considered as born in their father's lifetime; tutors, therefore, may by a parent's testament be given to posthumous children, as well as to those already born: provided always, that such posthumous children, if they had been born in their father's lifetime, would have been his proper heirs, and under his power.

Section V.—If a father, by his testament, give a tutor to his emancipated son, the appointment must have the ratification of the Magistrate; but that without further inquiry.

TITLE 14.

OF TUTORS APPOINTED BY TESTAMENT.

NOT only the father of a family, but the son also, may be appointed tutor by testament.

Section I.—A man may by testament appoint his own slave to be tutor; if, at the same time, he give him his liberty. But it must be remarked that if such slave be appointed tutor, without the express gift of liberty, he is still held to receive by implication an immediate emancipation; and can thus legally become a tutor. But if, however, he is appointed by mistake, from the testator imagining him to be already free, the appointment would be invalid. The absolute appointment of the slave belonging to another person as tutor is void: but if the appointment be made on the condition of the person appointed obtaining his freedom, then it becomes valid. To appoint one's own slave, with the like condition as to obtaining his liberty, is an invalid appointment.

Section II.—If an insane person, or one under twenty-five years of age, be appointed tutor, the one may begin to act when he comes to his right mind, and the other when he has completed his twenty-fifth year.

Section III.—There can be no doubt but that a testamentary tutor may be appointed either to a fixed time, or from a fixed time, or on certain conditions, or until the institution of an heir.

Section IV.—A tutor cannot be appointed for a special thing or business; for it is to a person, and not for a business or thing, that a tutor is appointed.

Section V.—If one nominate a tutor generally to his sons or daughters, he is held to nominate him also to his posthumous issue; for, under the name of son or daughter, a posthumous son or daughter is included. But, it may be asked, if there be grand-children, are tutors given to them also under an appointment to sons? Our answer is, that grand-children are included under an appointment to children, but not under one to sons; for the words son and grand-son differ widely in their signification. If, however, the testator's appointment of a tutor be to his posthumous descendants, then evidently not only his posthumous sons but all his other children, sons or grand-sons, are included.

TITLE 15.

OF GUARDIANSHIP BY AFFINITY OF BLOOD.

To those who have no tutor appointed by testament, the *Agnati* (relatives in the male line), are by the Law of the Twelve Tables appointed as tutors; and such are then called " legal tutors."

Section I.—*Agnati* are those who are related to each other by males; that is, such as are related through the father, as a brother by the same father, or the son of a brother, or the son of such a son. But those who are related through females are said not to be *Agnati*, but only *Cognati*, by reason of their natural relationship. Thus, the son of your father's sister is related to you not by agnation, but by cognation, and you also are in like manner, namely by cognation, related to him; and this, because children follow the family of their father, and not that of their mother.

Section II.—The Law of the Twelve Tables, when it calls upon the *Agnati*, in case of intestacy, to act as tutors, refers not only to the case of one who might have appointed a tutor, but dies without the execution of any testament at all; but to that, also, of one who has died intestate only in so far as regards the appointment of a tutor; a case which may occur when the tutor named in the testament, dies during the lifetime of the testator.

Section III.—The right of agnation is generally taken away by every diminution, or charge of civil standing; for agnation is a gift of the civil law. But the right of cognation is not lost by every diminution: because civil policy may, indeed, extinguish civil rights, but it can not deal in the like manner with natural rights.

TITLE 16.

OF SOCIAL DIMINUTION.

Social Diminution *(capitis diminutio)* is the change of a man's social standing (*status*), and may be effected in three ways: for it is either the greater diminution, or the less (called also the middle), or the least.

Section I.—The greater diminution is, when a man loses both his citizenship and his liberty. Such is the case of those who, by a most severe sentence, are pronounced the " Slaves of punishment;"—such also of freed-men, who are condemned to slavery for ingratitude towards their patrons;—and such, too, of those who suffer themselves to be sold, in order to become sharers in the sum obtained.

Section II.—The less, or middle diminution is, when a man loses his citizenship, but retains his liberty. Such is the case of one who suffers the interdiction of fire and water, or who is transported to some prescribed spot.

Section III.—The least diminution is, when a man's social standing is changed, but without forfeiture of either citizenship, or liberty. Such is the case of those who, being independent, become subject, by adoption or arrogation, to the power of another; or when the son of a family hath been emancipated by his father.

Section IV—A slave, however, who is manumitted does not thereby suffer diminution; because, before such manumission, he had no social standing, or civil capacity.

Section V.—They whose dignity, rather than their social standing is changed, suffer no diminution; so they, who are removed from the senatorial dignity, do not suffer diminution.

Section VI.—What was said, in the preceding title, as to the right of cognation remaining in spite of diminution, has reference only to the occurrence of the least diminution; in such case the cognation does subsist. For by the greater diminution, as, for example, if a cognate person become a slave, the right of cognation is destroyed utterly; even so as not to be recovered by manumission. The right of cognation, also, is lost by the less, or middle diminution, as when one is transported to any fixed spot.

Section VII.—Although the right of tutelage, belongs to the *agnati*, still it does not belong to all in common, but to those only who are in the nearest degree. If, however, there be several in the same degree of relationship it belongs to them all: for example, if there be several brothers, as they are all equal in degree, all of them are equally called upon to act as tutor.

TITLE 17.

OF THE LEGAL GUARDIANSHIP OF PATRONS.

By the afore-cited law of the Twelve Tables, the tutelage of freed-men and freed-women belongs to their patrons, and to the children of such patrons. And this is called a " legal tutelage," not that this particular law has any special clause on the subject, but because it has been as firmly settled, by interpretation, as if it had been introduced by express words. For, inasmuch as the law had commanded that patrons and patrons' children should succeed to the inheritance of such of their freed-men or freed-women as should die intestate, our ancient lawyers held that the law, by implication, intended that the tutelage also should belong to patrons and their descendants. Besides, when the law calls any of the *agnati* to inherit, it bids them also act as tutors; and generally, where lies the advantage of the succession, there ought also to lie the burthen of the tutelage. We use the word "generally," because, if a woman under years of puberty, be manumitted by a woman, she is indeed called to the inheritance, but another person, and a male, acts as tutor.

TITLE 18.

OF THE LEGAL GUARDIANSHIP OF PARENTS.

AFTER the similitude of the tutorship of patrons, is one of another kind, which also is called "legal": for if a parent emancipate a son or a daughter, a grand-son or a grand-daughter, the issue of that son, or any others descended in a right line from him, provided always they are within years of puberty, such parent is their legal tutor.

TITLE 19.

OF FIDUCIARY GUARDIANSHIP.

There is another kind of guardianship, which is called fiduciary; for if a parent emancipate a son or daughter, grandson or grand-daughter, or any other descendant below the age of puberty, such parent then becomes their legal tutor; but, at his death, the male children, him surviving, become the fiduciary tutors of their own sons, or brother, or sister, or other descendants who have been emancipated by the deceased. But if a patron, who is a legal tutor, die, his children also become legal tutors. The reason of this difference is, that the son, although never emancipated, becomes independent at the death of his father; and as he does not fall under power of his brother, so neither is he under his tutelage. But the freedman, if he had continued a slave, would still have been, after his master's death, the slave of that master's children. The persons aforesaid are however, not called upon to act as tutors unless they have attained their majority, (*i. e.*, 25 years); a rule which our Constitution hath universally ordered to be observed in the case of all tutors and curators.

TITLE 20.

OF GUARDIANSHIP BY MAGISTERIAL APPOINTMENT.

If any had no tutor at all, one was, in the city of Rome, assigned him by the Prætor and a majority of the plebeian Tribunes; this was by virtue of the *Lex Atilia*. In the provinces, tutors were, by the *Lex Julia et Titia*, appointed by the respective Governors of each province.

Section I.—If a testamentary tutor had been appointed conditionally, or to act from a fixed day, so long as the condition was unsatisfied, or until the day had arrived, another tutor might, under the above-named laws, be granted. Again, if a tutor had been assigned unconditionally, yet, so long as the heir by the testament deferred taking upon him the inheritance, another tutor might be assigned in the interval. But such assigned tutor ceased to hold office from the moment when the condition was satisfied, the day come, or the inheritance entered upon.

Section II.—If, again, a tutor were taken prisoner by the enemy, a fresh tutor might be applied for, under the terms of the two laws above cited. The office of such tutor, however, ceased when the first returned from his captivity; because the liberated man resumed his tutelage by the *jus postliminii*, or " right of return".

Section III.—Tutors, however, have ceased to be appointed under the terms of the laws above cited, from the time when the Consuls first began to assign tutors to pupils of either sex, after due investigation; and the Prætors were afterwards, by the imperial Constitutions, invested with like power. For, by above cited laws, no security was required from the tutors for the safe treatment of the pupil's property; nor were there any provisions which compelled them to act.

Section IV.—But our later usage is, that at Rome, either the Præfect of the city, or the Prætor, according to his jurisdiction, should assign tutors; while in the provinces the respective Governors may, in their own provinces, do the like; in all cases after strict investigation. At the command of a provincial Governor, an inferior Magistrate may also assign, if the pupil's property be but small.

Section V.—But we, by one of our Constitutions, to get rid of the distinctions of different persons, and to avoid the necessity of waiting for the sanction of the provincial Governor, have ordained, that if the property of the pupil or adult do not amount to more than 500 *solidi* (£527 1s. 8d.) tutors may be appointed by the Chief Magistrates of each city, acting in conjunction with the Chief Ecclesiastic of the place, or by any other official personages, that is by all who are in the Magistracy, or, in the city of Alexandria, by the Judge. But, in accordance with the terms of this same Constitution, security must be given; and that, be it understood, at the risk of those who accept it.

Section VI.—It is in accordance with the law of nature, that all who are not come to the age of puberty be under tutelage; so that whoso is of tender years may be under the fit government of some other.

Section VII.—As, therefore, tutors manage the property of their pupils, male and female, they may be compelled, by an action of tutelage, to render an account, when their pupils have arrived at puberty.

TITLE 21.

OF THE AUTHORITY OF GUARDIANS.

The confirmation by the tutor of the acts of his pupil is in some cases necessary, and in others not. When, for example, a pupil stipulates for something to be given him, the authority of the tutor is not necessary; but, if the pupil wish to bind himself by any obligation to others, the authority of the tutor is necessary. For it is an established rule, that the pupil may improve his condition without the tutor's authority; but cannot, without such authority, impair it. So, therefore, in all cases of reciprocal obligation, as in purchases, sales, lettings, hirings, bailments, deposits, if the tutor's authority be not obtained, they who contract with the pupil are bound, but the pupil is not bound.

Section I.—No pupil can, without his tutor's authority, enter upon an inheritance, nor demand the equitable authority of the Prætor to give him possession of property, nor take an inheritance in trust; and this, because though there be a chance of gain, they may incur a risk of loss.

Section II.—A tutor who wishes to lend his authority to any act, which he deems of service to his pupil, should lend it at the precise time when the act is going on, and in person. For the intervention of his authority, at a later period, or by messenger, or letter, is of no avail.

Section III.—When a suit is to be commenced between tutor and pupil, inasmuch as the former cannot authorize any thing in a matter pertaining to himself, a curator, and not, as was formerly the case, a *Prætorian tutor*, is appointed; and, by his intervention, the suit is carried on; but on the determination of such suit he ceases to be curator.

TITLE 22.

OF THE EXPIRATION OF GUARDIANSHIP.

Pupils, as well male as female, are freed from the authority of tutors when they arrive at puberty. Now, in the case of males, the ancients judged of puberty not by years alone, but also by the growth of their bodies. But our Imperial Majesty, from a regard to the purity of this our age, hath deemed that what was, of old, deemed immodest in the case of females, to wit inspection of the body, should be thought no less so in the case of males. We, therefore, by our sacred Constitution, have enacted, that puberty in males be considered to commence immediately on the completion of the fourteenth year. While, as to females, we have left unaltered that old and wholesome regulation, by which they are esteemed marriageable on the completion of their twelfth year.

Section I.—Tutelage is also determined if the pupil, before the age of puberty, be arrogated; suffer transportation; be reduced to slavery for ingratitude towards his patron; or be taken captive by the enemy.

Section II.—Also, if a person be appointed tutor by testament until a certain condition be completed, he ceases to act on the completion of such condition.

Section III.—Tutelage is, further, determined by the death either of tutor, or of pupil.

Section IV.—When a tutor suffers that diminution which we have called the "greater," by which he is deprived of both citizenship and liberty, his right of tutelage is wholly at an end. But if the tutor suffer only that diminution which we have called the "least," then the legal tutelage is alone extinguished; but other kinds are not affected. In the case of pupils, however, whether male or female, any diminution, even the least, destroys the tutelage.

Section V.—Tutors, also, who are by testament appointed to act for a term only, give up their tutelage at the expiration of such term.

Section VI.—Tutors also cease to act, who are removed from their tutelage on suspicion; or who excuse themselves from the burthen of tutelage on good grounds, and free themselves in accordance with the regulations, of which we shall hereafter treat.

TITLE 23.

OF CURATORS.

MALES at puberty, and females of marriageable age, receive curators, until they have completed their twenty-fifth year: for, although they have attained to puberty, they are nevertheless not of an age to take a proper care of their own affairs.

Section I.—Curators are appointed by the same Magistrates who appoint tutors. A curator, however, cannot be appointed absolutely by testament; but every such appointment must have the confirmation either of the Prætor, or of the Governor of the province.

Section II.—Persons, arrived at puberty, are not obliged, against their will, to accept curators, except when they were parties to lawsuits; for a curator may be assigned for any special purpose.

Section III.—Lunatics and spendthrifts, although past the age of twenty-five, are nevertheless, by a law of the Twelve Tables, placed under the curatorship of their *agnati*. [But if there are no *agnati*, or if those who exist are unqualified] curators are appointed for them, at Rome, by the City-Præfect, or the Prætor; and in the provinces, by the Governors, always after strict inquiry.

Section IV.—Persons, also, of weak intellect; those who are deaf and dumb; or who are subject to any incurable disease, inasmuch as they cannot take a proper care of their own affairs, must be placed under curators.

Section V.—Pupils even, sometimes, receive curators: as, for example, if the legal tutor be disqualified; and this, because he who has a tutor, cannot have another assigned. So also, if a tutor appointed by testament, or assigned by the Prætor or Governor, be incapable of administering his trust, even though he be guilty of no fraud, it is usual to assign a curator to act together with him. Curators, also, are wont to be assigned in the room of tutors, who are excused not wholly, but for a season only.

Section VI.—If a tutor be hindered by ill-health, or by any other cause, from administering the affairs of his pupil; and if the pupil be absent, or an infant, under seven years of age, then the Prætor or Governor of the province shall decree any one whom the tutor may select to be the pupil's agent; but such appointment shall be at the tutor's risk.

TITLE 24.

OF THE SECURITY REQUIRED OF GUARDIANS AND CURATORS.

To the end that the property of those who are under tutors, or under curators, may not be wasted or lessened by such tutors, or curators, the Prætor must see to it that tutors and curators give security against such waste. But this is not always necessary; for tutors, appointed by testament, are not obliged to give security; inasmuch as their good faith and carefulness have been sufficiently approved of by the testator. Also tutors, or curators, granted after strict inquiry, are not called upon to give security, because they have been chosen on account of their fitness.

Section I.—If, by testament, or by a Magistrate after strict inquiry, two or more are appointed as tutors, or curators, any one of them may offer security for the indemnification of the pupil, or minor, and be preferred to his co-tutor, or co-curator, so as to have the sole administration, or he may oblige his co-tutor, or co-curator to give security, if he himself wish to gain the preference and have the sole administration. So that a man cannot demand security of his co-tutor or co-curator; he must himself offer it, and leave his co-tutor or co-curator the choice of receiving or giving security. And if none of them offer security, if any one have been appointed by the testator to act, he must act; but, if no such appointment have been made, then he whom the majority shall choose, must have the administration; and this, in accordance with the Prætorian edict. But if the tutors themselves disagree as to the selection of the person or persons who are to administer, then the Prætor must interpose his authority. The same course must be adopted when several are appointed by the Magistrate after strict inquiry; that is, a majority of them may appoint one of their number, by whom the administration shall be conducted.

Section II.—It is well to be known, also, that not only are tutors and curators responsible for the administration of the affairs of pupils, minors, and others under their protection; but, as a final safeguard, a subsidiary action, *i. e.*, one for neglect of duty, may be brought against the Magistrate who accepted the security. Such subsidiary action, then, may be brought against a Magistrate who has either omitted to take any security at all from the tutors or curators, or who has taken such as is insufficient. And this action, in accordance with the answers of the jurists, as well as by our imperial Constitutions, lies even against the heirs of such Magistrates.

Section III.—By our imperial Constitutions, it is also enacted that tutors and curators who do not give security, may be forced so to do; their goods being seized as pledges.

Section IV.—Neither the City Præfect, nor the Prætor, nor Governor of a province, nor any other high officer who has power to assign tutors shall be subject to this subsidiary action; but those Magistrates only, whose business it is to exact security.

TITLE 25.

OF THE EXEMPTIONS OF GUARDIANS AND CURATORS.

TUTORS and curators are excused from acting on different grounds; the most general plea is that of having children, whether in their power or emancipated. For, if a man in Rome have three children living, in Italy four, or in the Provinces five, he may claim exemption from the office of tutor, or curator, as well as from other public employments: for the office both of tutor and curator is considered as public. But adopted children are of no avail; for, though given in adoption, they count in favor of their natural father. Also, grand-children by a son, when they succeed in place of their father, will excuse their grand-father; but grand-children by a daughter will not excuse him. Again, it is only children yet alive who can excuse a man from tutelage or curatorship; those who are dead avail him nothing. But a question has arisen as to whether those who have fallen in battle may not be reckoned. The decision is, that a man may avail himself of those only of his dead children who have fallen in battle; for they who have fallen, on behalf of father-land, are deemed to live for ever in their high renown.

Section I.—The Emperor Marcus declared by Rescript in his *Semestria* (half-yearly council), that a person employed in the public treasury should be excused from acting as tutor or curator, so long as he is so employed.

Section II.—Those who are absent on the business of the State are excused from acting as tutors or curators; and if those who have already been appointed tutors or curators, should afterwards be absent on the business of the State, they are excused during such their absence, and other curators are appointed in their room. But on their return, they must again assume the burthen of tutelage; nor are they entitled, as Papinian held, in the fifth book of his answers, to the privilege of a year's vacation; that term is granted only to those who are appointed, on their return, to a new tutelage.

Section III.—By a Rescript of the Emperor Marcus, all inferior Magistrates may claim exemption; but, when once they have undertaken the trust, they cannot desert it.

Section IV.—Further, no tutor or curator can excuse himself from acting, by the plea that there is a lawsuit pending between him and the pupil or minor; unless, indeed, the suit have reference to the whole property, or to all the inheritance of such pupil or minor.

Section V.—Also, three tutelages or curatorships, if unsued for, will, during their continuance, exempt a man from the burthen of a fourth. But the tutelage or curatorship of several pupils or minors, under one and the same patrimony, as in the case of brethren, is reckoned only as one.

Section VI.—The Emperors Marcus and Lucius Verus jointly, and Marcus singly, have enacted by their Rescripts, that poverty, also, is a sufficient excuse; provided a man can prove that he is unable to sustain the burthen imposed upon him.

Section VII.—Illness, also, is allowed to be a ground of excuse, if a man be unable to look after even his own affairs.

Section VIII.—So, also, by a Rescript of the Emperor Antoninus Pius, persons who cannot read must be excused; although in some cases, men who cannot read are capable of the administration.

Section IX.—Also if, through ill-will, a father by testament appoint any one as tutor, such motive alone will form a sufficient excuse: as, on the other hand, they who have given their promise to the father of the pupils, cannot be excused.

Section X.—The two Emperors above-named have enacted by their Rescript, that it is not alone to be admitted as sufficient excuse, that the tutor was personally unknown to the father of the pupils.

Section XI.—An enmity against the father of the pupil or minor, if really of the bitterest kind, and if no reconciliation has intervened, is usually looked on as a good excuse from acting as either tutor or curator.

Section XII.—So, too, if a man's social standing have been called in question by the father of the pupil, he is excused from acting as tutor.

Section XIII.—A person, also, above seventy years of age, may claim exemption both from tutelage and curatorship. Minors, that is all under twenty-five years of age, were also formerly excused; but now, by our Constitution, they are forbidden to aspire to such trusts; so that, of course, there is now no need of any formal excuse. It is also enacted, by the same Constitution, that neither a pupil, nor a minor, shall be called even to a legal tutelage. For it were ridiculous, that they who are themselves under governors, and are known to need help in the administration of their own affairs, should notwithstanding act as the tutors and curators of others.

Section XIV.—And it must be observed, also, that no member of the military profession can, even though he be willing, be admitted to the office of tutor or curator.

Section XV.—Grammarians, rhetoricians, and physicians practising whether in Rome, or in their own provinces, and being within the number authorized by law, have exemption from both tutelage and curatorship.

Section XV.—Whoso wishes to claim exemption, and has several grounds of excuse, may, even though some have been disallowed, urge others; provided always he do so within the time prescribed. But tutors and curators, of what kind soever they may be, that is, however they have been appointed, ought not, if they wish to claim exemption, to appeal directly, but should offer their excuses within the fifty days next after they have known of their appointment; that is, supposing they are within an hundred miles of the place where they were nominated. If, however, they live at a distance of more than an hundred miles, an allowance is made of a day for every twenty miles, and thirty days besides; the time, however, as Scævola said, should never be less than fifty days.

Section XVII.—A tutor when appointed, is considered as appointed to administer the whole patrimony.

Section XVIII.—He who has acted as tutor to a minor, cannot, against his will, be compelled to become his curator; so much so that, by a Rescript of the Emperors Severus and Antoninus Caracalla, even though a father appoint a tutor by testament, and add that he nominates the same person as curator, the person so appointed is not, against his will, compelled to take upon him the office of curator.

Section XIX.—The same Emperors enacted, by Rescript, that a husband appointed as curator to his wife, may claim exemption; and this, even though he may have begun to act.

Section XX.—If, however, any person have gained exemption from acting as tutor, by false allegations, he is not thereby discharged from the burthen of this office.

TITLE 26.

OF TUTORS AND CURATORS UNDER SUSPICION OF FRAUD.

The right of accusing a tutor or curator who is under suspicion is derived from the law of the Twelve Tables.

Section I.—At Rome, the power of removing suspected tutors belongs to the Prætor; and in the provinces, to the Governors, or to the Legate of the Proconsul.

Section II.—We have shown what Magistrates can take cognizance of persons under suspicion; let us now inquire what persons may become suspected. And first, all tutors may become so, and this whether appointed by will, or in any other way soever; wherefore also, an accusation will lie against a legal tutor. But how is it in the case of a patron? He, also, may be accused; we must only bear in mind that, even though he be removed from his trust as suspected, his reputation must be spared.

Section III.—The next point is, to consider who have the right of accusing such as are suspected. And first, be it known, that an accusation of the sort is of a public nature; that is, it is open to all. Yea, by a Rescript of the Emperor Severus, women even are admitted as accusers; nevertheless they only are admitted, who are induced by feelings of affection, as in the case of a mother, or nurse, a grand-mother or a sister. But the Prætor can, at his discretion, admit, to make the accusation, any other woman also in whom he perceives a genuine affection, and who, without overstepping the modesty of her sex, is, by this same affection, induced to an impatience of the pupil's wrongs.

Section IV.—Pupils cannot themselves bring an accusation against their tutors as suspected: but minors may, in accordance with a Rescript of the Emperors Severus and Antoninus, accuse their curators; provided they do so under the advice of their near relations.

Section V.—A tutor who does not faithfully fulfil his trust is, as Julian writes, under suspicion; and this though he be in circumstances to answer damages. And the same Julian is also of opinion, (and an imperial Constitution has been framed in accordance with such opinion), that even before he enters upon his office, the tutor may be removed, as suspected.

Section VI.—He who is suspected, and removed on account of fraud, incurs that civil degradation called " infamy;" but not so he who is removed for neglect alone.

Section VII.—If an accusation of suspicion be brought against any one, his administration is, according to Papinian, held in suspense, while the charge is under consideration.

Section VIII.—If an action be commenced against a tutor or curator, as suspected, and the accused die pending the examination, then such action is extinguished.

Section IX.—It is provided by a Rescript of the Emperors Severus and Antoninus that, if a tutor fail to appear in court, to fix the amount to be allowed for the pupil's maintenance, the pupil shall be put in possession of his tutor's goods; and, on the appointment of a curator, those things, which are perishable, may be forthwith sold. Any tutor, therefore, may be removed, as under suspicion, who does not make a due allowance for the maintenance of his pupil.

Section X.—But, if a tutor do personally appear in court, and aver that, by reason of the smallness of the estate, no maintenance allowance can be made; if such averment be untrue such tutor shall be handed over, for punishment, to the City Præfect; and be treated just as is he, who has gotten a tutorship by bribery.

Section XI.—A freedman, also, who is proved to have fraudulently administered the tutelage of the son, or grand-son of his patron, must be handed over for punishment to the Præfect of the City.

Section XII.—Lastly, it is to be observed, that tutors and curators who unfaithfully administer their trust must be removed from it, even though they tender sufficient security. For the giving security, does not alter the fraudulent intention of the tutor, but only gives him an opportunity of injuring the estate for a longer period.

Section XIII.—We also hold every man suspected, whose moral conduct is such that we needs must have him in suspicion. But a tutor, or curator, who, though poor, is faithful and painstaking, is not to be set aside as a suspected person, simply by reason of his poverty.

END OF BOOK I.

BOOK II.

TITLE 1.

OF THE CLASSIFICATION OF THINGS; AND THE ACQUISITION OF PROPERTY.

In the foregoing book, we have treated of the Law of Persons; let us now inquire concerning Things. Things, then, are either in the patrimony of some one, or are not in the patrimony of any one. For some things are, by the Law of Nature, common to all; some are public; some belong to corporate, or politic bodies; and some belong to no one. Most things are the property of individuals; and these acquired by each person in different ways, as will be seen hereafter.

Section I.—These things are, by the Law of Nature, common to all mankind,—air, running water, the sea, and consequently the shores of the sea. No one, therefore, is forbidden to approach the shore of the sea, provided he abstain from injuring houses, monuments and buildings, for these are not of common right, as is the sea.

Section II.—All rivers, also, and ports are public property, therefore all men have a common right to fish in a port, or in rivers.

Section III.—Sea-shore, is that tract of land over which the highest winter's tide extends itself.

Section IV.—By the Law of Nations, the use of the banks of a river is public, just as is that of the river itself. Thus every one has a right to bring his vessel to the bank; to tie ropes to the trees that grow there, or to place any portion of his cargo on it, just as much as he has to navigate the river itself. But still, the property of the banks is vested in those who are proprietors of the land which they adjoin; for which reason, the trees which grow upon them belong to those proprietors.

Section V.—The use of the shores of the sea is as public, and common to all men as is the sea itself; therefore any person is permitted to build a house there, for his habitation, or to dry his nets, and draw up anything from the sea upon the shore. The property of the shore, however, must be understood to be vested in no individual, but to partake of the same legal nature as the sea itself, and the soil or sand which is beneath it.

Section VI.—Certain things belong to bodies corporate, and not to individuals; as, for example, in cities, theatres, race-courses, and other like places, which are the common property of the whole city.

Section VII.—Things sacred, religious, or holy, belong to no individual, for that which is of divine right, is the property of no man.

Section VIII.—Things sacred, are such as have been duly consecrated, and that too by the Pontiffs, as sacred buildings, and offerings, in due form dedicated to the service of God. Which things we, by our Imperial Constitution, have forbidden to be sold or mortgaged, save for the purpose of purchasing the freedom of captives. But, if a man merely by his own authority presume to consecrate a building, it is not thereby sacred, but profane only. The site, however, on which a consecrated building has been raised, continues sacred even though the building be itself destroyed; and this is the written opinion of Papinian.

Section IX.—Of things religious; any one may at his pleasure, make a place religious, by burying a dead body in land belonging to himself: but when land is held in joint proprietorship and has hitherto been unused for such a purpose, it is not lawful to bury, without the consent of a co-proprietor. But, if a burying ground be held in common, any one co-proprietor may bury in it, even though the rest dissent. So, if one have the usufruct, and another the ownership, the owner may not, without the consent of him who has the usufruct, make the ground religious. But it is lawful to bury in the ground of another, provided that other consent: and though he should withdraw his assent, after the burial, still the place is religious.

Section X.—Things holy, also, as the walls and gates of a city, are, in some sort, subject to divine law, and are therefore no part of the property of any individual. The walls of a city are said, by us, to be holy, because capital punishment is decreed against those who do them any injury; so, also, those portions of the laws, wherein penalties are established against transgressors, we call "*sanctions.*"

Section XI.—Things become the property of individuals in various ways; of some we acquire the ownership by the Law of Nature, which, as we have observed, is also called the Law of Nations; and of others, we acquire it by the Civil Law. It will be more convenient to begin with the more ancient law; and it is most clear that the law, which nature herself established at the first origin of the human race, is the more ancient; for Civil Laws could only first exist when States were founded, Magistracies created, and Laws written.

Section XII.—Wild animals, therefore, and birds, and fishes, and all living things which are produced in the sea, the heavens, and the earth, so soon as they are taken possession of by any one, become the property of him that captures them; and this by the Law of Nations; for natural reason gives that which was the property of no one, to him that first occupies it. Nor does it matter whether a man take wild animals or birds upon his own premises, or upon those of another. Undoubtedly he who enters the land of another for the purpose of hunting or fowling may be warned off by the owner, if he should perceive the purpose of entering. All that of this kind you take, is considered as your property so long as it is under the restraint of your custody; but so soon as it has escaped from such custody, and regained its natural liberty, it ceases to be yours, and again becomes the property of him that captures it. The animal is considered to regain its natural liberty when it has either vanished from your sight, or is before your eyes under such circumstances that pursuit would be difficult.

Section XIII.—The question has been mooted, whether, if you have so wounded a wild animal, that it might with ease be taken, it is understood to be forthwith your property. According to the opinion of some, it becomes your property so soon as you have wounded it, and continues to be yours, so long as you continue to pursue it: but if you cease to pursue it, is ceases to be yours, and becomes again the property of him that first can capture it. Others have held that it becomes yours only on condition of your capturing it. And we confirm the latter opinion, for many mischances may occur to hinder you from capturing it.

Section XIV.—Bees, also, are wild by nature. Those, therefore, which swarm upon your tree, before you have hived them, are no more deemed your property, than are the birds which build their nest there; so, therefore, if any other hives them, he becomes their owner. Furthermore, if they have made honeycombs, any one is at liberty to take them. But clearly if, before the comb be touched, you see any one entering on your ground, you have full right to stop his entrance. A swarm also, which has flown from your hive, is looked upon as your property, so long as it is in sight, and may without difficulty be pursued: otherwise it becomes the property of him who first can capture it.

Section XV.—Peacocks, also, and pigeons are wild by nature; nor is it a valid objection to say, that after every flight they are wont to come back; for bees do the like, and that they are naturally wild, is on all hands admitted. So, also, some people have deer so tame, that they go regularly into the woods, and as regularly return; yet no one denies but that deer are wild by nature. But, in the case of animals which are in the habit of going and returning at regular periods, the rule observed is, that they are considered yours so long as they retain the disposition to return; but if they cease to have this disposition, they cease also to be your property, and become that of him who first can capture them. Now animals are held to have lost the disposition, when they have lost the habit of returning.

Section XVI.—But fowls and geese are not by nature wild; and this we perceive from the fact that there are particular kinds of fowls and geese, which we call wild. If, therefore, your geese or fowls, being disturbed and frightened, take to flight, they are still considered as your property, wherever they may be, and that although you have lost sight of them; and he who takes possession of such animals, with intent to appropriate them, is guilty of theft.

Section XVII.—All those things which we take from our enemies become immediately our own, by the Law of Nations; so far even, that freemen are, in this manner, reduced to slavery under us. But, so soon as they escape from our power, and have got back to their own people, they regain their former social standing.

Section XVIII.—Precious stones and gems, and other

valuables which are found upon the sea-shore, become instantly, by natural law, the property of him that finds then.

Section XIX.—The offspring of animals of which you are the owner becomes, by the same natural law, your property.

Section XX.—Moreover, the soil which a river hath added by alluvial increase, to your estate, becomes yours by the Law of Nations. Now an alluvial is an imperceptible increase; and that is held to be added by alluvial increase, which is so gradually joined on that it is impossible to determine how much is added in each moment of time.

Section XXI.—But if the violence of a river carry off any portion of your land, and join it on to the estate of your neighbour, it undoubtedly still remains yours. But, if it should remain joined to his estate for a considerable space of time, and if the trees, which it swept with it, should strike their roots into his land, then both it, and the trees upon it, become, from that time, part of your neighbour's estate.

Section XXII.—An island which rises in the sea, a thing of rare occurrence, is the property of him that first occupies it, for it is held, before occupation, to be the property of no one. But, if an island be formed in a river, a thing of frequent occurrence, if it be exactly in the middle of the stream, it becomes the common property of those who, on each side of it, possess the lands on the river-banks; and they take in proportion to the extent of each man's property, as it adjoins the banks. But, if the island be nearer to one side than the other, it is the sole property of those who own lands near the river-bank on that side. Also, if a river be divided at one place, into branches, and afterwards lower down the stream such branches reunite, and thus any one's land is enclosed, in the form of an island, such land still continues the property of the former owner.

Section XXIII.—If a river, leaving utterly its natural bed, begin to flow in another direction, the old bed is the property of those who have lands along its banks; always in proportion to the extent of land which each has adjoining to the banks. The new bed, however, becomes public. And if, after some time, the river again return to its former channel, the new bed again becomes the property of those who own the lands along its banks.

Section XXIV.—If, however, a man's whole field be flooded only, the case is wholly different; for a flood does not alter the nature of the land; when, therefore, the waters have subsided, the land is still indisputably the property of its former owner.

Section XXV.—When one man has made any thing with the materials of another, a question often arises, as to which ought, according to natural reason, to be considered the proprietor; he, namely, who gave the form, or he who owned the materials. As, for example, if a man have made wine, or oil, or flour, from the grapes, olives, or wheat-ears of another; or have cast a vessel, out of gold, silver, or brass, the property of another; or have brewed mead with another man's wine and honey; or have composed a plaster, or an eye-salve, with another man's drugs; or have made a robe, with another's wool; or have built a ship, a chest, or a bench, with another man's timber. Now, after much discussion between the Proculeans and Sabinians, it has seemed good to us to adopt a middle course, or compromise, between the conflicting authorities, and to make the following distinction. If the thing wrought can be reduced to its original raw materials, then he who owned the said materials is deemed the owner of the thing made; but, if the thing wrought cannot be so reduced, then he who made it is adjudged proprietor. For example, a vessel when cast, may be reduced, with ease, to its raw materials of brass, of silver, or of gold; wine, oil and flour, on the other hand, cannot be again converted into grapes, olives, or wheat-ears; nor can mead, even, be resolved into wine and honey. But, if a man have made any fresh thing, out of materials partly belonging to another; as, for instance, if he have brewed mead, with his own wine and some one else's honey; or a plaster or eye-salve, with drugs partly his own, and partly those of another; or a robe, with a mixture of his wool with that of another; there can be no doubt but that, in such cases, the maker of the thing is its proprietor; since he not only gave his labour, but contributed also a share of the materials.

Section XXVI.—If, however, a man have woven the purple belonging to another man into his own vestment; then, the purple, although it be more valuable than the cloth, still belongs to the vestment as an accession. And he who was the owner of the purple can sue him who stole it from him both in an action of theft, and in that personal action, called a *condiction;* and this whether the vestment were made by him who committed the theft, or by some other. For although things which have become, as it were, extinct by change of form, cannot be recovered identically,—*i. e.*, by a real action or *vindication,*—still a personal action, or *condiction,* for the recovery of their value may be brought either against the thief, or against any other possessor.

Section XXVII.—If the materials of two proprietors be mixed together by their joint consent, the whole mass which results from such mixture is the common property of both owners; as, for example, if they have mixed their wines, or fused together their gold, or their silver. The same rule is observed, where different elements are so used in the admixture, as to form one new substance; as when mead is made of wine and honey; or an electrum by the fusion together of gold and silver; for in this case, also, it cannot be doubted that the new substance is common. The same rule holds, too, when materials, whether of like kinds or unlike, are mixed together accidentally, and without the consent of the proprietors.

Section XXVIII.—If, with your consent, the wheat of Titius have been mixed with yours, the mixed heap is the common property of both; and this, because, each grain of corn, which was before the property of one or other of you, has, by your will and consent, been made common property. But if such admixture was the result of accident, or brought about by Titius without your consent, then the mixed wheat does not appear to be the common property of you both, for the single grains still remain distinct, and retain their proper substance. In such case, the corn is no more held to be common, than would a flock, if the sheep of Titius were mixed with yours. But, supposing the whole mass of mixed wheat to be detained, by either party, the other party has his real action for the amount of wheat which belongs to him; and it is part of the duty of the judge to assess the quantity, or value of the wheat belonging to each party.

Section XXIX.—When a man hath built upon his own ground, using materials belonging to another, he is looked upon as the owner of the building, because all that is built on the soil, accedes to, or follows the soil. The owner of the materials does, nevertheless, not thereby cease to be so; he cannot, however, claim the materials, nor bring his action for the exhibition of them; being prevented by a law of the Twelve Tables, which provides, that no man shall be compelled to remove from his house a beam *(tignum)* which belongs to another; but he may be forced, by an action called " *de tigno juncto*," to pay twice the value of the materials; and under this general term *tignum*—literally, a " beam,"—all building materials are included. The aim of this provision was, to prevent the necessity of buildings being pulled down. If, however, from any cause, a building should be pulled down, the owner of the materials, provided he have not already obtained his double value, may then demand to have the identical materials, and bring his action for their exhibition.

Section XXX.—So, on the other hand, if a man have built with his own materials on the ground of another, the building becomes the property of him to whom the ground belongs. But in this case, the owner of the materials loses his right of property in them, for he is understood to have made a voluntary alienation of them; that is, if he were well aware that he was building upon another's land. Therefore, if even the building should be destroyed, he cannot prefer any claim to the materials. But it is indisputable, that if the man who builds be in actual possession of the soil, and if the owner of the soil claim the building, but refuse to pay the cost of the materials, and the wages of the workpeople, such owner may be repelled by the exception, or bar of fraud,—provided always, he who built was in *bonâ fide* possession. But it may justly be objected to any man, who well know that the ground belonged to another, that he had rashly built upon ground which he knew to belong to another.

Section XXXI.—If Titius, in his own ground, have set the plant of another, such plant will belong to Titius; if, on the other hand, Titius have set his own plant in the ground of Mævius, that plant will belong to Mævius, provided always, in both one case and the other, the plant has taken root; for before it has done so, it continues the property of its former owner. But, from the very instant when a plant has cast its roots into the ground, the right of property in it is changed; so that, if a neighbour's tree border so closely on the ground of Titius as to take root in it, we may affirm, that such tree is the property of Titius. For reason does not allow,—that a tree should be deemed the property of any, save of him in whose ground it has taken root; if, therefore, a tree planted near the boundaries of one man's land, extend its roots, also, into the lands of a neighbour, such tree becomes the common property of both land-owners.

Section XXXII.—On the same principle that plants, rooted

in the soil, are accessories to the soil; so grains of corn, when sowed, are considered to accede to, or follow the soil. But as he, who built upon another's ground, may (as was before said) defend himself by an exception of fraud, if the owner of the ground claim the building; so also, he who at his own cost, and *bonâ fide* hath sowed his grain in another's land, may claim protection by the like exception.

Section XXXIII.—Writings, also, even though the characters be of gold, are accessories of, and follow the papers or parchments on which they are written; precisely as what is built on, or sowed in, the soil, accedes to, and follows the soil. So, then, if on your paper, or parchment, Titius have written a poem, a history, or an oration, you, not Titius, are the owner of the written paper. But, if you sue for your books or parchments from Titius, and at the same time refuse to pay for the expenses of writing, then Titius can claim protection by an action of fraud; provided always he was in possession of such papers or parchments *bonâ fide;* that is honestly, and believing them to be his own.

Section XXXIV.—If a man have painted on another man's canvass, some hold that the canvass is an accessory of the painting, while others hold, that the painting, whatever be its value, is an accessory of the canvass. To us it seems the better opinion, that the canvass is accessory to the painting; for it were ridiculous that a painting of an Apelles, or a Parrhasius should be but the accessory of a worthless canvass. But, if the owner of the canvass have got possession of the picture, the artist who claims it from him, and yet refuses to pay the cost of the canvass, may be repelled by an exception of fraud. If, however, the artist have possession of the picture, it follows that the proprietor of the canvass may sue him in what is called, "a beneficial action"—(*actio utilis*)—; and if, in this case, the plaintiff do not first pay the expense of the painting, he also may be repelled by an exception of fraud; that is, if the painter had *a bonâ fide* possession of the canvass. But it is also clear, that if either the painter, or any one else have feloniously taken a canvass, the owner of such canvass will be entitled to his remedy in an action of theft.

Section XXXV.—If a man have *bonâ fide* purchased an estate from one whom he believed to be the owner, but who in fact was not; or have, also *bonâ fide*, acquired it from such a person, by gift, or any other lawful means, it is in accordance with natural reason, that the produce, which he has gathered, shall be his, as a return for his care and cultivation. If, therefore, at an after period, the real owner shall arrive, and claim his lands, he can sustain no action for the produce, which the *bonâ fide* possessor has consumed. But the like exemption, from such action, is not conceded to the man, who, of his knowledge, has taken possession of another man's estate; he, therefore, is compelled to restore, together with the estate, all the produce, or its value, if it have been consumed.

Section XXXVI.—He, however, to whom the mere usufruct of lands belongs, does not gain a property in the fruits of such lands until he has actually gathered them; if, therefore, he should die, while the fruits, although ripe, are still ungathered, such fruits do not belong to his heirs, but are the property of the owner of the lands. The same may, in general, be said of the tenant-farmer.

Section XXXVII.—In estimating the fruits of animals, we reckon their young, as well as their milk, hair and wool; thus lambs, kids, calves, colts, and young pigs are, of natural right, the property of the usufructuary. The offspring, however, of a female slave is not reckoned as a fruit, but belongs to him in whom the property of such female slave is vested; for it appeared absurd that a human being should be reckoned as a fruit; when all kinds of fruits are provided by nature for the benefit of man.

Section XXXVIII.—He who has the usufruct of a flock should keep up the original number, by supplying out of the young, the place of such as chance to die; such was the opinion of Julian. In the room, also, of dead vines, or trees, the usufructuary should plant others; for he should cultivate with care, and act in every thing as would a careful father of a family.

Section XXXIX.—The Emperor Hadrian, in accordance with natural equity, granted treasure, which a man found in his own land, to the finder; and made a similar grant in the care of him who, accidentally, found a treasure in a sacred or religious place. Also, if a person, without express search, but by chance, found a treasure in land belonging to another, he granted half to the finder, and half to the owner of the land. Consequently, if any thing be found in the Imperial demesnes, he ordained that half should go to the finder, and half to the Emperor. In like manner, if a man find any thing in a spot, the property of the treasury, the public, or the State, one-half should belong to the finder, and the other to the treasury or the State.

Section XL.—Things, also, are acquired, according to natural law, by tradition, or delivery; nothing can be more in accordance with natural law than to give effect to the will of a proprietor, who desires to transfer his property to another. Consequently, any corporeal thing, whatever be its nature, may be passed by tradition, or livery, and when so passed it is alienated by the proprietor. Stipendiary and tributary lands (those which are situated in the provinces are so called) may be alienated in this manner; for between these lands and those of Italy, there is now, by our Imperial Constitution, no difference; but if, for the purpose of a gift, a jointure, or any other object, they are passed by tradition, or livery, without doubt the property in them is transferred.

Section XLI.—Things sold and delivered do not, however, become, by acquisition, the property of the buyer until he have either paid the seller his price, or satisfied him in some way or other, as by procuring some one as security, or by giving him a pledge. And, though this is so ordained by a law of the Twelve Tables, it may properly be said to spring from the Law of Nations, that is, from the Law of Nature. If, however, the vendor have given credit to the purchaser, we must hold that the thing then becomes at once the property of the latter.

Section XLII.—It makes no difference whether the owner himself give livery of the thing; or whether another, to whom its custody has been entrusted, do so with the owner's consent. Therefore, if a man be entrusted by an owner with the uncontrolled administration of his goods, and if such committee sell and pass by delivery, any portion of such goods, he passes the property in that portion to him who receives it.

Section XLIII.—In some cases, the mere will of the proprietor, without delivery, serves to pass the property in a thing, as when a person has sent a thing to you, or let it, or left it in your care, and afterwards either sells, or gives, or lets you have it as a marriage portion. For, although he has not delivered it to you for any of these ends, so soon as it is, by his consent, reported to be yours, you have instantly acquired in it a property, as full as if it had been formally delivered, for the purpose of passing the property.

Section XLIV.—Also, if any one have sold merchandize in a warehouse, he transfers the right of property in it to the purchaser, so soon as he has delivered over to him the keys of the warehouse.

Section XLV.—The will of an owner, directed towards a person even who is not specified, passes the property in a thing: as, for example, when the Prætors and Consuls cast their largesses among the crowd, they know not what any particular man will get; still, because their will is, that what each man gets should be his own, they make him forthwith master of that which he may get.

Section XLVI.—By similar reasoning, it seems quite true to say that, if a thing which has been cast away, and made a derelict, by its owner, be seized by some other person, it becomes at once the property of him who so gets possession of it. Now a thing is looked on as derelict, which an owner has cast away, with the express purpose to have it no longer, as a part of his effects; and therefore, from that moment, it ceases to be his.

Section XLVII.—The law is different in the case of those things which are thrown overboard in a storm, for the purpose of lightening a ship; such things remain the property of their owners, inasmuch as it is clear that they were not thrown away from a wish to be rid of them, but that both owners, and ship too, might the more easily escape the perils of the sea. For which reason, if a man, with a view to gain, carry them off when washed on shore, or even when found on the high seas, he is guilty of theft. Not very different from these, is the case of those things which have dropped from a carriage in motion, without the knowledge of the owners.

TITLE 2.

OF THINGS CORPOREAL AND INCORPOREAL.

Some things, again, are corporeal; and some others incorporeal.

Section I.—Corporeal things are those which are tangible by their nature; as land, slaves, raiment, gold, silver and other things out of number.

Section II.—Incorporeal things are those which are not tangible, but consist in right; as rights of inheritance, usufructs, uses, and all obligations, however contracted. Nor does it make any difference that the inheritance contains corporeal things; for fruits gathered by the usufructuary are corporeal; and that which is due to us by virtue of an obligation is generally corporeal, as land, slaves, money; but the very right of inheritance, and right of usufruct, and right of obligation are incorporeal.

Section III.—Of things incorporeal are, also, those rights over estates, urban and rural, which are called Servitudes.

TITLE 3.

OF SERVITUDES.

SERVITUDES of rural estates are these; a foot-path, a horse-road, a highway, and an aqueduct. The first—the foot-path—is the right of way for human creatures, but not for driving a beast or cart. The second—the horse-road—is the right of way for driving a beast or cart; consequently, he who has the first, or simple right of way, has not the right of passage for beasts or vehicles; but he who has the second, has the former also, and may use it even though he have no beasts with him. The third—the highway—is the right of way, with beasts and vehicles, or afoot; it comprehends, therefore, the first two, namely, the foot-path, and the horse-road. The fourth—the aqueduct—is the right of having a passage, or conduit for water through the land of another.

Section I.—Servitudes of urban estates are proper to buildings; and they are called servitudes of urban estates, because we call all buildings "urban" messuages, even though they be built in the country. Now the following are the servitudes of urban property; (1) the right of making a neighbour's house support an adjoining building; (2) the right of fixing a beam, or joist in a neighbour's house; (3) the right of permitting, or of refusing to permit, the drip and flow from the gutter-pipes of another man's house, to run upon one's own buildings, or into one's court or drain; (4) the right of restraining a man from raising his house in height, so as to obstruct his neighbour's lights.

Section II.—Some think that among the servitudes of rural estates ought properly to be reckoned, the right of drawing water; of watering and feeding cattle; of burning lime; and of digging sand.

Section III.— All these are called *real* servitudes, because they cannot exist without real property to support them. For none can either acquire or own a servitude of an estate, rural or urban, unless he have an estate in his possession.

Section IV.—If a man be desirous of creating a servitude in favour of a neighbour, he may do it by contracts and stipulations. A person can, also, by his testament, prohibit his heir from heightening his house, so as to obstruct his neighbour's lights; or may bind his heir to allow a neighbour to insert a beam into his wall; or to receive upon his house the drippings of another's; or to suffer a neighbour to walk or drive across his land, or to have a water-conduit through it.

TITLE 4.

OF USUFRUCT.

USUFRUCT is the right of using and enjoying the fruits of things which belong to others, without destruction of their substance. It is a right over a corporeal thing; and if this cease to exist, the right is necessarily extinguished.

Section I.—The usufruct is separated from the property; and this separation may be effected in many ways;—if the usufruct be bequeathed by testament; for the heir has then the bare ownership, while the legatee has the usufruct; or, on the contrary, if an estate be bequeathed subject to the deduction of the usufruct, the legatee has the bare ownership and the heir has the usufruct. So too, a testator may leave the usufruct to one, and the estate, less the usufruct, to another. If, however, he wish to constitute an usufruct otherwise than by testament, he must do it by contract and stipulations. Lest, however, property should be rendered wholly valueless, by the usufruct being for ever detached, it has been deemed expedient to frame certain methods whereby the mere usufruct should become extinguished, and revert to the property.

Section II.—Usufruct may be constituted not only in lands and buildings, but in slaves, also, in beasts of burthen, and in all other things, save those which are consumed by use: for in these the separation of the usufruct is incompatible with either natural or civil reason. Of such may be reckoned wine, oil, wheat, clothes; money, also, may be added as being very similar; for, by constant use, and frequent change of owners, it is in a manner consumed by use. But the Senate deemed it matter of expediency, that a certain usufruct might, even in such things, be constituted; provided always, sufficient security were given to the heir. If, therefore, the usufruct of money be left by testament, such money is considered as given to the legatee in strict ownership; but he must give security to the heir, for the repayment of a like sum in case of his death, or of his suffering diminution. Other things, of consumable nature, are, in case of bequest, delivered to the legatee so as to become his property; but a valuation of them is effected, and security given for the payment of the amount of such valuation, in the event of the death of the legatee, or of his diminution. The Senate, then, has not created an absolute usufruct in things of this nature, for that were an impossibility, but has, by demanding security, established what may be called quasi-usufruct.

Section III.—Usufruct terminates by the death of the usufructuary; also, by his suffering the greater, or middle diminution; and lastly, by his lack of use, according to the manner, and in the time prescribed; all which points are set forth in our Constitution. The usufruct, also, expires by surrender from the usufructuary to the owner of the property (for surrender to a stranger has no such effect); or, on the other hand, by the acquisition of the property by the usufructuary; and this union of the usufruct with the property, is called consolidation. Further, it is evident that if buildings have been burnt down, or fall to pieces, whether through earthquake or decay, the usufruct in them is wholly destroyed; and no usufruct is due, even of the ground on which they stood, to the former usufructuary.

Section IV.—When the whole right of usufruct is extinguished, it then reverts to the property; and thenceforth, he who had before the bare ownership, acquires full power over the thing.

TITLE 5.

OF USE AND HABITATION.

THE bare use, and the usufruct are both constituted, and both terminated by the same means.

Section I.—The right of use is, however, of less extent than is that of usufruct. For he who has the bare use of lands, is understood to have nothing more than the right of taking such herbs, fruit, flowers, hay, straw and fuel as shall suffice for his daily requirements. He is allowed to remain on the land, also, so long only as he neither harasses the owner, nor is a hindrance to those who are engaged in the cultivation of the soil; but he has not the power—which the usufructuary has, to transfer his privileges to another, whether by lease, or sale, or gift.

Section II.—Also, he who hath the mere use of a house, is understood to have in it only such a right as to enable him to inhabit it himself, but he cannot transfer this right to another; and there has been great doubt as to whether he can let it to a lodger. He has however the right to live in it, with his wife, and children, and freed-men, and such other free persons as are as much in his service as are his slaves. So, in like manner, a wife who has the use of a house, may dwell in it with her husband.

Section III.—He, also, who has merely the use of a slave; has the right to avail himself only of the labour and service of such slave; but he is by no means permitted to transfer his right to another. The same rule prevails as to beasts of burthen.

Section IV.—If the use of a herd of sheep or cattle be left by testament, he who has the use cannot take either milk, lambs or wool; for these are part of the fruits. He may, however, clearly use the manure for the improvement of his ground.

Section V.—The right of habitation, whether given by will or constituted by any other means, seems to be neither use nor usufruct, but a right, as it were, peculiar to itself. With regard, therefore, to general expediency, and in accordance with an opinion of Marcellus, we have published a decision whereby we have permitted all such as have this right of habitation, not only themselves to dwell in the place over which such right extends, but also to transfer that right by lease to others.

Section VI.—What we have here said of servitudes, usufruct, use, and habitation may, at present, be enough. Of inheritances and obligation we shall treat in their proper places. We have already briefly explained how things are acquired according to the Law of Nations: let us now see how they are acquired according to the Civil Law.

TITLE 6.

OF TITLE BY PRESCRIPTION.

By the Civil Law it was anciently provided, that he who, by purchase, gift, or any other legal means, had obtained a thing from one who was not the owner, but whom he deemed so, should acquire, by use, a title to such thing; provided that in the case of a moveable, he had been in *bonâ fide* possession for the space of one year, either in Italy or the provinces; and for the space of two years, in the case of an immoveable, but only if held within the limits of Italy. This was provided in order to prevent the ownership of things remaining in uncertainty. Now these, by our more ancient legislators, were thought terms of sufficient length to enable owners to make search for their property; we, however, have come to a better decision, as well from a desire to protect lawful owners from being too quickly defrauded of their property, as to prevent this boon of acquisition from being confined to any set locality. We, therefore, have published a Constitution as to this matter, wherein it is provided, that the property in things moveable shall be acquired by the use of them for the space of three years; and that in things immoveable by the " possession of long time," that is, ten years, for persons present (*i. e.*, living in the same province), and twenty years for persons absent (*i. e.*, in different provinces.) By these means, if a just ground of possession precede, the property in things may be acquired, and this not in Italy alone, but in every country subject to our imperial sway.

Section I.—In certain cases, however, although a man have been in possession with indisputably good faith, yet use, however long, will never found a prescription: as in the case of one who has in his possession a free person, a thing sacred or religious, or a runaway slave.

Section II.—Things stolen, also, and such as have been taken with violence, cannot be acquired by use, although they have been held in *bonâ fide* possession during the length of time required by our Constitution: for prescription to such things as have been stolen, is forbidden both by a Law of the Twelve Tables, and also by the *Lex Atinia*; and, as to such as have been taken with violence, by the *Lex Julia et Plautia*.

When, however, it is said that the title by prescription to things which have been stolen, or seized with violence is forbidden by these laws, it is not meant that the thief only, or the disseisor, cannot so acquire the property, because such are incompetent to take by prescription, for another reason, namely, that their possession is not *bonâ fide*; the meaning is, that no other person, although he may have obtained them *bonâ fide*, by purchase, or otherwise, is able to acquire the property by use. Wherefore, in the case of moveables, it cannot easily happen that a *bonâ fide* possessor should gain the property in them by use. For he who sells, or in any other way makes over a thing which belongs to another, is guilty of a theft upon that other.

But even this rule, however, is sometimes liable to exceptions. For example, if an heir deeming a particular movable to be part of the inheritance, but which in reality had been only lent, let to, or deposited with the deceased, shall have sold, given, or passed it as dowry to one who receives it *bonâ fide*, there can be no doubt but that he who so received, can acquire the property in it by use. Because, the thing itself is not tainted with the vice of theft, as the heir who *bonâ fide* alienated it as his own, committed no theft.

So, also, if he who has the usufruct of a slave-girl, should sell or give away her child, in the full belief that it belonged to him, he is guilty of no theft: for theft cannot be constituted without the intention to commit it.

It may happen, also, in many other ways, that a person may, without the commission of theft, transfer the property of another, and give a right of property by use to the possessor.

With reference, however, to immoveables, prescription may more easily accrue; as, in the case of a person who, without violence, takes possession of an estate vacant, by reason either of the absence or negligence of the owner, or of his death without heirs. Now, although his own possession is not *bonâ fide*, for he is well aware that he has seized upon land not his own, if he make a transfer to one who takes it *bonâ fide*, this latter may, by long possession, acquire the property in it, because what he has received has neither been stolen, nor seized by violence. For the opinion of certain of our ancient lawyers, that there could be a theft of lands, or things immoveable, is now abandoned; and it is, therefore, provided by the Imperial Constitutions, that the benefits of long and undoubted possession shall not be taken away from those who are in possession of immoveables.

Section III.—A title by prescription may, sometimes, be founded even in a thing which has been taken, or seized by violence; as, for example, if it have come again into the power of the true owner; for then, the thing is reported purged from the contamination of theft, and acquisition by use may take place.

Section IV.—Things belonging to the imperial treasury cannot be acquired by use. But Papinian held that if, before *bonâ vacantia,—i. e.,* things escheatable—have been duly reported to the treasury, a *bonâ fide* purchaser has livery of any of them, he may acquire a title by prescription. The Emperor Antoninus Pius, and the Emperors Severus and Antoninus have issued Rescripts confirming this opinion.

Section V.—It is lastly to be observed that, in order to give a title by prescription to one who has purchased a thing *bonâ fide,* or got possession by any other legal method, the thing itself must be free from all taint of " vice," that is, liability to exception.

Section VI.—The mistake of thinking a bad cause of possession to be a good one, does not give rise to acquisition by use; as when a person is in possession, under the belief that he has bought, when he has really not bought; or that the thing was a gift, when it has never really been given him.

Section VII.—Long possession, which has begun to reckon in favour of a deceased, is continued in favour of the heir, or of him who has the equitable inheritance, even though he may know the immoveable to be the property of another. But if the possession of the deceased had no just, or *bonâ fide* commencement, the possession is of no avail to heir, or equitable inheritor, though he were ignorant of the vicious possession of the deceased. A similar enactment in our Imperial Constitutions provides, that the time of usucapion, or prescription to moveables also, shall be continued in the same way from the deceased to his successor.

Section VIII.—As between vendor and purchaser, the Emperors Severus and Antoninus have ordained by Rescript that the time of possession of the vendor, shall be conjoined with that of the purchaser.

Section IX.—By an edict of the Emperor Marcus Aurelius, it is enacted that he who purchases from the public treasury a thing belonging to another, may repel the true owner by an exception of prescription, provided five full years have elapsed since the sale. But the Emperor Zeno, of sacred memory, has by a Constitution of his, fully provided that those who receive any thing from the public treasury, by sale, gift or any other title, may be at once secure, and certain of success, whether they sue, or are sued in any action. While those who imagine that they have grounds of action, either as proprietors, or mortgagors of things aliened, may commence a suit against the public treasury at any time within four years. Also in an Imperial Constitution, which we ourselves have lately published, we have made, with reference to those who have received any thing from our household, or from that of the Empress, a provision similar to that in the abovementioned Constitution of Zeno, as to things alienated from the public treasury.

TITLE 7.

OF DONATIONS.

Another way of acquiring property is by Donation; of which there are two kinds: the one, donation *mortis causâ* —that is, made in contemplation of death; and the other, *non mortis causâ*—that is, not made in contemplation of death.

Section I.—A donation *mortis causâ*, is that which is made under an apprehension of death; as when a man gives a thing upon condition, that if the donor die, the donee shall possess it absolutely; but that, if the donor should survive, or repent him of the gift, he shall recover his property in it; and the like also in the event of the donor out-living the donee. Donations *mortis causâ* are now made strictly analogous to legacies. For, since it was a moot point with jurists, as to whether they should be considered in the light of gifts, or of legacies, partaking as they do in certain respects of the nature of both; and since some classed them under the one head, and some under the other, we have, by our Constitution, decreed that such donations be reckoned, in almost every respect, amongst legacies, and be made in such manner and form as our said Constitution directs. In few words, then, a donation *mortis causâ* is effected when a man so gives, as to show that he had rather the thing given should remain in his possession, than that the donee should have it; but still wishes such donee to have it, in preference to his heir. Of this kind is the donation which, in Homer, Telemachus makes to Piræus:—

> He (when Piræus ask'd for slaves, to bring
> The gifts and treasures of the Spartan king)
> Thus, thoughtful, answered; Those we shall not move,
> Dark, and unconscious of the will of Jove.
> We know not yet the full event of all:
> Stabb'd in his palace, if your prince must fall,
> Us and our house, if treason must o'erthrow,
> Better a friend possess them than a foe.
> But on my foes should vengeance Heaven decree,
> Riches are welcome then, not else, to me;
> Till then, retain the gifts.
>
> *Pope's Odyssey*, B. XVII.

Section II.—The other kind of donations are those made in no apprehension of death, and are called donations *inter vivos*— *i. e.*, between living persons. These admit of no comparison with legacies; and, if duly perfected, cannot be revoked at pleasure. Now they are said to be duly perfected, if the donor have manifested his will either in writing, or otherwise. Also our Constitution has enacted, that a donation *inter vivos* shall, like a sale, involve the necessity of delivery; in such wise, however, that even if delivery be not made, it may have the fullest and most absolute effect, and render it incumbent on the donor to make delivery of it. And although the Constitutions of previous Emperors have enacted that these donations should be registered in the public rolls, if they exceeded 200 *solidi* (£210 16ˢ. 8*d.*) in value, our enactment has raised the limit to 500 *solidi*; so that, for a gift which does not exceed this sum, registration is unnecessary: it alludes, also, to certain donations which have no need of registration at all, but have the most complete validity of themselves. We have passed, also, many other fresh rules for the more unfettered extension of donations; all of which may be collected from those of our Constitutions which we have published on this subject. It remains, however, to be observed, that even though donations be made in the most perfect and absolute manner, if those on whom the bounty has been conferred prove ungrateful, we have, by our Constitution, granted permission to donors in certain specified cases, to revoke such donations: and this is to the end, that they who have bestowed their property on others may not suffer, at their hands, loss and injury, of the kind set forth in our Constitution.

Section III.—There is, also, another kind of donation *inter vivos*, which was wholly unknown to the ancient jurists, but was introduced by some of the later Emperors. It was called the donation *ante nuptias*—or, " before marriage;" and involved the tacit condition that it should take effect so soon only as the marriage had been celebrated. It was *ante nuptias*, therefore, because it preceded marriage, and never took place after the celebration. But, as it was permitted to increase dowries even after marriage, our father, the Emperor Justin, was, by a Constitution, the first to permit donations *ante nuptias* to be also increased during marriage; but the donation still kept what was now an unmeaning name, for it was still called ante-nuptial, while this increase had been made to it during marriage. We therefore, being minded to make our imperial sanctions as complete as possible, and wishing to give things names fitted to them, have enacted that such donations may not only be increased during marriage, but may then also first be made; and that they shall be known, not as donations *ante-nuptias*, but *propter nuptias* (*i. e.*, on account of marriage); and that they shall thus be made like dowries in this respect, that while dowries may not only be increased, but also first made during marriage, so donations *propter nuptias* may now not only precede marriage, but, after its celebration, may be increased, or even made.

Section IV.—There was formerly another mode of acquiring property by the civil law, namely, by survivorship; thus if one who owned a slave in common with Titius, had himself alone enfranchised that slave, whether by the *vindicta*, or by testament, in such case his share in such slave was forfeited, and accrued to Titius. But, as it was an example of most injurious tendency, that both the slave should be barred of liberty, and masters of more humane dispositions should suffer loss, while the more harsh were gainers, we have deemed it expedient, by our Imperial Constitution, to apply a pious curative to what seemed so full of objections; we, then, have devised a way, whereby as well the owner who grants manumission, as his co-proprietor, and the enfranchised slave, may all share in our beneficence. Liberty, then, in favour whereof even former legislators have clearly often broken through strict rules, shall in reality be granted to the slave; he, too, who has granted this gift of liberty, shall be gladdened by seeing it upheld; while the co-proprietor shall be indemnified by receiving a value for the slave, in proportion to his share in him, and in accordance with the rates which we, in our Constitution, have set down.

TITLE 8.

OF THE POWER TO ALIENATE.

In some cases it happens that he, who is the owner of a thing, has not the power to alienate it; while, in others, he who is not the owner, has that power. For instance, the husband is forbidden, by the *Lex Julia*, to alienate the lands which form a wife's portion, without the consent of the wife; although such lands belong to him, having been given him as a marriage portion with his wife. But we, by certain amendments in this *Lex Julia*, have made it more truly efficacious. For while that law had reference only to immoveables situated in Italy, and forbade alienations made against a wife's will, or mortgages of such possessions even with her will; we have amended all these points, by enacting, that any such alienation or charge shall be forbidden in the case of property situated even in the provinces; and that no such alienation or charge shall be lawful even if made with the consent of the wife, lest the weakness of the female sex be made an instrument for the detriment of their interests.

Section I.—On the other hand, however, a creditor may, in accordance with the terms of an agreement, alienate a pledge, although the thing is not his own property. This power, however, may perhaps be considered to arise from the will of the debtor, who when he first made the contract agreed that the creditor should have the power to sell the thing pledged, if the money advanced were not repaid. But lest, on the one hand, creditors should be hindered in the acquisition of that which is their due, or on the other, debtors should seem to lose their property too easily, we have provided, by our Imperial Constitution, that there shall be a certain fixed method of procedure, by which the sale of pledges may lawfully be effected; and by the tenor of this enactment, abundant provision is made for the interests as well of creditors as debtors.

Section II.—It must now be observed that a pupil, male or female, has power to make any alienation without the authority of the tutor. If, therefore, a pupil lend money to any one, without the authority of the tutor, such pupil contracts no obligation; because he has not the power to vest the property of the money in the borrower. Such monies, therefore, if they still exist, can be recovered by a real action, or *vindication.* But if the monies so lent, have been consumed by the borrower, and that too *bonâ fide*, they may be recovered by a personal action, or *condiction.* If, in the latter case, they have been consumed *malâ fide*, then the borrower may be sued in an action *ad exhibendum*—*i. e.*, for production of the thing borrowed.

Section III.—On the other hand, pupils, of either sex, may lawfully acquire a property in anything whatsoever, without the authority of their tutors. When, therefore, a debtor makes a payment to a pupil, such debtor must have the authority of the tutor; or otherwise he is not legally discharged. Now this point was, on the clearest grounds, decided by us, in an Imperial Constitution which we published to the advocates of Cæsarea, at the suggestion of that very eminent man, Tribonian, Quæstor of our sacred palace: wherein it was enacted, that the debtor of a pupil might legally make a payment to the tutor or curator of such pupil, provided he gained permission, by the certificate of a judge previously obtained, free of all expense to the minor; and that, if all these forms were observed, a payment in accordance with the judge's decree, should afford the fullest security to the debtor. If, however, payment have been made to a pupil, otherwise than we have sanctioned, the pupil who has the money still safe in his custody, or has become the richer by it, may, if he again make claim for the same sum, be defeated by an exception of fraud. But if he have foolishly squandered the money, or lost it by theft, an exception of fraud will stand the debtor in no stead, because he made his payment inconsiderately, without the tutor's authority, and in contravention of our rules. On the other hand, pupils of either sex can make no payments without the tutor's anthority; for that which they do pay, without such authority, does not become the property of him who receives it; inasmuch as they have the privilege of alienating no single thing without such authority.

TITLE 9.

OF THE PERSONS BY WHOM PROPERTY MAY BE ACQUIRED.

THINGS may be acquired not by ourselves alone, but by those also who are under our power; by slaves, of whom we have the usufruct; by freemen also, and by slaves belonging to others whom we possess *bond fide*. Let us now, therefore, examine carefully as to all these persons.

Section I.—Formerly, then, all that children, of either sex, who were under the power of their parents, acquired, excepting only the *peculium castrense* (*i. e.*, property acquired by the son in war), was acquired, without distinction, for their parents. And these rights were so strictly vested in the parents, that they had full power to give, sell or transfer in such manner as they pleased, anything that had been acquired through one of their children; and such gift, sale, or transfer might be either to another child, or to a perfect stranger. As this rule seemed to us inhuman, we have, by the publication of a general Constitution, given relief to children, and yet upheld that honour which is due to parents. Our enactment, therefore, is, that anything accrues to the child, by means of the fortune of the father, shall, in accordance with the ancient usage, be acquired absolutely for the father; for what hardship can there be in enacting, that the wealth which has sprung from the father's supplies should revert to him? But what thing soever the son of a family acquires, in any other way, he shall acquire the usufruct for his father, but the absolute property shall remain in the son; so that what one has gained by hard labour, or by good fortune, shall not to his detriment, be transferred to another.

Section II.—We have also laid down some rules with respect to the interest of children in their emancipation; for, in accordance with former Constitutions, the father had the power, if he so willed, on the emancipation of his children, to retain for himself one-third of the things which were exempt from paternal acquisition, deducting it as the price of emancipation. Now it seemed, in sooth, a cruel thing that a son should, by emancipation, be deprived of a third part of his property, and that he should lose in fortune, what he gained in honour, by becoming independent through emancipation. We, therefore, have enacted, that the parent shall henceforth retain one-half, in lieu of one-third of such acquisitions; but retain it as usufructuary, and not as proprietor. So, therefore, the whole property will remain in the son, without any diminution, while the father will enjoy the benefits of a share larger than before, of a half, namely, in lieu of a third.

Section III.—Whatever, also, our slaves acquire, whether by delivery, contract, or in any other way, is acquired for us; and this, even though we are ignorant of, or averse to, such acquisitions; for the slave himself, being in the power of another, can have no property of his own. Also, if he be instituted heir, he cannot enter on the inheritance save at his master's bidding; and if, at the bidding of his master, he do enter, the master acquires the inheritance, precisely as if he himself had been instituted heir. In like manner, a legacy left to a slave is acquired by the master. Further it is to be observed that, by those who are in our power, we acquire not the property alone, but also the possession. For what thing soever they have acquired in possession, that also we are deemed to possess; wherefore, through their means, we may acquire a title by long use and prescription.

Section IV.—In regard to those slaves in whom we have the usufruct only, it has been held, that whatever they acquire by means of our property, or by their own labour, shall belong to us; but that what they have acquired from any other source, shall belong to their real owner. Thus, if a slave be instituted heir, or receive a legacy, or gift, the inheritance, legacy, or gift will belong not to the usufructuary, but to the proprietor. The same rule holds with regard to any one who is *bonâ fide* in our possession, whether he be free, or another man's slave; for the rule which holds as to the usufructuary, holds also as to the *bonâ fide* possessor; therefore, whatever is by such acquired, other than from the two sources above-mentioned, becomes the property of the man himself, if he be free, or of his master, if he be a slave. A *bonâ fide* possessor who, by long use or prescription, has gained the property in a slave, acquires, as absolute owner, all that the slave acquires. But the usufructuary master can gain no property in his slave by use or prescription; first, because he has not the strict possession, but merely the right of usufruct; and secondly, because he knows that the slave belongs to another. But what we acquire by means of those slaves in whom we have the usufruct, or of those whom we possess *bonâ fide*, or by means even of any free person, who acts *bonâ fide* as our slave, we acquire not in ownership alone, but in possession. We say this, both as to slaves and freemen, with reference only to the distinction before laid down, and speak but of those acquisitions which they have made, either by means of our property, or by their own labour.

Section V.—From the above remarks it is clear, that we can by no means acquire by free persons not under our power, and whom we do not possess *bonâ fide*; nor can we do so, by slaves belonging to other people, of whom we have neither the usufruct, nor the just possession. And this is the meaning of the assertion, that no acquisition can be made by means of a stranger; except, indeed, that in accordance with a Constitution of the Emperor Severus, possession may be acquired for us by a free person, as for instance by an agent or procurator, not only with, but even without, our knowledge; and by this possession, we acquire the property, provided it were the owner who delivered the thing; or a title by use and prescription if it were not.

Section VI.—The remarks which have been made, as to the modes of acquiring property in particular things, will suffice for the present. For, afterwards, we shall more conveniently treat of legacies, by which, also, we acquire a property in particular things, and of *fidei-commissa*—bequests in trust—by which particular things are left to us. Let us now show by what means things may be acquired *per universitatem*—that is, wholly, and in gross. If, for example, we are made heir, or if we sue for possession of the property of another, or arrogate a son, or if the goods of any are adjudged to us in order to preserve his liberty, in all these cases all that did belong to the person passes to us, whole and entire. First, then, let us treat of inheritances, which are of two kinds, such, namely, as accrue to us by testament, and such as come by intestacy. We will first treat of those which come to us by testament; and in doing this, it is necessary to begin by an explanation of the formalities required in making testaments.

TITLE 10.

OF TESTAMENTS.

THE word "Testament," is derived from the Latin *testatio mentis*—an evidence of the will.

Section I.—Now, that nothing of ancient usage be absolutely forgotten, it is needful to remark that in former days two kinds of testament were in use; whereof the one was used in times of peace and quiet, and was named *calatis comitiis, i. e.* from the convention of the *comitia:* the other was used at the moment of setting out to battle, and was called *procinctum;* a third kind was afterwards added, called the testament *per æs et libram,*—*i. e.*, " by brass and balance," which was effected by emancipation, that is, by a fictitious sale in the presence of five witnesses and of the *libripens*—or, " balance-holder"—all Roman citizens who had arrived at years of puberty—and also in the presence of him who was called *emptor familiæ*—" the purchaser of the inheritance." The two former kinds of testaments fell into disuse, in very distant times; and that " by brass and balance," although it continued longer in use, has still in great measure ceased to be observed.

Section II.—The three kinds of testament before named had their origin in the Civil Law: afterwards, however, in accordance with the Prætor's edict, another kind was used. For by the Honorary Law, or edicts of the Curule Magistrate, the signature of seven witnesses was deemed enough, without the requirement of any emancipation. By the Civil Law, however, the signature of witnesses was not essential.

Section III.—But when, in course of time, partly by custom and partly by reforms in the Imperial Constitutions, the Civil and Prætorian Law began to be blended together, it became established, that every testament should be drawn up at one and the same time, as the Civil Law required; that there should be seven witnesses present, who should subscribe their names, as was brought into usage by the Constitutions; and that these seven should affix their seals to the will, in compliance with the Prætor's edict. The law, therefore, concerning testaments seems to be tripartite; the necessity for witnesses, and for their presence at one, and the same time, in order to give validity to a testament, springs from the Civil Law; the subscriptions of testator and witnesses, are demanded in compliance with the Imperial Constitutions; while the sealings of the witnesses, and their number, are ordained by the Prætorian edict.

Section IV.—To all these solemn forms, however, we have exacted by our Constitution, that for the better security of testaments, and the prevention of frauds, there be this addition; to wit, that the name of the heir be inserted in the handwriting either of the testator, or of the witnesses; and that there be a full observance of all the forms set forth in that our Constitution.

Section V.—All the witnesses may use the same stamp in affixing their seals to a testament. For, as says Pomponius, what if the device on all seven stamps were the same? A witness, also, may use another person's seal.

Section VI.—They may be allowed to act as witnesses who are in possession of *testamenti factio*,—*i. e.*, who can legally take or dispose of property by will. But no woman, person under puberty, slave, madman, person deaf and dumb, prodigal restrained from spending his own property, nor one whom the laws have branded as worthless and incompetent to witness, can be admitted as witness to a testament.

Section VII.—If, however, one of the witnesses to a testament, were thought to be free at the time of attestation, but afterwards appeared to have been then a slave, the Emperor Hadrian, in a Rescript to Catonius Verus, and afterwards the Emperors Severus and Antoninus, by their Rescript, in like case decreed, that they, of their imperial generosity, would aid such a defect in a testament, and cause it to be esteemed as valid, as if it had been regularly made; and this because, when the signatures were affixed to the testament, this witness was taken, in the estimation of all men, to be free; and there was, at that time, no one to dispute his social standing.

Section VIII.—A father, and a son under his power; or two brothers, under the power of the same father, may both be witness to the same testament; for there can be nothing to hinder several persons, from one and the same household, acting as witnesses in a business which affects none of their family.

Section IX.—No one, however, can be admitted as a witness, who is under the power of the testator. And if a son, after he has obtained his discharge from the army, make a will wherein he bequeaths his *castrense peculium*,—*i. e.*, that private property which he has acquired in war — neither his father, nor any one under his father's power, can legally be a witness. For, in this case, the attestation of members of the same family is disallowed.

Section X.—An heir cannot be admitted to attest the testament wherein he is appointed heir; nor can his father, in whose power he is; nor his brothers, if they are under the power of the same father; and this, because the whole business of making a testament is now-a-days considered as a transaction between the testator on the one part, and the heir on the other. Formerly, however, there was great confusion; for although the ancients never would admit the attestation of the *emptor familiæ*—i. e., "purchaser of the inheritance"—nor of any of those who were connected with by subjection to the family authority, still they permitted the real heir to attest, as also any of those connected with him by the ties of family. Still, however, they who so granted this privilege, exhorted such witnesses to be most careful not to abuse it. We, however, by a correction of this usage, have brought within the strictness of legal enactments, that which they sought to curb by mere persuasion. For in imitation of the ancient law with reference to the *emptor familiæ*,—the mere purchaser of the inheritance—we now refuse to admit, as witnesses in their own behalf, either the proper heir, who represents the ancient *emptor familiæ*, or any person allied to him by the ties of family. On this account it is that we have suffered the former Imperial Constitutions on this subject, to be inserted in our code.

Section XI.—We do not, however, refuse the attestation of legatees, or of those for whose benefit trusts (*fidei-commissa*) are made; or of any who are allied to them; and this, because they are not universal heirs and successors. Nay, in one of our Constitutions, we have specially accorded this privilege to legatees, and to those who are to benefit by trusts; and we accord it, with still more readiness, to those who are in the power of such, and to those in whose power they are.

Section XII.—It matters not whether a testament be written upon tablets, paper, parchment, or any other substance.

Section XIII.—A person, also, may execute any number of copies of the same testament; provided in every case the forms prescribed be duly observed. This is at times a necessary thing: as, when a man about to embark on a voyage, is anxious both to take with him, and also to leave at home, the declaration of his last wishes: the same may occur in numberless other circumstances, arising from the several necessities of mankind.

Section XIV.—This then, may suffice with reference to such testaments as are in writing. If, however, any one be desirous to make a testament, valid by the Civil Law, but still without writing; let such an one be well assured, that if in the presence of seven witnesses, he signify his will by nuncupation—*i. e.*, verbal declaration,—such declaration, will constitute a testament perfectly valid according to the civil law, and confirmed by Imperial Rescripts.

TITLE 11.

OF THE TESTAMENTS OF SOLDIERS.

THE aforementioned strict observation of all due formalities in the construction of testaments, has been dispensed with by the Imperial Constitutions, in favour of military persons, on account of their excessive lack of skill in such matters. For, although such persons neither employ the legal number of witnesses, nor observe any other prescribed solemnity, still their testament is valid, provided it be made when they are upon actual service; a provision, on good grounds, introduced by a Constitution of our own. Thus in what manner soever a soldier's last will is expressed, whether in writing or not in writing, the testament prevails in accordance with his intention. But during such times as soldiers are not on actual service, but when they are living in their own homes or elsewhere, they are by no means entitled to claim this privilege. Soldiers also, though sons of a family, and so under power, gain from military service the right of making a testament; but according to the general law, the same formalities must be observed which we have just now spoken of as essential to the testaments of civilians.

Section I.—As to the testaments of soldiers, the Emperor Trajan wrote as follows, in his Rescript to Statilius Severus: "The privilege accorded to soldiers, that their testaments, "however made, shall be deemed valid, must be interpreted to "mean, that it must first be evident, that a testament of "some sort has been made; for an unwritten testament may "be made even by those who are not soldiers. If, therefore, "it should appear that the soldier, as to whose property the "action, now pending before you, was brought, did, in the "presence of the witnesses, expressly summoned, testify his "intentions, and declare by word of mouth whom he wished "to be his heir, and what slave he desired to have enfranchised, "he shall thus be deemed to have made a testament without "writing, and his desires shall be upheld. But, if he merely "said to some one, as in conversation it often happens, 'I "'appoint you my heir,' or 'I leave you all my property,' such "expressions must not be regarded as a testament. And none "can be more deeply interested than the soldiers themselves, "that a precedent of this sort should not be allowed; or other-"wise witnesses might readily be forthcoming after the death "of any soldier, who would declare that they had heard him "leave his property to any one they pleased to name; and "thus the real intentions of the deceased might easily be "defeated."

Section II.—A soldier, though deaf and dumb, may make a testament.

Section III.—But this privilege is accorded by the Imperial Constitutions to soldiers, so long only as they are on service, and in camp. If, therefore, veterans after their discharge, or those who are still soldiers but not in camp, wish to make their testaments, they must fulfil all the forms required in general of every Roman citizen. Also, if a soldier make his testament in camp by a mere expression of will, and without the usual formalities, such testament will remain valid for one year only after the maker's discharge. How, then, will it be in the case of a soldier who, having made a military testament, dies within a year of his discharge, while the condition upon which the heir is instituted is not accomplished until after the year; will such a testament be valid as that of a soldier? We decide that it will be so valid.

Section IV.—If a man, before entering the army, have made an informal testament, and afterwards when in the army, and on service should open it, and either add something to, or erase something from, it; or, if in any other way his will is manifested, that such testament should be valid; it must needs be affirmed to be so, seeing that it is a re-publication of a soldier's wishes.

Section V.—If a soldier should be given in arrogation; or, being the son of a family, should be emancipated, his testament continues valid, as though it were the re-publication of a soldier's wishes; nor is to be considered as invalidated by the diminution he has undergone.

Section VI.—We may here make it known, that in imitation of the *castrense peculium*—or military estate—both ancient laws and Imperial Constitutions have permitted certain persons to hold a *quasi-castrense peculium*—or quasi-military estate,—and some of these have been permitted to make their testaments, even when under the power of others. We, therefore, by our Constitution have more widely extended this privilege; granting it to all who have this kind of *peculium*, provided the testaments themselves are drawn up in accordance with the ordinary legal formalities. He, however, who carefully reads this our Constitution, may make himself acquainted with every point which has reference to the aforesaid privilege.

TITLE 12.

OF THOSE WHO MAY NOT MAKE TESTAMENTS.

To make a testament is not in the power of all. First, then, those who are in the power of others have not this privilege; insomuch that, even though the parents have granted them leave, they still are barred from making a valid testament. Exception, however, must be made of those whom we have already enumerated, and especially of soldiers who are in the power of their parents, for they have, by the Imperial Constitutions, permission to dispose by testament of all that they have acquired in actual service. This privilege was first granted by the Emperors Augustus and Nerva, and by the illustrious Trajan, also, to soldiers only on actual service; afterwards, however, by an epistle of the Emperor Hadrian, it was extended to veterans, or those who had obtained their discharge. If, therefore, the son of a family bequeath his *peculium castrense*, or military estate, it will pass to him who is, in the testament, named heir; but, if he die intestate, and have neither children nor brothers him surviving, his military estate aforesaid will then, in accordance with the general rule, pass to his father, or to him in whose power he is. Whence we may conclude, that such property as a soldier, though under power, has acquired, in actual service, cannot be taken from him even by his father; nor can his father's creditors sell, or otherwise disturb the son in his possession; nor, on his father's death, is he forced to share it with his brothers, but it remains the sole property of him who acquired it. And this, although by the Civil Law the *peculia*—or estates, of those under power of parents, are reckoned as part of the property of the parents; just as the *peculium* of a slave is reckoned among the goods of his master; excepting always those particular kinds of *peculium* which, in accordance with the Constitutions of the Emperors, and especially of ourselves, are prohibited, for diverse reasons, from being so acquired for parents. With the exception, then, of those sons of a family, who have a *castrense*, or *quasi-castrense peculium*,—*i. e.*, a military,. or quasi-military estate,—none can make a testament, or if he do so, it is invalid, even though, before his death, he became independent of paternal authority.

Section I.—Persons, moreover, within the age of puberty, cannot make a testament, because they have not the mental judgment which is needed; nor can madmen, for they are reft of their senses. The will of one, under puberty, does not become valid, although he arrives at full age before his death; nor does that of a madman, although he afterwards regain his senses, and then dies. But, if a madman make a testament during a lucid interval, he is then a legal testator; and assuredly a testament made before the madness seized him is good; for an after-fit of frenzy can neither invalidate a previous testament made with all due formalities; nor can it injure the force of any other former act in which the rules of law have strictly been observed.

Section II.—A spendthrift also, who is interdicted from the management of his own estate, cannot make a testament: but a testament made before the publication of such interdiction will be valid.

Section III.—A person deaf and dumb, is not always capable of making a testament. When, however, we speak of a deaf person, we mean one who is absolutely unable to hear at all, not one who does hear, but with difficulty: so, also, by dumb, we mean one who cannot speak at all, not one who does speak, but with difficulty. For it, not unfrequently, happens, that well-read and learned persons, by various accidents, lose the power of hearing, and of speech. A Constitution published by us, comes, then, to the assistance of such; so that, through its provisions, they are enabled, in certain cases, and with certain forms, to make testaments, and execute also certain other acts. But if a person, through ill-health, or any other misfortune, should become deaf and dumb, after having made his testament, such testament will nevertheless continue valid.

Section IV.—A blind man cannot make a testament; unless he observe those forms which the law of our father, the Emperor Justin, has introduced.

Section V.—The testament of one who is in the hands of an enemy, if made during the continuance of his captivity, is not valid, even though he live to return. But that testament which he made while still in his own country holds good, either by the *jus postliminii* — "the right of return," — if he do come back; or, by the *Lex Cornelia,* if he perish in captivity.

TITLE 13.

OF THE DISINHERISON OF DESCENDANTS.

The observance of all the formalities before laid down will not alone suffice to give validity to a testament; but he who has a son in his power, must take care either to institute him heir, or by name to disinherit him. Otherwise, if he pass him in silence by, the testament will be inoperative; and this so absolutely, that if such son were to die, while his father was yet alive, no one could be heir under that testament; and this, because it was null and void from the first. In olden times, this rule was not observed with respect to daughters, or grand-children of either sex, though descended through the male line; for though they, whether male or female, were neither instituted heirs, nor disinherited, the testament was not invalidated, but they were entitled to join themselves with the instituted heirs, and so receive a share of the inheritance. Parents, also, were not compelled to disinherit these descendants by name, but might include them all as *cæteri*—" the remainder." A child is formally, and by name disinherited, if the words in the will run thus—" let Titius, my son, be disinherited"; or thus—" let my son be disinherited," without the addition of the proper name, if the testator have no other son alive.

Section I.—Posthumous children, also, must either be instituted heirs, or formally disinherited; and, in this, the condition of all the children is the same; but, if a posthumous son, or any posthumous descendant of either sex, be passed over, the testament is still valid, at the time of making; but becomes wholly void by the subsequent birth of a child of either sex.

If, therefore, a woman who is expected to have a posthumous child, should miscarry, nothing can prevent the heirs instituted by testament from entering upon the inheritance Female posthumous children may either be expressly disinherited, or by using the general term *cæteri*. If, however, they are disinherited by the use of the general term, some legacy must be bequeathed to them, to show they were not passed over through forgetfulness. But male posthumous children, *i. e.*, sons, and their descendants cannot be disinherited otherwise than nominally; to wit, in the form following: "whatever son hereafter may be born to me, let him be disinherited."

Section II.—They, also, are to be reckoned as posthumous children, who, by succeeding in the stead of the proper heirs, become, as by a quasi-birth, heirs to their parents. As for example; if a man have under his power a son, and by him a grand-son or grand-daughter, the son, as first in degree, has the sole rights of real heir; although the grand-son, or grand-daughter by that son, are subject to the same parental power. But, if such son should, in his father's life-time die, or by any means cease to be under his power, the grand-son, or grand-daughter would at once succeed in his place; and would thus, by what may be called a quasi-birth, obtain the rights of a proper heir. To the end, therefore, that his testament be not invalidated, the testator who is obliged either to institute his son, or to disinherit him by name, if he would have his testament upheld, is no less obliged to institute or disinherit his grand-son or grand-daughter by that son; lest if the son should die during the testator's life-time, the grand-son or grand-daughter, by succeeding to his place, should by such a quasi-birth, annul the testament. This case has been provided for by the *Lex Julia Velleia*, wherein is given a form of disinherison, similar to that for the disinherison of posthumous children.

Section III.—By the Civil Law, it is not necessary in a testament either to institute or disinherit children who have been emancipated; because, being no longer in the father's family, they are no longer proper heirs. But the Prætor ordains, that all children, of either sex, if not instituted heirs, shall be disinherited; the males by name, and the females under the general term *cæteri,*—" the rest". For, if children have been neither instituted heirs, nor expressly disinherited, the Prætor admits them to possession of the property, in opposition even to the provisions of the testament.

Section IV.—Adopted children, so long as they are under the power of their adoptive father, have the same legal rights as they who are born in lawful wedlock; they, therefore, must be instituted heirs, or disinherited, in accordance with the rules laid down in regard to natural children. But neither by Civil Law, nor Prætorian edict, are children who are emancipated by an adoptive father, numbered as of his natural children. Whence it comes, that children while living in their adoptive family, are, so far as regards their natural parents, deemed aliens, whom parents are not compelled either to institute as heirs, or to disinherit; but, when emancipated by their adoptive father, they are then in that position wherein they would have been, if emancipated by their natural father.

Section V.—Such were the rules which the ancient jurists introduced. But thinking that no reasonable distinction can, in this respect, be made between the sexes, since each has its share in the propagation of the species, and because, by the ancient Law of the Twelve Tables, all children alike were called to the succession in case of intestacy, a law which the Prætors seem to have had regard to, we have made the law plain, and similar in regard both to sons and daughters, and to all the other descendants in the male line, whether actually born, or posthumous; thus all children, whether proper heirs, or emancipated, must either be instituted as heirs, or be disinherited by name; and their omission shall have the same effect in annulling the testaments of the parents, and in taking the inheritance away from the instituted heirs, as would the omission of proper heirs, or emancipated children, whether actually born, or conceived and born afterwards. With reference to adopted children, we have laid down a certain distinction between them, which is explained in our Constitution on Adoptions.

Section VI.—If, however, a soldier, on actual service, make a testament, and omit to disinherit by name, his children, born or posthumous, but pass them by in silence, and that not from ignorance that he has such children, it is provided by the Imperial Constitutions that his silence shall be equivalent to a disinherison by name.

Section VII.—Neither a mother, nor a maternal grand-father is compelled either to institute their children heirs, but may pass them by in silence: for the silence of a mother, a maternal grand-father, and of all other ascendants on the mother's side, is equivalent to express disinherison by the father. For that a mother should be obliged to disinherit her children if she does not institute them her heirs, or a maternal grand-father to disinherit his grand-children by a daughter, is required neither by the Civil Law, nor by the Prætorian edict which gives possession of goods, in contravention of a testament, to those children who have been passed over in silence. But children are, in this case, provided with another remedy against the testament, which shall be set forth hereafter.

TITLE 14.

OF THE INSTITUTION OF HEIRS.

A MAN may institute as his heirs as well slaves as freemen; and such slaves may belong to another as well as to himself. Still, according to the general opinion, no master was formerly able to institute his own slaves, unless he also gave them their liberty; but, at present, by virtue of our Constitution, a master may institute his slave as heir, without any express emancipation of him. This rule we have introduced not from any love of innovation, but because it seemed more equitable; and Paulus, in his commentaries on Massurius, Sabinus and Plautius, mentions that such also was the opinion of Atilicinus. Also by the expression " our slave," is meant even one in whom the testator had the bare ownership while another had the usufruct. One case, however, there is, in which the institution of a slave by his mistress is void, although his liberty be expressly granted; it is that provided for by a Constitution of the Emperors Severus and Antoninus, in the following words:—" Reason ordains that a slave, accused of adultery with his mistress, shall not be enfranchised by that mistress, who is so alleged to have been the sharer in his guilt; not, at least, before sentence has been pronounced." It, therefore, follows that the institution as heir of such a slave by his mistress, is null and void. Also, the expression "slave, of another," is used to denote a slave of whom the testator had the usufruct, though not the property.

Section I.—When a slave has been instituted heir by his master, and continues still a slave; at his master's death, by virtue of the testament, he obtains his freedom, and becomes the necessary heir; if, however, such slave have been manumitted in his master's lifetime, he may use his pleasure in accepting or refusing the inheritance; for he does not become a necessary heir, as he does not by his master's testament get both freedom, and the inheritance. But, if such slave have been aliened, he must enter upon the inheritance at the bidding of his new master, who thus, by means of his slave, becomes the heir of the testator. For a slave who has been aliened, cannot, by virtue of the testament of the master who aliened him, obtain either liberty, or an inheritance to his own use, even though freedom were expressly given by such testament; because the master who aliened him, has shown that he has, thereby, given up all intention of giving him his liberty. The slave, also, of another, when appointed heir, if he remain in the same condition, must enter upon the inheritance at his master's bidding; and if such slave be aliened, either, in the lifetime of the testator, or after his death, and before he has actually entered upon the inheritance, he must then enter upon it at the bidding of his new master. But, if such slave have received manumission, either during the testator's lifetime, or after his death, and before he has entered upon the inheritance, he is at liberty to use his pleasure in its acceptance or refusal.

Section II.—The slave of another may be legally instituted heir after the death of his master; for the slaves of an inheritance not entered upon, are capable of taking by testament; and this, because an inheritance not entered upon, represents the person of the deceased, and not that of the future heir. Thus the slave even of a child in the womb, may be instituted heir.

Section III.—When a slave, the property of several masters, all capable of taking by testament, is instituted heir by a stranger, such slave acquires for each master at whose command he took it, a share of the inheritance, corresponding to their several interests in him.

Section IV.—A testator may institute one heir, or several; the number being restricted by his wishes only.

Section V.—An inheritance is generally considered as divided into twelve parts, called *unciæ*, or ounces; the whole, which comprehends, and is composed of these fractional parts, is called an *as*, or pound. Each of these parts, from the *uncia*, or single fraction, up to the *as*, or full unit, has its peculiar name; *e. g.*

Uncia,	=	$\frac{1}{12}$	= one ounce.
Sextans,	=	$\frac{1}{6}$	= two ounces.
Quadrans,	=	$\frac{1}{4}$	= three ounces.
Triens,	=	$\frac{1}{3}$	= four ounces.
Quincunx,			= five ounces.
Semis,	=	$\frac{1}{2}$	= six ounces.
Septunx,			= seven ounces.
Bes (bistriens,)	=	$\frac{2}{3}$	= eight ounces.
Dodrans,	=	$\frac{3}{4}$	= nine ounces.
Dextans,			= ten ounces.
Deunx,			= eleven ounces.
As,	=	1	= twelve ounces.

It is not, however, essential that this *as*, or total, should be always divided into twelve parts; for the *as*, may consist of as many of these divisions as the testator wishes. If, for example, a testator institute but one heir, and style his inheritance *semis*, or of six parts; these six parts will still make up the whole *as*; and this, because no one can die in part testate, and in part intestate, unless it be a soldier, in the consideration of whose testament intention only is looked to. So, on the contrary, a testator may divide the *as*, or total of his estate, into as great a number of parts as he will.

Section VI.—If a testator have instituted several heirs, it is essential that he make a division of his effects, specifying what shares he intends for each, provided he does not intend that all the heirs should take equal shares. It is, however, clear, that if no special division be made, all the heirs will take equally. Also, if the shares of some be expressly stated, but another, who is nominated heir, has no portion assigned to him, he will take that fractional part which may be lacking to complete the *as*. Also, if several nominated heirs have no share allotted them, they will take, and share among them, such remaining fraction as may exist as aforesaid. If, however, the whole *as* be given among certain of the nominated heirs, and there be no fraction left for such as have no shares specified, then shall such be entitled to one moiety of the whole estate, while they whose shares are specified, shall take only the remaining moiety. And if an heir, whose share under a will is not specified, be nominated in the testament in the first place, or the middle, or the last; that place is wholly immaterial, such part as is not specifically bequeathed in the testament is invariably looked upon as his.

Section VII.—Let us now inquire what the law would direct in the event of a part of an inheritance remaining unbequeathed, while each of the instituted heirs has got his share assigned him; as, for instance, if three heirs were instituted, and a fourth given to each. It is clear that here, the undisposed part would vest in each of the three, in proportion to the share bequeathed him, and it would be exactly as if each had been nominated heir of a third. So, on the other hand, if several heirs be instituted, and the shares specifically bequeathed to each exceed the *as*, each heir must submit to a proportionate reduction; as, for example, if four heirs be instituted, and to each a third bequeathed, it will in reality be the same, as if each of the heirs had been instituted to a fourth only.

Section VIII.—Again, if more ounces, or parts of an estate, than twelve have been bequeathed, he who is instituted heir, but has no express share, shall be entitled to such amount as shall be wanting to make up the second *as*,—or, *dupondius* —of twenty-four parts. So, if more than twenty-four parts be specified, he will be entitled to the amount necessary to make up the third *as*—or, *tripondius*—of thirty-six parts. But all these parts, however numerous, are afterwards reduced to the ordinary *as*, with its regular division, twelve ounces.

Section IX.—The institution of an heir may be absolute, or conditional; but it cannot be *from*, or *to* a fixed time; as, for instance, "five years after the date of my death," or "from the calends of such," or, "to the calends of such a month." The time thus added is looked upon as surplusage, and the institution operates as though unconditional.

Section X.—An impossible condition in the institution of heirs, the disposition of legacies, the creation of trusts, and the conferring of liberty, is considered as if not inserted at all.

Section XI.—When several conditions are attached to the institution, and placed conjunctively; as, for example, "if this be done, *and* also that *and* that": in such case, all the conditions must be complied with. But if they are placed disjunctively; as, "if this *or* that be done"; it will be, sufficient to obey any or either.

Section XII.—A testator may institute as his heirs, persons whom he has never seen; as, for instance, his brother's sons, born in a foreign land, and perfectly unknown to him; for such want of knowledge on his part will not serve to make the institution null.

TITLE 15.

OF VULGAR SUBSTITUTION.

A MAN may, by testament, appoint several degrees of heirs; as, for instance, " if Titius will not be my heir, let Mævius be so"; and he may proceed in such substitutions so long as he thinks fit; nay, in the last place, he may, in default of others, institute a slave as necessary heir.

Section I.—A testator may substitute many in the place of one; or one in the place of many; or one in the place of each of the instituted heirs; or, lastly, he may, of the instituted heirs, substitute each reciprocally to the other.

Section II.—A testator, who has instituted several heirs with unequal portions, and who substitutes them reciprocally, each for other, but makes no mention of the shares they are to take in the substitution, is considered to have given implicitly by substitution, the same shares which he did give in the institution; and such was held by the Emperor Antoninus in his Rescript.

Section III.—If to an instituted heir, a co-heir be substituted, and again a third person substituted to that co-heir, the Emperors Severus and Antoninus have by Rescript ordained, that such substituted heir shall be admitted to the portions of both co-heirs, without distinction.

Section IV.—If a testator institute as his heir, the slave of another man, being under the belief that such slave was enfranchised; and if, in case such slave do not take the inheritance, he substitute Mævius in his room; then, if the slave, at his master's bidding, were to enter upon the inheritance,

Mævius, the substitute, would be admitted to a moiety. For the words " if he do not become my heir," in the case of one whom a testator knew to be under the power of another, are held to mean, " if he will neither become my heir himself, nor cause another to be my heir"; but in the case of one whom the testator believed to be a free-man, the words mean " if my heir will neither acquire the inheritance for himself nor for him to whose power he may afterwards become subject." Such was the decision of the Emperor Tiberius, in the case of his own slave Parthenius.

TITLE 16.

OF PUPILLARY SUBSTITUTION.

A TESTATOR can substitute an heir in place of his children, under puberty, and in his power, not only in the manner before-mentioned, namely, by appointing some other to be his heir, if his own children will not be so; but further, if his children do become his heirs, yet die within years of puberty, he may substitute another heir; as though he were to say;—
" Let Titius, my son, be my heir; but if he should not become my heir, or becoming so, should die before he ceases to be under tutelage, (*i. e.* within years of puberty), then let Seius be my heir." Here, if the son do not become his father's heir, the substitute becomes heir to the father; if, however, the son do enter upon the inheritance, but die within years of puberty, then the substitute is heir to the son. For usage has ordained, that parents may make testaments

for their children, when such children are not of age sufficient to make them for themselves.

Section I.—Influenced by like reasons, we have inserted into our code a Constitution, which provides, that such as have children, grand-children or great-grand-children, of unsound mind of whatever sex or rank, may make a substitution of certain persons as heirs to such children, after the example of a pupillary substitution, even though they have arrived at years of puberty. But if they should recover, such substitution shall be void, after the analogy of pupillary institution, which has no force when the minor comes to puberty.

Section II.—In a pupillary substitution, then, made in the manner above-mentioned, there are, so to say, two testaments, the one of the father, the other of the son; as though the son had instituted an heir for himself; or, at least, there is one testament referring to two subjects, to wit, two inheritances.

Section III.—If, however, a testator be apprehensive lest, after his death, his son, being yet a minor, should be exposed to the risk of foul play, from having another heir openly given as his substitute; such testator should openly make a vulgar substitution, and insert that in the first portion of his testament; but, as for the substitution, whereby a substituted heir is named, if his son, being an heir, should die within years of puberty, he ought to write it at the latter part of the testament, and this part should be separately bound and sealed; it were well also to insert a clause in the first part of the testament, with an admonition that the latter part should not be unsealed so long as his son was yet alive, and under years of puberty. It is, however, undoubtedly true, that the substitution of an heir to a son within years of puberty, is not the less valid because written on the same tablet of the testament in which he is instituted heir; although, however, it may be fraught with danger to the minor.

Section IV.—Parents may not only so grant a substitute to their children, under years of puberty, as that even though such children enter upon the inheritance, but die within years of puberty, the heir shall be he whom the testators will; but they can make a like substitution in regard to disinherited children. In such case, therefore, whatever a disinherited child, within years of puberty, may have acquired by inheritance, by legacies, or by the gifts of friends and relatives, the whole will be the property of the substituted heir. Whatsoever we have said of the substitution of minors, whether they be instituted heirs or disinherited children, is to be understood also as including posthumous children.

Section V.—No one, however, can make a testament for his children, unless he make one for himself also; for the testament of a child within puberty, is part and parcel of the parent's testament; insomuch that, if the father's testament be invalid, that also of the son will be of no avail.

Section VI.—A pupillary substitution may be made either to each one of a testator's children, or to him only who last dies, within the age of puberty. To each, if the parent be minded that none of them die intestate; to the last who dies within puberty, if he wish that the strict order of legitimate succession be maintained among them.

Section VII.—A substitution may be made to a child under puberty, either by name, as thus: "If my son become my heir, and die a minor, let Titius be heir": or generally, as thus: "Whoever may be my heir, let him be substitute to my son, if he die within puberty." By these latter general words all those are called to the inheritance by substitution, on the son's death, as aforesaid, who having been instituted heir, have entered upon the father's inheritance; and each is entitled to a share in the son's inheritance, proportionate to that assigned him in the father's.

Section VIII.—A pupillary substitution may be made to males up to fourteen; and to females up to twelve years of age. But when they exceed either of these ages, the substitution becomes extinct.

Section IX.—A testator cannot substitute to a stranger, or son of ripe years, whom he has instituted; by declaring that if such stranger, or son, enter upon the inheritance, and then die within a certain time, another shall be his heir. The sole permission is, for the testator to bind the person instituted by a *fidei-commissum*—*i. e.* bequest in trust,—to give up all, or a part, to some third person: of the law on this point, however, we will treat in the proper place.

TITLE 17.

OF THE AVOIDANCE OF TESTAMENTS.

A Testament, legally made, continues valid, until it be either revoked, or annulled.

Section I.—A testament is said to be revoked when the effect of the instrument is destroyed, while the testator still retains his social standing. For, if a man, after making his testament, were to arrogate an independent person, by licence from the Emperor, or, in presence of the Prætor, and in conformity with our Constitution, were to adopt a child under the power of its natural parent, then, by such quasi-birth of a proper heir, there would be a revocation of his testament.

Section II.—A former testament is revoked by a subsequent one, made in conformity with the law's directions; nor is it material whether, under the new testament, any one becomes heir or not; the only point to be looked to is this, whether the nominated heir might have entered upon the inheritance. If, therefore, an heir instituted under the new testament, refuse to enter upon the inheritance; or die, whether during the testator's lifetime, or after his death and before he himself could enter upon the inheritance; or if there be a failure of the condition, under which he was instituted heir; then, in any of these cases, the testator is held to be intestate. Because the first testament would be invalid, as being revoked by the second; while the second is, for lack of an heir, of just as small avail.

Section III.—If a man who has made already a legally perfect testament, make afterwards another just as legally perfect, and in this latter institute an heir for certain particular things only, the Emperors Severus and Antoninus have, by their Rescript, decided that the first testament is thereby revoked. We have commanded the actual words of this Constitution to be here inserted; the rather as it contains also another provision :—

" The Emperors Severus and Antoninus to Cocceius Campa-
" nus. We ordain, that a second testament, although the heir
" named in it is not universal, but appointed for particular things
" alone, shall be as good in law as if such particular things
" had not been specified; but the heir so instituted must,
" beyond all doubt, content himself either with the particular
" things so given him, or with the fourth part permitted by
" the *Lex Falcidia;* and must be compelled to restore the
" remainder of the inheritance to the heirs named in the first
" testament; and this, by reason of those words in the second
" instrument, which declare expressly that the first shall be
" still held binding." Thus, then, a testament may be said to be broken or revoked.

Section IV.—Testaments, legally made, become also ineffectual in another way; to wit, if the testator suffer diminution, *i. e.*, loss of social position. In our First Book we have set forth the circumstances under which this may happen.

Section V.—Testaments made void by diminution are technically called "*irrita*"—*i. e.*, "ineffectual;" although, strictly speaking, those which are broken or revoked, or which were invalid from the very first, are also in fact ineffectual. Thus, also, we may speak of those testaments as revoked, which have become ineffectual by diminution. Still, as it is evidently more convenient to distinguish by different names, effects produced by different causes; we speak of testaments irregularly made, as "*null*"; of testaments regularly made, if voided by the testator's revocatory act, as "*broken*" or "*revoked*"; and of the like legal testaments voided by the testator's diminution, as "*ineffectual*".

Section VI.—Testaments, however, which at first were legally made, and afterwards become ineffectual by diminution, are not absolutely void. For if they have been attested by the seals of seven witnesses, the written heir can obtain possession of the goods, by virtue of the testament, provided it appear that the deceased was a Roman citizen, and not under power at the time of death. But, if a testament become ineffectual, because the testator has lost the rights of citizenship, or his liberty, or has given himself in adoption and was at the time of death, still under the power of his adoptive father, then the written heir cannot sue for possession of the goods, by virtue of the testament.

Section VII.—A testament cannot be rendered invalid, by the mere after-wish of the testator that it should be invalid; so that, if a man, after making one testament, should begin another, but, whether prevented by death, or change of mind, should not perfect it, it is decided in a senatorial address of the Emperor Pertinax, that the former testament shall not be revoked, unless the after one be regularly made and perfect: for an imperfect testament is null beyond all doubt.

Section VIII.—The Emperor Pertinax, in the same oration, declared, that, he would not accept the inheritance of any testator who, by reason of a lawsuit pending, made him, the Emperor, his heir; that, he would never establish a will, deficient in point of form, if, by reason of such deficiency, and to gloss it over, he himself were instituted heir; that, he would not suffer himself to be appointed heir, by word of mouth alone; and that, he would never reap an advantage by virtue of any document, unauthorized by the strict letter of the law. To like purport the Emperors Severus and Antoninus have published their Rescripts, over and over again: " For though," say they, " We be above the laws, still we do live in obedience to them."

TITLE 18.

OF UNNATURAL TESTAMENTS.

FORASMUCH as parents often disinherit children, or omit them from their testaments, without just cause, a law has been introduced, whereby children who complain that they have been unjustly disinherited, or unjustly omitted from the testaments of their parents, may bring an action to set aside such testaments as unnatural, and contrary to natural affection; and this, by a legal fiction, on the allegation that their parents, when they made them, were not of sane mind. By this, however, it is not meant to allege, that the testator was really of unsound mind, but merely that though he may have made his will in regular form, still it is at variance with that duty of natural affection, which every parent owes. Because, if the testator were actually insane at the time of making his testament, the document is clearly, on that ground, null.

Section I.—Not only have children the right to attack the testaments of their parents, as unnatural; but parents also are permitted to attack, on like grounds, those of their children. Also, the brothers and sisters of a testator are, by the Imperial Constitutions, preferred to persons of bad character, if such have been instituted heirs; still brothers and sisters are not therefore allowed to bring an action of this kind, against *any* heir who may be instituted. No collateral, beyond brothers and sisters, can (if opposed) bring an action to set aside a will as unnatural; or if they should, being unopposed, bring such an action, not they, but those nearest in succession upon an intestacy, will be the gainers.

Section II.—Natural children, as well as those adopted by ascendants, according to the distinction laid down in our Constitution, can only attack a testament as unnatural when they can obtain the goods of the deceased in no other way; for, such as are able to obtain the whole of the inheritance, or a part, by any other means, are not at liberty to impugn the testament, by action, as unnatural. Posthumous children, also, if unable to obtain their inheritance by any other method, may pursue this remedy.

Section III.—What has now been said, is to be understood to hold in cases only where nothing has, by the testator's will, been left to those who complain; and this is a provision which we have introduced, by our Constitution, out of respect to the natural right of parents. If, however, the very smallest portion of the inheritance, or any single thing, have been bequeathed to them, they are barred from complaint against the testator's will as unnatural; but, if near enough in blood, they are entitled to sue for such amount as is wanting to raise the sum bequeathed them to that fourth part, or legitimate portion, which they would have had, in case of the intestacy of the deceased; and they are entitled to this, even though the testator did not add to his gift any special direction, that this their fourth, legitimate portion, should be made up to them in accordance with the estimate of some approved arbitrator.

Section IV.—If a tutor, in the name of the pupil under his charge, accept a legacy given in the testament of the tutor's own father, while to such tutor nothing has, in that testament, been left; he may, notwithstanding, in his own name, attack his father's testament as unnatural.

Section V.—So, on the contrary, if a tutor, in the name of his pupil to whom nothing has been left, attack,* and that without success, the testament of his pupil's father as unnatural, such tutor does not forfeit any thing that may have been left to him personally in the same testament.

Section VI.—To bar a person, near enough in blood, from bringing this complaint of a will being unnatural, he must have already received his fourth, or legitimate portion; whether as heir, or by legacy, or by trust for his use, or by gift in anticipation of death, or by gift in the testator's life-time (in those cases set forth in our Constitution), or by any other of the modes, which are stated in our Constitutions. What we have said of this fourth, or legitimate portion, must be taken in the sense following; namely, that if there be one person, or if there be several, who bring their action to set aside a testament as unnatural, one-fourth only is to be awarded; and such one-fourth is to be divided in due proportion among them all; that is, each will receive the fourth of his proper share.

TITLE 19.

OF THE SEVERAL KINDS OF HEIRS.

Heirs are said be of three kinds—(1) necessary; (2) under power of the testator, and also necessary; (3) extraneous, not in the power of the testator, and not necessary, but voluntary.

Section I.—A "necessary" heir is a slave who is instituted heir; and he is so called because, whether he will or no, at the death of the testator he is straightway free, and compelled to enter upon the inheritance. Persons, therefore, who have doubt as to their own solvency, are wont to institute a slave, as heir in the first, second, or some other place; so that, if they do not leave assets sufficient to satisfy their debts, the goods seized, sold, or shared among the creditors, may seem rather those of the heir than of the testator. A slave, however, to compensate for this disgrace, enjoys the privilege of having reserved to him, such things as he may have acquired after the death of the testator; for even though the effects of the deceased are insufficient to satisfy the creditors, still the property so acquired, from other sources, by the slave, is not liable to be sold.

Section II.—Heirs "under power of the testator, and also necessary," or "family heirs", are sons, daughters, grand-sons grand-daughters by a son, or other descendants in the right line; provided they were actually under power of the testator at the time of his death. But in order to constitute grand-children heirs of this sort, it is not enough that they should be under their grand-father's power at the time of his decease; it is further requisite, that their father should have ceased to be a proper or family heir in the life-time of his father, having been freed, by death, or otherwise, from the paternal authority; because, in such case, the grand-son or grand-daughter succeeds in the place of their father. Heirs of this kind get their name (*sui* — *i. e.*, belonging to) because they " belong to" the family, and even during their father's life-time are considered, in some sort, owners of the inheritance. Wherefore, if a man die intestate, his children are preferred to all others in the succession. They are also called " necessary" heirs, because, whether they will it or will it not, whether by a testament, or by reason of an intestacy, they must become heirs. Still, if the children desire it, the Prætor allows them to abstain from the inheritance; that the goods, if taken in execution by the creditors, may be the property rather of their parents, than of themselves.

Section III.—" Extraneous" heirs, are all those who are not under power of the testator; thus, even those of our children, who are not under our power, are, if we institute them in our testament, " extraneous" heirs. Similarly, children who are instituted heirs by their mother are to be reported extraneous; because women have not their children under their power. A slave, also, whom his master has instituted by testament, and afterwards manumitted, is reckoned as of those heirs who are extraneous.

Section IV.—With regard to extraneous heirs, it is requisite that they have *testamenti factio*,—*i. e.*, power to make, take by, or witness a testament; — and this whether they themselves, or whether those under their power, are instituted heirs. Now this capability is needed at two several times; at the making of the testament, that the institution may be valid; and at the testator's death, that the institution may operate. Further, the heir should have this capability at the time of entering upon the inheritance; and this, whether his institution be simple or conditional; for his right as heir, and capacity to take, is principally examined at the time of his acquiring the possession.

But in the time which intervenes between the making of the testament and the death of the testator, or the satisfaction of the condition of the institution, a charge of social standing will not prejudice the heir; because, as we have said, the times important to be regarded, are the three which we have named. But not only is a man said to have the *testamenti factio*, or capability aforesaid, who can make a testament, but he also has it who, by virtue of another's testament, can either take for his own benefit, or acquire for that of another, even though he cannot himself make a testament; therefore mad people, and dumb, posthumous children, infants, sons under power, and slaves belonging to another, may be said to possess this capability. For although such persons are incapable of making a testament, still they can, by testament, acquire either for themselves or others.

Section V.—Extraneous heirs have the power to deliberate whether they will, or will not, enter upon an inheritance. But if a proper, or family heir, who has the liberty of abstaining, should intermeddle with the property of the inheritance, or an extraneous heir, who is permitted to deliberate, should once enter upon the inheritance, neither will afterwards be able to renounce it; unless indeed he were under the age of twenty-five years; for the Prætor, who in all other cases relieves minors who have been deceived, does so also when they have rashly entered upon an injurious inheritance.

Section VI.—Here, too, it may be noted that the Emperor Hadrian, once gave permission to a person even of full years, to relinquish an inheritance, when it proved to be hampered with a heavy debt, the existence of which had been concealed at the time when he entered upon the inheritance. This, however, was accorded by the Emperor as a special favour; the Emperor Gordian, however, afterwards granted it as a settled privilege, but to soldiers only. Our kindly feeling, however, has prompted us to make the benefit common to all our subjects, and to promulgate a Constitution as equitable as illustrious, by virtue of which, heirs who will strictly observe its conditions, may enter upon their inheritance and be held liable only so far as the value of the estate extends; so that now they are no longer obliged to have recourse to deliberation; unless, by omitting to observe our Constitution, they choose rather to deliberate, and expose themselves to the liabilities which attend the acceptance of an inheritance according to the ancient rule.

Section VII.—An extraneous heir, instituted by testament, or called by law to a succession in case of intestacy, may actually become heir, either by doing some act as such, or by a bare expression of his wish to accept the inheritance. Now a man is held to act as heir who treats the goods of the inheritance as his own, either by selling any portion of it, by tilling the land, by letting it, or by any actual declaration, whether by deed or word, of his will to enter upon the inheritance; provided always, he be well assured that the person, over whose property he acts the heir, is really dead, either testate or intestate, and that he is himself the heir. For to act as heir, is to act as proprietor; and, in former days, men used the word heir, when they meant to denote the proprietor. Again, as the extraneous heir is the creature of mere intention; so by a contrary intention, he is at once barred from the inheritance. There is nothing to hinder a person deaf and dumb, whether so born, or who afterwards becomes so, from acting as heir, and acquiring the inheritance, provided only he understand the effect of his actions.

TITLE 20.

OF LEGACIES.

Let us now proceed to treat of legacies. This branch of the law may, indeed, not seem to fall within the limits of our present subject, to wit, the inquiry as to the legal methods by which things may be acquired, not singly, but universally, and in the gross: since, however, we have just been treating of testaments, and those who take under testaments, it seems not unreasonable that, in the next place, we go on to treat of legacies.

Section I.—A legacy, then, is a species of donation, bequeathed by a deceased person, and to be delivered to the legatee by the heir.

Section II.—Anciently there were four kinds of legacies in use, namely; (1) *per vindicationem,*—*i. e.*, by direct bequest, to be enforced by a *vindication*, or real action: (2) *per damnationem,*—*i. e.*, by obligation on the heir: (3) *sinendi modo,*—*i. e.*, by injunction on the heir to permit: (4) *per præceptionem,*—*i. e.*, by authority to the legatee to pre-occupy, or take before partition of the property.

To each of these a certain form of words was assigned by which one was distinguished from another. But these ordained forms have been wholly abolished by Imperial Constitutions. We also, by a Constitution composed with great care and study, from an earnest desire to give avail to the wishes of deceased persons, and with a regard to their intentions rather than to their words, have enacted that, henceforth, the nature of all legacies be one and the same; and, further, that legatees, by what words soever constituted, may be entitled to sue for that which is left them, not only by personal but also by real, or by hypothecary actions. The well-digested matter of the Constitution may, however, best be seen by an actual perusal of its provisions.

Section III.—But, we have not deemed it expedient that our reforms should be limited by the terms of this Constitution; for when we observed that the ancients bound legacies by the strictest rules, but accorded a far greater latitude to gifts in trust, as springing more directly from the wishes of the deceased, we deemed it essential that all legacies should be placed on the same footing with gifts in trust, and that no practical difference should subsist between them. That, therefore, which is deficient in the nature of the legacies shall be supplied from the nature of trusts; and that wherein legacies may be more amply furnished, shall be deemed an addition to the nature of trusts. But not by an explanation of these two subjects jointly, to raise a difficulty in the minds of the young, at their first entrance upon the study of the law, we have deemed it worth while to treat separately, first of legacies, and afterwards of trusts, that, when the nature of each is known, the student so grounded may more easily understand the joint relations and intermixture.

Section IV.—Not only the property of the testator, or of the heir, but that also of a third party may be bequeathed as a legacy; and the heir is, in such case, bound to purchase that property and deliver it to the legatee; or, if he be unable to purchase it, he must pay an equivalent in lieu of the specific thing. If, however, the thing bequeathed be such as, in its nature, cannot be bought or sold, then no equivalent is due; as though a man were to bequeath the *Campus Martius*, the imperial palaces, the temples, or any of these things set apart for public purposes, for such a legacy is absolutely null. But our assertion, that the property of a third party may be legally bequeathed, must be understood as confined to the case, where the deceased was well aware that what he bequeathed did belong to another, and does not apply to the case where he was ignorant that it was another's. The reason of this distinction being, that if he had known that what he bequeathed was the property of another, he would probably have made no such bequest; and this is so decided by a Rescript of the Emperor Antoninus. It is, however, incumbent upon him who claims, to wit, the legatee, to prove that the deceased well knew that what he bequeathed belonged to a third party; and not upon the heir to prove him to have been ignorant of that fact. And this is conformably to the general rule that the burthen of proof always lies upon him who claims.

Section V.—Also, if a man bequeath a thing which he has given in pledge to a creditor, the heir is found to redeem it. Still in this case, as in the former one of the property of a third party, the heir is not bound to redeem, unless the deceased well knew that the thing was pledged: and this the Emperors Severus and Antoninus have, by their Rescript, settled. If, however, the deceased wished that the legatee should himself redeem the thing, and have expressly said so, the burthen of redemption lies no longer on the heir.

Section VI.—If a thing belonging to a third party be given as legacy, and if the legatee become its proprietor while the testator is still alive, it is expedient to know how it became the property of the legatee: for if he acquired his title by purchase, he may recover the value, by an action on the testament; but, if he acquired it by a lucrative title, as by donation or the like, he has no ground of action; for it is a received maxim, that two lucrative titles to the same thing can never concur in the same person. Similarly, if one and the same thing be, by two testaments, given to the same person, it is of the greatest importance to know whether the legatee who sues under one testament, has, by virtue of the other, obtained the specific thing, or the value of it. For if he be already in possession of the thing itself, he has no ground of action, because he has acquired it by a lucrative title; if, however, he have received the value only, he may bring his action for the thing.

Section VII.—A thing which has no present existence, but which one day will have, may be legally bequeathed; as, for instance, the fruits which shall grow on such a farm, or the child which shall be born of a particular slave.

Section VIII.—If the same specific legacy be given to two persons, either conjointly or disjunctively, and if both be willing to accept the legacy, it is shared between them; if, however, one of them fail to take, either by refusing to accept it, or by dying in the testator's life-time, or otherwise, the whole vests in his co-legatee. A legacy is given conjointly when thus worded:—" I give and bequeath my slave Stichus to Titius and Seius"; and disjunctively as thus;—" I give and bequeath my slave Stichus to Titius; I give and bequeath my slave Stichus to Seius." And even though the testator say that he gives *the same* slave, Stichus, the legacy will still be held to be disjunctive.

Section IX.—If land, the property of a third party, be left by testament, and the legatee have purchased the bare ownership, while the usufruct accrues to him (by a lucrative title); if, afterwards, he sue under the testament, Julian affirms, that his claim to the land is sound and good; because, in such claim, the usufruct is regarded merely as a servitude. In this case, the duty of the judge is, to order the value of the land, less the usufruct, to be paid over to the legatee.

Section X.—If a testator give as legacy, a thing which already belongs to the legatee, such legacy is null; for that which is already the property of the legatee cannot become more so. And although the legatee may (after the bequest) have aliened the thing bequeathed, still he has no legal claim either to the specific thing, or to its value.

Section XI.—If a testator give, as a legacy, that which is his own, as though it were the property of another, the legacy is valid; for the real state of a case outweighs any opinion of it. And even though the testator believe that what he gives is already the property of the legatee, yet, if it do not, the legacy is valid, because the wishes of the deceased may thus be carried out.

Section XII.—If a testator give as a legacy, a thing which does belong to him, but which he afterwards alienates, Celsus holds, that the legacy is still due to the legatee, if the testator did not sell with intent to revoke the legacy: the Emperors Severus and Antoninus held the same in their Rescript. The same Emperors, also, have ordained by Rescript, that a man who, after making his testament, has pledged immoveables therein given as a legacy, is not to be held to have revoked the legacy; and that the legatee may bring his action against the heir, and compel him to redeem the property. Also, if a testator have alienated a portion of the thing given as a legacy, the legatee is, beyond all doubt, entitled to that which is unalienated; and the alienated portion is also due to him, if it can be proved that the alienation was not made by the testator with the design to revoke the legacy.

Section XIII.—If a testator give, as a legacy, a discharge to his debtor, the legacy is valid; and the heir can bring no suit to recover the debt against the debtor, his heir, or any one who represents that heir. But, on the other hand, the heir of the testator may be legally summoned by the debtor, and compelled to grant him his discharge. A testator may also command his heir not to sue a debtor within a time fixed.

Section XIV.—On the other hand, if a debtor give as a legacy to a creditor the money which he owes him, the legacy is null, if its amount be not greater than that of the debt; and this, because the creditor gains nothing by his legacy. If, however, a debtor give absolutely as a legacy to his creditor, an amount which was due only on a certain day, or on the accomplishment of a certain condition, such legacy is valid, because it becomes due immediately, and before the debt. Papinian, indeed, holds that, even though the day arrive, or the condition be fulfilled in the life-time of the testator, the legacy would still be valid, because it once was good; and this is true. For we coincide not in the opinion of those who imagine that a legacy once good, can become invalid, because it has been brought, by circumstances, to a condition which, if originally existing, would have rendered it ineffectual.

Section XV.—If a man retnrn to his wife, by legacy, her marriage portion, the legacy is good, because the legacy is of more advantage to her, than the action which she might bring for the recovery of her portion. If, however, a husband, give as a legacy to his wife her marriage portion, while he has never actually received it, the Emperors Severus and Antoninus have decided by a Rescript, that if the bequest be of the portion only, without specifying any actual amount, the legacy is void; if, however, any certain sum or thing, of the actual amount stated in the dowry deed, be specified as to be paid by way of legacy, before it could be recovered, in the shape of dowry, the legacy is effectual.

Section XVI.—If a thing left as a legacy be destroyed, without the act of the heir, the loss falls upon the legatee. Also, if the slave of another man, given as a legacy, should be enfranchised, without the privity of the heir, the heir is not liable. But, if a testator leave, as a legacy, the slave of his heir, and if the heir should afterwards enfranchise that slave, he is, says Julian, liable: nor is it material whether he knew or did not know, that the slave had been left away from him. And, even, if he have given the slave to some other, and that other have enfranchised him, still the heir is liable, even though he were wholly ignorant of the bequest.

Section XVII.—If a testator give, by legacy, his female slaves and their issue; then, even though the mothers die, the issue passes to the legatee. So also if ordinary, or domestic slaves, are bequeathed together with the vicarial slaves, who are their attendants, even though the ordinary slaves should die, the vicarial slaves will still pass to the legatee. If, however, a slave be bequeathed with his *peculium*—or perquisites,—on his death, manumission, or alienation, the legacy of the *peculium* becomes void. The like is the case of the legacy of a piece of land, with the implements of husbandry upon it; for, if the testator alien the land, the legacy of the instruments becomes extinct.

Section XVIII.—If a flock be given as a legacy, and be afterwards brought down to a single sheep, that sheep may be claimed by the legatee; also, if a flock be given as a legacy, Julian holds, that such sheep as are added to it after the making of the testament, will pass to the legatee. Because, a flock is but one body, consisting of several members; as a house is considered as one body, composed of several stones wrought together.

Section XIX.—Also, when a building is given as a legacy, the marble or pillars which may be added after making of the testament must, as we declare, pass under the general legacy.

Section XX.—If the *peculium* —" perquisites"—of a slave be subject of a legacy, there is no doubt but that if it be increased, or lessened, in the life of the testator, the gain or loss accrues to the legatee. And if the *peculium* of a slave be left to himself, together with his liberty, whatever he may acquire after the death of his master, and before the inheritance has been entered upon, will, in the opinion of Julian, pass to him as legatee; for such a legacy is not vested in the legatee, until the inheritance be entered upon. But, if this *peculium* have been left to a stranger, or extraneous heir, then any increase acquired within the time aforesaid will not pass by the legacy, unless such increase has been made by means of something appertaining to the *peculium*. The *peculium* of a slave enfranchised by testament, does not belong to him, unless expressly so stated; although, if a master in his life-time manumit his slave, the *peculium* will pass as of course, unless the master expressly forbid it; and to this effect wrote the Emperors Severus and Antoninus, in their Rescript. The same Emperors, by Rescript, have decreed, that when his *peculium* is given by legacy to a slave, it does not seem to be intended that he should claim such monies as he has expended for his master's purposes. The same Emperors have decided, that a slave appears to be entitled to his *peculium*, when freedom is left him as a legacy, on the condition of his producing his accounts, and making up any deficiency in them, out of his *peculium*.

Section XXI.—Things incorporeal may be given as legacies as well as things corporeal. Thus a debt due to a testator, may be given by him as a legacy, so that the heir is bound to assign his right of action to the legatee; unless, indeed, the testator, when alive, exacted payment, for in such case the legacy is become void. A legacy such as the following would also be valid;—"let my heir be bound to re-build the house of Titius; or to free him from his debts."

Section XXII.—If either a slave, or any other thing, be bequeathed generally, that is, without specifying any particular slave, or other thing; the legatee has the choice, unless the testator has expressed a contrary intention.

Section XXIII.—The legacy of choice, is that where the testator bids the legatee choose any one from among his slaves, or any other specified class of things; a legacy of this kind was formerly held to imply the condition, that if the legatee did not make the choice during his life-time, he could not transmit the legacy to his heir. Our Constitution, however, has introduced a reform in this matter, and now the heir of the legatee has the right of even choice, though the legatee in his life-time neglected to use it. And after a still closer investigation of the subject we have further, in the same Constitution, added that, if there be several legatees to whom the right of choice is given, and they cannot agree in their selection, or if there be several heirs of one such legatee,—who are also unable to agree, one desiring to select one thing, and one another, then lest the legacy should become invalid (as most of the ancient lawyers, contrary to all equity, held would be the case,) fortune must be the judge; the dispute must be decided by lot, so that he who has the lot, shall have the ruling voice in the selection.

Section XXIV.—A legacy can be given to those only who have the *testamenti factio*,—i. e., the capability to take by, make, or witness a testament.

Section XXV.—Formerly, neither legacies nor gifts in trust could be bequeathed to uncertain persons; and even a soldier was not permitted to leave anything to an uncertain person, as the Emperor Hadrian decided by Rescript. An "uncertain person", is reported to be one of whom the testator has but an ill-defined imagination, as though he were thus to express himself:—"To that person, be he who he may, who shall give his daughter in marriage to my son, let my heir deliver up such a piece of ground." A legacy, likewise, given to the persons first appointed consuls after making of the will, was held to be a legacy to uncertain persons; and there are divers other examples of the like kind. Liberty, also, could not be conferred upon an uncertain person; for it was necessary that every slave should be enfranchised by name. But, if the legacy were given with a certain amount of identification, that is, to a person uncertain, one of a number of persons certain, it was valid; for instance, if the expressions were as follow;—"To him, of my collateral relatives, who shall marry my daughter, let my heir give such a thing." If, however, a legacy or gift in trust to uncertain persons, had been paid by mistake, the Imperial Constitutions provided that no restitution could be claimed.

Section XXVI.—Formerly, also, a legacy could not be effectually given to a posthumous stranger: a posthumous stranger is one who, if he had been born during the life-time of the testator, would not have been numbered among his proper, or family heirs; therefore, a posthumous grand-son, by an emancipated son, was a posthumous stranger with regard to his grand-father.

Section XXVII.—But these points, also, have not been left without due reform; for in our codes has been inserted a Constitution, whereby we have remedied the law as to uncertain persons, not only as regards inheritances, but also as regards legacies and gifts in trust. The alterations will be more clearly seen by a perusal of the Constitution. Still, even by this our Constitution, the nomination of an uncertain tutor is not permitted, for it is incumbent upon every parent, by fixed and determinate appointment, to appoint a tutor for his offspring.

Section XXVIII.—A posthumous stranger could formerly, and may now, be instituted heir; unless he have been conceived by a woman who could not have been legally married to his father.

Section XXIX.—Although a testator have made a mistake in the *nomen, cognomen,* or *prænomen,*—*i. e.* in the clan,—family,—or personal—name,—of a legatee, still, if the identity be clearly ascertained, the legacy will be valid. The same latitude is observed in regard to heirs, and with great reason; for names are of use only to make out, and distinguish individuals; and if their identity can be made out, by any other mode, it matters not.

Section XXX.—A rule of law which comes very near to the foregoing is, that a legacy is not annulled by a false

description. For instance, if a legacy were to run thus:—
" I give and bequeath Stichus, my slave, who was born in my family"; in this case, although Stichus was not born in the family of the testator, but bought by him, still if there be a certainty as to the person meant, the legacy is good. So, in like manner, if the identification were,—" Stichus, my slave, whom I bought of Seius"; then, although he was really bought of some one else, the legacy would be valid, if no doubt existed as to the slave intended to be given.

Section XXXI.—Still less is a legacy rendered invalid, by the assignment of an untrue reason for making it; as if a testator were to say—" I give and bequeath my slave Stichus to Titius, because he took charge of my business during my absence; or, because I was acquitted upon a capital charge, thanks to his undertaking my defence"; though Titius had never taken charge of the business of the deceased, and though the testator had never been acquitted upon any capital charge, thanks to the defence of Titius, the legacy will be effectual. But if the cause alleged be put conditionally, the case is quite different, as thus,—" I give and bequeath to Titius such a piece of ground, if it is shall appear that he has taken charge of my business."

Section XXXII.—It has been a question whether a legacy can legally be given to the slave of an heir. It is, however, clear beyond all doubt that such a legacy is ineffectual; nor can it avail aught, that the slave was freed, during the testator's life-time, from the power of the heir: for a bequest which would have been null, if the testator had died immediately after he had made his testament, ought not to become valid, simply because he chanced to enjoy a longer life. A legacy may, however, be given under a condition to the slave of an instituted heir; and then, we have to inquire whether at the time when the condition is fulfilled, and the legacy becomes vested in the legatee, he has ceased to be under the power of the heir.

Section XXXIII.—On the contrary, it cannot be doubted but that, if a slave be appointed heir, an unconditional legacy may, by the same testament, be given to his master. For, even though the testator should die immediately after making his testament; yet, at that time, the right to the legacy is not immediately vested in the heir. For here a distinction is drawn between the inheritance and the legacy, and another master may, by means of this slave, become heir, if, before he have entered upon the inheritance at the bidding of his master, he be transferred into the power of a new master; or he may himself become the heir, by manumission; and, in both cases, the legacy is effectual. If, however, the slave remain in the same state, and enter upon the inheritance by order of the legatee, his master, the legacy becomes extinct.

Section XXXIV.—Formerly, a legacy given before the institution of an heir was void; because, a testament gets its whole force and efficacy from the institution of the heir; which, therefore, is looked upon as its head and its foundation. Likewise, a gift of freedom could not be made, in a testament, before the institution of an heir. But we have deemed it absurd, that the mere order of the composition should be looked to, in opposition to the wishes of the testator; a thing which even the ancients seem to have thought unpardonably wrong. We, therefore, by our Constitution, have introduced a reform in this matter; so that now, either before the institution of the heir, if there be but one, or among the institutions of heirs, if there be several, a legacy, or grant of liberty, a gift always favoured, may legally be made.

Section XXXV.—A legacy to take effect after the death of an heir, or legatee, was also formerly ineffectual; as, if a testator had said,—"When my heir is dead, I give and bequeath such a legacy"; or, "I give and bequeath such a sum to be paid on the day before that of the death of my heir, or of my legatee." But here, also, we have introduced a reform, giving to all such legacies the same force, which is possessed by gifts in trust; to the end, that gifts in trust should not, in this case, be more favoured than legacies.

Section XXXVI.—Legacies also made by way of penalty, could former be neither made, revoked, nor transferred effectually. Now, a legacy is reputed as bequeathed by way of penalty, if it be given with intent to compel the heir to do, or not to do, a certain act; as, if the testator said,—" If my heir give his daughter in marriage to Titius", or, " if he do not give his daughter in marriage to Titius, let him pay ten golden pieces to Seius"; or thus, " if my heir shall alienate my slave Stichus", or, " if my heir shall not alienate my slave Stichus, let him pay ten golden pieces to Titius." And this rule was so strictly observed, that it was expressly ordained by many of the Imperial Constitutions, that even the Emperor would receive no legacy, which was given by way of penalty. And even in the testaments of soldiers, legacies of this kind were of no avail; although, in all other respects, the intentions of soldiers in making their testaments were strictly followed out. Nay, even freedom itself could not be given by way of penalty; still less, in the opinion of Sabinus, could another heir be added, as a penalty; as if a testator were to say,— " Let Titius be my heir; but if he give his daughter in marriage to Seius, let Seius also be my heir". For if Titius, the heir, were laid under restraint, it mattered not by what means, whether by the gift of a legacy, or by the addition of an heir. But this over-scrupulous nicety accorded not with our views, and we, therefore, have ordained that, as a general rule, things by testament, left, revoked, or transferred, shall be treated, in all respects, as other legacies; with the exception, however, of such as are either impossible, forbidden by law, or likely to cause scandal; for the moral principle of the age in which we live will not endure testamentary dispositions of such a character.

TITLE 21.

OF THE REVOCATION AND TRANSFER OF LEGACIES.

The revocation of a legacy is valid, whether it be inserted in the testament itself, or in a codicil. It is also immaterial whether it be made in terms directly contrary to those of the bequest; as when a testator who gives a legacy in these terms,—" I give and bequeath", revokes it by adding,—" I do not give and bequeath"; or else, in terms not contrary, that is by any other form of words.

Section I.—A legacy may also be transferred from one person to another; as thus,—" I give and bequeath to Seius, my slave Stichus, whom I have given and bequeathed to Titius." This also may be done either in the testament itself, or in a codicil; and thus, at one and the same time, a legacy is taken from Titius, and given to Seius.

TITLE 22.

OF THE FALCIDIAN LAW.

It remains for us to speak of the Falcidian Law, by which legacies have received their latest regulations. In former days, in accordance with a law of the Twelve Tables, the right of disposing of property by legacy was wholly unrestrained, a man, indeed, might dispose of his whole patrimony in legacies, for the words of the law were;—" As a man has disposed of his property, so let the law be"; it has, however, seemed fit to put some check upon this licence. And this has been provided for the benefit of the testators themselves, inasmuch as they frequently died intestate, the heirs whom they had instituted, refusing to enter upon an inheritance, whence the profit they could glean would be but small, if there were any at all. To remedy this were introduced first the Fusian Law, and afterwards the Voconian; and, as neither of these appeared adequate to meet the requirements of the case, last of all was enacted the Falcidian Law. This last law forbids a testator to give more than three-fourths of his property in legacies; so that whether there be one heir or several, there must now remain for him, or them, an entire fourth part of the whole.

Section I.—The following question has been raised, in the case of the institution of two heirs, say Titius and Seius. If the share of Titius in the inheritance be either wholly exhausted, or heavily incumbered with legacies expressly charged upon it, and if, the share of Seius be either wholly unincumbered, or have legacies charged upon it only up to half its amount; would, now, the fact of Seius having a clear fourth, or even larger share of the whole inheritance, bar Titius from keeping back out of the legacies charged upon his share, enough to secure the fourth part of his own moiety? It has been held that Titius may retain the fourth part of his own moiety; for the principle of the Falcidian Law applies to each heir individually.

Section II.—The Falcidian Law has regard to the quantity of the estate at the time of the testator's death. Thus, for example, if he, who at the time of his death is worth but an hundred golden pieces, bequeath them all in legacies; the legatees will be no gainers, though the estate should, before the inheritance is entered upon, be so much increased in value, by the acquisition of slaves, new-born children of female slaves, or produce of cattle, that, even after full payment of the hundred pieces to the legatees, a clear fourth of the whole estate would remain to the heir; because one-fourth of the said hundred pieces would be still due to him, and the legacies would remain liable to such an abatement. If, on the other hand, the testator gave in legacies seventy-five golden pieces only (being worth an hundred at his death), then, although before the entrance of the heir the estate should be so wasted, by fire, shipwreck, or loss of slaves, as to be worth not more than seventy-five pieces, and probably less, yet the legacies would still be due without abatement. This is, however, in no way prejudicial to the heir, as he is at full liberty to decline to enter upon the inheritance; it does, however, virtually oblige the legatees to come to some agreement with the heir, so as to get a part, lest, by his refusal to act, they should forfeit the whole of their legacies.

Section III.—In the valuation of an estate, under the Falcidian Law, a deduction is first made of the testator's debts, funeral expenses, and the cost of manumitting slaves; then the residue is divided, so that one-fourth part remains for the heir, and the other three parts are shared among the legatees, in proportion to the amount of their respective legacies. Thus, let us suppose that four hundred golden pieces have been given in legacies, and that the whole value of the estate, from which such legacies are to issue, does not exceed that sum; then each legatee must suffer his legacy to be abated by one-fourth. But, if the testator gave in legacies three hundred and fifty pieces, and there remained after debts paid four hundred, an eighth only ought to be abated from each legacy. And if he gave in legacies five hundred, and there remained, after debts paid, four hundred only, a fifth must be abated from every legacy, and afterwards a fourth. For that which is above the full value of the goods of the deceased must first be abated, and afterwards comes the abatement of what is due to the heir.

TITLE 23.

OF BEQUESTS IN TRUST.

LET us now go on to Trusts. And first, let us speak of fiduciary inheritances; or inheritances in trust.

Section I.—We must first observe that all trusts (*fidei-commissa*) were originally of small avail, for no one could be forced, against his will, to execute the trust, which he was merely asked to fulfil. For when testators were minded to give an inheritance, or legacies to those who could not legally be made heirs or legatees, they entrusted their gifts to the honour and good faith of some person capable of taking by testament. These species of inheritances and legacies were called *fidei-commissa*,—*i. e.* trusts to good faith,—because they were sanctioned by no bond of law, but rested only upon the honour and good faith of those to whom the request was addressed. In later days, however, the Emperor Augustus, whether from having been frequently influenced by a desire to relieve particular persons, or because he was earnestly adjured by testators in the name of his imperial safety, or being moved with indignation at some peculiarly gross breach of faith, ordered the Consuls to interpose their authority in these matters. And since this intervention of the Consuls was both just and popular, it soon assumed the form of a settled jurisdiction; and that jurisdiction became so high in public favour, that in course of time a special Prætor was appointed to adjudicate in cases of the sort; and he was thence called *Prætor Fidei-commissarius*,—*i. e.*, Prætor Commissary of Trusts.

Section II.—First, we must again remark, that in every testament it is absolutely necessary that some one be duly instituted heir; but it may be left to the good faith of such heir, to give back the inheritance to some one else; a testament, however, which contains no appointment of an heir, is absolutely ineffectual. When, therefore, a testator has said, "let Lucius Titius be my heir", he may add, "and I ask thee, Lucius Titius, as soon as thou canst enter upon my inheritance to return and give it up to Caius Seius." A testator may also ask his heir to restore a portion only of the inheritance; and may also leave the gift in trust absolutely, conditionally, or on the expiration of a certain day.

Section III.—An heir who has restored an inheritance, in obedience to the trust reposed in him, still remains the heir. He, however, who has actually received the inheritance from such fiduciary heir, is considered at times in the light of heir, and at times of legatee.

Section IV.—In the reign of the Emperor Nero, when Trebellius Maximus and Annæus Seneca were Consuls, it was provided by a decree of the Senate, that so soon as an inheritance, under a testamentary trust, had been restored, all actions, which by the Civil Law might be brought by, or against the heir, should be permitted to, or against him, to whom, by virtue of the trust, the inheritance had been restored. After the passing of this decree, therefore, the Prætor began to grant equitable actions to and against him who so took the inheritance, precisely as though he were the heir.

Section V.—But, as instituted heirs were very frequently asked to restore the whole, or well-nigh the whole of an inheritance, they used to refuse to accept it, since they could receive little or no profit; and so it happened that testamentary trusts were oftentimes extinguished. Afterwards, however, in the reign of the Emperor Vespasian, when Pegasus and Pusio were Consuls, the Senate decreed, that the heir, who was requested to return an inheritance, might retain a fourth; just as he was permitted to do in the case of legacies by the Falcidian Law. And the heir may make a like deduction in the case of specific things, left him by testament in trust for another. For some time after this decree the heir alone bore the burthen of the inheritance; but afterwards any one who received a share or part of an inheritance under a testamentary trust, was looked upon as a part legatee; that is, as a legatee who had a legacy not of particular thing, but of a share or part of the property. Now this species of legacy was called partition, because the legatee took his part of the inheritance together with the heir. Whence it came about that such stipulations as were formerly in use between the heir and the part-legatee, were afterwards made between the heir and the person benefitted under the testamentary trust; the intent, in both cases, being that both the profit and the loss accruing from the estate of the testator, should be shared between them, in proportion to their respective interests.

Section VI.—If, therefore, an instituted heir were requested to restore a share, not exceeding three-fourths of the inheritance, he was obliged to make such restitution by virtue of the Trebellian decree; and all actions having reference to the inheritance might, according to their respective shares, be brought against the heir, by the Civil Law, and against him who virtually received the inheritance, as though against an heir, by the Trebellian decree. If, however, the instituted heir were requested to restore the whole inheritance, or a share exceeding three-fourths, then the Pegasian decree was applicable; and the heir who once entered upon the inheritance, provided he did so of his free will, was obliged to bear all charges of the inheritance; and this, whether he had retained, or had declined to retain the fourth to which he was entitled. When, however, the heir did retain his fourth, he and the person taking under the trust (the *fidei-commissary*, or *cestui-que-trust*) entered into those stipulations for the apportionment of charges, technically called *partis et pro parte*, which we have above said were made between the part-legatee and the heir. Again, when the heir declined to retain his fourth, and transferred the whole amount left to the person benefitted by the trust, then the stipulations called *emptæ et venditæ hæreditatis*,—i. e. for the bargain and sale of the whole inheritance, were entered into between them. But if the nominated heir refused to enter upon the inheritance, on the allegation that he feared it would prove a loss to him, it was provided, by the Pegasian decree, that, on the petition of him to whom he had been requested to restore the inheritance, such heir should be compelled, under a Prætor's order, to enter upon the inheritance, and to restore it; and that, afterwards, all actions should be brought by, or against him who so received the inheritance, in accordance with the provisions of the Trebellian decree. And in this latter event there is no need of formal stipulations; for, by this one act, ample security is afforded to the heir, who restores the inheritance, and all actions as to such inheritance, whether for or against, are transferred to him who has received it; there is, therefore, in this case, a concurrent application of both the Trebellian and Pegasian decrees.

Section VII.—But, as the formal stipulations, which sprang from the Pegasian decree, were misliked even by the ancient jurists themselves; insomuch that Papinian, a man of real ability, deems them in some cases absolutely quibbling; and, as we are of those who prefer plainness to needless obscurity in matters of law, it has pleased us, on a comparison of the points of agreement and disagreement in each decree, to annul the Pegasian, which was passed later than the other, and to transfer exclusive authority to the Trebellian decree; by virtue of which all testamentary bequests in trust shall, for the future, be restored, whether the testator have given by his testament, to the nominated heir, either a fourth, more or less than that portion, or even nothing at all; so that where either nothing, or a portion less than a fourth, is given to the heir, it may be competent to him either to retain a fourth, or so much as shall be needed to make up the deficiency, by virtue of our authority, or even to demand a re-payment of it, if he has paid it over in his own wrong; all actions lie as well as against the heirs, as against the *fidei-commissary* (or *cestui-que-trust*) according to their respective shares, as they did under the Trebellian decree. If, however, the heir, of his free will, give up the whole inheritance, all actions, having reference thereto, must be brought either by or against the *fidei-commissary*. And, seeing that the peculiar provision of the Pegasian decree was, that when an instituted heir refused to accept an inheritance, he might be compelled to enter upon and give it up to the *fidei-commissary*, at his instance, and to transfer all actions to and against him, we have carried this whole provision over to the Trebellian decree. So that, now, this is the only law, whereby an obligation of entering upon the inheritance is imposed upon the heir, in the event of his refusal, and of the *fidei-commissary* being anxious that restoration should be made to him; and, in this case, neither loss nor gain can accrue to the heir.

Section VIII.—Further also, it matters not whether an heir, who is instituted to the whole of an inheritance, be requested to give up the whole or a part, or whether one instituted to a part only, be requested to give up that entire part, or only a portion of it; for we have ordained that, in the latter case, the like rules be observed, which we have laid down with reference to the restitution of the whole.

Section IX.—If an heir be requested, by a testator, to give up an inheritance, after deducting or excepting some specific thing, amounting to a fourth of the whole, as a piece of land, or any thing else, he will be called upon to make restitution, under the Trebellian decree, precisely as if he had been requested to give up the remainder of an inheritance, after the reservation to himself of a fourth. There is, however, this difference in the two cases: in the first, when the inheritance is given up after the deduction or exception of some particular thing, then, by virtue of the decree aforesaid, actions of all sorts are transferred to the *fidei-commissary*; and the specified portion, which remains to the heir, is free from all incumbrance, just as though he had acquired it by legacy. In the second, however, when the heir is requested to give up an inheritance, after the reservation to himself of a fourth, all actions are proportionably divided, those which refer to three-fourths of the estate are transferred to the *fidei-commissary*, while those which refer to the other fourth continue with the heir. And, even though an heir be requested to give up an inheritance, after deducting or excepting some specified thing, whereof the value may amount to the greatest part of the whole estate, still actions of all sorts are transferred to the *fidei-commissary*; he, therefore, ought well to consider whether it will, or will not be expedient that the inheritance should be given up to him. And the same principles are observed, whether an heir be requested to give up an inheritance after the deduction, or exception, of two, or more specific things; the like holds equally if the deduction be of a certain sum of money, which amounts to a fourth, or even to the principal part of the inheritance. What, also, we have said of an heir who is instituted to the whole, applies with equal force to him who is instituted only to a part of an inheritance.

Section X.—Further, one who has made no will, may, when about to die, make a request of him, to whom he believes that his estate will pass, either by the Civil or Prætorian Law, that he will give up, to a certain third person named, either the whole inheritance, or a part of it, or some specific thing in it, as a farm, a share, or a sum of money. Legacies, on the contrary, are valid only if given by testament.

Section XI.—A *fidei-commissary,* himself may also be requested, in his turn, to give up to another, either the whole, or a portion of what he receives; or even to give some other thing in lieu of it.

Section XII.—All testamentary bequests in trust depended, originally, upon the good faith of the heir; and from this "*fides*"—"good faith"—they gained as well their name as properties. The Emperor Augustus first brought them within the cognizance of the law; and we, more recently, have striven to out-vie that Prince. At the instance, therefore, of Tribonian, that most illustrious man and Quæstor of our sacred palace, and in consequence of a special instance laid by him before us, we have framed a Constitution, whereby we have enacted that; if a testator have trusted to his heir to make surrender of an inheritance, or any specific thing; and if the fact of such trust having been imposed, can be proved neither by any written document, nor by the evidence of five witnesses;—a number, known as that which the law, in such cases will demand,—if then, the witnesses were fewer than five, or perhaps not at all were present, in such case, whether it were the father, or whether any other person who has trusted to the good faith of the heir, and begged him to give up the inheritance, if such heir should perfidiously refuse to give it up, and repudiate the whole affair, the *fidei-commissary,* having himself first taken the oath of calumny, may insist on having an oath administered to the heir; he may thus compel such heir either to deny, upon his solemn oath, that he has ever received such a trust, or to fulfil it, though against his will, whether it relate to the whole inheritance, or some specific thing. This is permitted lest the last wishes of a testator should be defeated, when entrusted to the good faith of his heir. We have ordained that the same remedy should be available against a legatee, or even *fidei-commissary*, to whom a testator has left anything with a request to give it up. And if any man, so charged, confess the trust, but strive to find shelter in the subtle turns of the law, he may nevertheless, be forced to fulfil his duty.

TITLE 24.

OF INDIVIDUAL THINGS BEQUEATHED IN TRUST.

A TESTATOR may also leave particular things in trust, as a piece of land, a slave, a robe, gold, silver, coins; and may either request his heir to give them up, or even a legatee, though a legatee cannot be made chargeable with a legacy.

Section I.—A testator may not only leave his own property in trust, but that also of his heir, of his legatee, of his *fidei-commissary*, or of any other; thus a legatee, or a *fidei-commissary*, may not only be requested to give up that which hath been bequeathed him, but what is absolutely his own property, or even what belongs to another. The only caution necessary to be observed by the testator is, not to ask any one to give up more than he has actually taken under the testament; for what exceeds the value of that so given, will be disposed of ineffectually. Also, when another man's property is left, by testament in trust, the fiduciary trustee, or person requested to give it up, must either procure the actual thing from him who owns it, or else must pay its estimated worth.

Section II.—Freedom, also, may be given to a slave by virtue of a testamentary trust; for an heir, a legatee, or a *fidei-commissary*, may be requested to give him manumission; nor is it material, whether the testator request the enfranchisement of his own slave, or of the slave of his heir, or of that of his legatee, or of that of a stranger; therefore, even a slave who belongs not to the testator, must, if possible, be bought and set free. If, however, the proprietor of such slave refuse to sell him, as he may, if he have taken nothing under the testament, still the freedom granted by the trust is not extinguished, but put off only; for it may become possible, in course of time, when an opportunity of purchasing the slave has presented itself, that the boon of liberty may be afforded him. The slave, however, who is enfranchised in pursuance of a testamentary trust, does not become the freedman of the testator, even though he were the testator's own slave, but he becomes the freedman of him who manumits him. That slave, however, who gives his freedman by a direct bequest in the testament, becomes the freedman of the testator, and is called *Orcinus*,—the freedman of one in *Orcus*;— no slave, however, can obtain his liberty by direct bequest, who was not the property of the testator, both at the time of the making of his testament, and also of his death. A direct gift of liberty is said to be made, when a testator does not request that his slave may be manumitted by some other person, but when he wills that liberty shall accrue to him instantly by virtue of his testament.

Section III.—The terms usually employed in the expression of testamentary trusts, are the following: I beg, I ask, I wish, I commit, I entrust to thy good faith; and of these, each singly is as binding, as if all were conjoined.

TITLE 25.

OF CODICILS.

It is certain, that codicils were not in use before the time of Augustus; as Lucius Lentulus, to whom also the first use of testamentary trusts may be traced, introduced them. For, when about to die in Africa, he wrote sundry codicils, confirmed, by anticipation, in a testament of earlier date; and in these codicils, he requested the Emperor Augustus, by way of testamentary trust, to do something therein expressed. The Emperor Augustus carried his wishes into effect; and afterwards many other persons, influenced by the Emperor's example, discharged trusts which had been committed to them: the daughter, also, of Lentulus paid certain legacies, which she could not legally have been compelled to pay. Augustus, then, is said to have convoked an assembly of the learned, among whom was Trebatius, whose opinion had, at that time, the very greatest weight, and to have put the question as to whether this practice could be admitted, and whether codicils were not inconsistent with the principles and policy of law. Trebatius, however, advised Augustus to declare that the practice in question was most useful and even necessary to the citizens, by reason of the long journeys frequently undertaken at that time, when they might execute codicils, though it would be impossible to make a testament. After this time, when Labeo himself had executed codicils, no one entertained any doubt but that those instruments were perfectly valid.

Section I.—Not only is he permitted to make codicils, who nas already made his testament, but even one who dies intestate, may commit his property in trust to others, by way of codicil. But when codicils are made before a testament, they cannot, according to Papinian, take effect, unless specially confirmed by the subsequent testament. The Emperors Severus and Antoninus have, however, decided by Rescript, that a thing left in trust by codicils, made before a testament, may legally be demanded by the *fidei-commissary*, provided it be clearly shown that the testator has not drawn back from that wish which he originally expressed in his codicils.

Section II.—In codicils, however, an inheritance can neither be given, nor taken away; and this is, to prevent confusion, in the consideration of the respective operations of testaments and codicils. It is, however, only in direct terms, that no inheritance can, by codicils, be either given or taken away; for it may legally be alienated in codicils, by means of a trust. By codicils, again, no condition can be imposed upon an instituted heir; nor can a direct substitution be made by them.

Section III.—A man may make many codicils; and they need no solemnities in form or execution.

END OF BOOK II.

BOOK III.

TITLE 1.

OF INHERITANCES IN CASES OF INTESTACY.

He dies intestate, who has either made no will at all, or one which is invalid; or whose will, though valid at its execution, is revoked or cancelled afterwards, or becomes of none effect, for lack of an heir to enter upon the inheritance.

Section I.—Inheritances of intestates belong, according to the law of the Twelve Tables, in the first place to the proper, or family heirs.

Section II.—Proper, or family heirs, as we have before observed, are those who are under power of the deceased, at the time of his death; as a son or a daughter, a grand-son or grand-daughter by a son, a great-grand-son or great-grand-daughter by the grand-son of a son; and it matters not whether those children be natural or adopted. Together with the above, are to be reckoned also, those who, though not born in lawful wedlock, are, nevertheless, in accordance with the tenor of the Imperial Constitutions, entitled to the privileges of proper or family heirs, by being admitted into the order of the Curials, and so rendered liable to be chosen Decurions. And we must further add, all those comprised in the provisions of those of our own Imperial Constitutions which enact, that if a man have lived in intercourse with a woman, whom he at first did not intend to marry, but with whom he might lawfully contract marriage; and if he have had children by her, and afterwards, in obedience to the dictates of affection, shall marry that woman, and so have other children by her, sons or daughters, then not only shall those children be legitimate and under the power of their father, who are born after the celebration of the marriage, but those also who, though born before, gave occasion to the legitimacy of the after issue. And we have deemed it expedient to make this rule, as to children born before marriage, hold and obtain, even though there should be no issue after marriage, or though such as had been born be dead. But a grand-son or grand-daughter, a great-grand-son or great-grand-daughter, is not reckoned in the number of proper, or family heirs, unless the person preceding them in degree have ceased to be under the power of the ascendant, whether by death, or by some other mode, as by emancipation. For if, when a man died, his son was under his power, his grand-son, by that son, cannot be the proper, and family heir of him, the grand-father; and the same must be understood to be the case with reference to all other descendants. Posthumous children, also, who would have been under their father's power, if they had been born during his life-time, are esteemed as proper, or family heirs.

Section III.—Persons may become proper heirs, without their knowledge, and even though they be insane; for in all cases where inheritances may be acquired without our knowledge, in all such also may they be acquired by the insane. The ownership in an inheritance is not broken at the father's death, but immediately carried on and continued in the heir; the authority of a tutor, therefore, is not needed to enable a pupil to inherit, for proper or family heirs may acquire inheritances even without their knowledge; and an insane person, also, inherits, not by assent of his curator, but by reason of his own indefeasible right.

Section IV.—Sometimes, however, a child becomes a proper heir, although he was not under power at the death of his parent. Such is the case of one, who returns from captivity after the death of his father; he is at once made a proper heir, by virtue of the *jus postliminii,* or right of return.

Section V.—On the contrary, it may happen that a child, who was under the power of his parent, at the time of his death, does not become his proper heir; as, for instance, when a father, after his decease, has been adjudged guilty of treason, and his memory in consequence rendered infamous; such an one can have no proper heir, inasmuch as the public treasury succeeds to his estate. Still a son may, in such case, be said in strictness to have been in his own right a proper heir, although afterwards he ceased to be so.

Section VI.—A son or a daughter, and a grand-son or grand-daughter, the issue of another son, are all equally called to the inheritance; nor does the nearer in degree exclude the more remote; for it appears a just thing, to permit grand-sons and grand-daughters to succeed in the place of their father. For like reasons a grand-son or grand-daughter by a son, and great-grand-children by a grand-son are all equally called. And since it has been held that grand-sons and grand-daughters, great-grand-sons and great-grand-daughters should succeed in the place of their parent, it seemed a necessary conclusion that the inheritance should be divided, not *per capita,*—*i. e.,* by the head, in equal shares to each individual descendant,—but *per stirpes,*—*i. e.,* by the roots, or stock, in such shares, to each sub-division of the original family, as would have accrued to the head of such sub-division, if he had been living. Thus, where there is a son, and also grand-children by another son (no longer living,) the inheritance will be divided equally between them; the son will take the one-half, and the other will go to the grand-children, whether two or more, as representatives of their father. So again, if two sons die, leaving a father and children them surviving, if there be one child or perhaps two, of one brother, and three or four, of the other, then the inheritance of the grand-father will be equally divided, half will go to the single grand-child or two grand-children by the one son; and half to the three or four grand-children by the other son.

Section VII.—When it is asked, whether any particular person is a proper heir; we must proceed to inquire at what time it was certain that the deceased died without a testament; and he may be said to have so died, if his testament were abandoned. Thus, if a son be disinherited, and a stranger instituted heir; and if, after the death of the son, it become certain that the instituted heir did not in fact enter upon the inheritance, either because he was unable, or unwilling so to do, then the grand-son of the deceased will be the proper heir of his grand-father; for at the time when it became certain that the deceased died intestate, there was no other heir but the grand-child; and this is a point well settled.

Section VIII.—And, even if a child be born after the death of his grand-father, yet provided he were conceived in his life-time, he will, at the death of his father, and after his grand-father's testament has been abandoned, become the proper heir of his grand-father. If, however, the child be both conceived and born after the death of his grand-father, then, although his father should die, and his grand-father's testament be abandoned, he could not be the proper heir; for he was never actually allied to his grand-father by any tie of relationship. So, again, he who has been adopted by an emancipated son, is not to be reckoned as among the proper heirs of the father of his adoptive father. The adopted children, therefore, of an emancipated son, as they are not proper heirs of their adopter's father, so far as regards the inheritance, are also unable to sue for possession of the goods, as next of kin. So much then, of proper, or family heirs.

Section IX.—Emancipated children have, according to the Civil Law, no legal claim to the inheritance of their parents; because, as they have ceased to be under the paternal authority, they are no longer proper or family heirs, and they are not called upon to inherit, on any other title, by the law of the Twelve Tables. But the Prætor, in obedience to the dictates of natural justice, grants them that possession of the goods, which, from the first words of the edict, is known as *unde liberi*, precisely as if they had been under the power of their father, at the time of his death; and this grant is made whether they are alone, or whether there are other children, who are proper heirs. Thus if there be two sons, the one emancipated, and the other under power at the father's death, the latter is, according to the Civil Law, alone the heir, that is, alone the proper heir; but as, thanks to the equitable jurisdiction of the Prætor, the emancipated son is admitted to his share, the result is, that the proper heir becomes actual heir of his own share only.

Section X.—Children, however, who after emancipation have given themselves in adoption, are not admitted, as children, to possession of the goods of their natural father; that is, not if, when he dies, they are still in the adoptive family. But, if they have been emancipated by their adoptive father, and that during the life-time of their natural father, they are admitted, by Prætorian equity, to take the goods of their natural father, precisely as though they had been merely emancipated by him, and had never been members of the adoptive family. Thus, as a necessary consequence, they are, with regard to their adoptive father, looked upon as perfect strangers. If, however, they are emancipated by the adoptive, after the death of the natural father, they are still equally looked upon as strangers to their adoptive father; and with regard to the effects of their natural father, make no advance toward regaining their portion as children. And this has been so settled, because it was most unjust to permit that a mere adoptive father, should have it in his power to decide to whom the inheritance of the natural father should belong, whether to his children, or to his agnates.

Section XI.—Adopted children have, therefore, fewer privileges than have natural children; for natural children, when emancipated, retain the rank of children, thanks to the equitable jurisdiction of the Prætor, although they lose it by the Civil Law; but adopted children, when emancipated, lose the rank of children by the Civil Law, and can sue for no relief from the Prætor. And this is most reasonable; for civil policy cannot put an end to natural rights; nor can natural children cease to hold the relations of sons and daughters, of grand-sons and grand-daughters, simply because they cease to be proper heirs. But adopted children, when they are emancipated, begin forthwith to be as though mere strangers; because by one ceremony of the Civil Law, to wit, emancipation, they lose utterly that which they had obtained by another ceremony of the Civil Law, to wit, adoption.

Section XII.—The same rules are observed, also, in that possession of goods which the Prætor, contrary to the letter of the testament, grants to children who have been left unmentioned; that is to such as have been neither formally instituted, nor formally disinherited. For the Prætor calls, to share in this possession, upon all the children who were under the power of their father at his death, and upon those also who were emancipated; but he excludes those who were members of an adoptive family at the time of the death of their natural parent. And as the Prætor does not permit those adopted children who have been emancipated by their adoptive father, to succeed him in case of dying intestate, much less does he permit them to take possession of his goods, contrary to the letter of his testament; because, by emancipation, they cease to be in the number of his children.

Section XIII.—We must, however, observe, that those children who remain in an adoptive family, or who have been emancipated by their adoptive father, after the decease of their natural father, who dies intestate, although not admitted by that part of the Prætorian edict which calls children to the possession of goods, are still by another part admitted; by that, namely, whereby the *cognati*—*i. e.* the relatives through females —of the deceased are called. By such latter part of the edict, however, they are called only when there are no proper heirs, no emancipated children, and no *agnati*, or relatives through males. For the Prætor first calls the children, whether proper heirs or emancipated; then the *agnati*, who being appointed by virtue of the law of the Twelve Tables, and also by the Constitutions, were thence called "legitimate" heirs; and lastly the *cognati*, in the earlier degrees.

Section XIV.—These then were the rules which obtained in former times; but they have been in some sort reformed by that Constitution of ours, which refers to those who are given in adoption by their natural parents. For we have been made acquainted with certain instances, wherein sons have, by adoption, forfeited the right of succession to their natural parents; and also, through the case whereby the tie of adoption is dissolved by emancipation, have lost the right of succession to their adoptive, and thus, to either parent. We, therefore, with our wonted wish to set right what is wrong, have promulgated a Constitution which enacts, that when a natural father has given his son in adoption, the rights of such son shall still be preserved entire, precisely as if he had continued in the power of his natural father, and as if no adoption had taken place; with, indeed, this sole exception, namely, that the person adopted may succeed to his adoptive father, in the event of his dying intestate. If, however, the adoptive father make his testament, (and omit the name of the adopted son), the son can, neither by Civil Law nor by Prætorian Edict, acquire any portion of the inheritance, whether he sue for possession of the goods, in opposition to the letter of the testament, or whether he seek to set the instrument itself aside as being unnatural; for there is no obligation which renders it incumbent on an adoptive father either to institute as heir, or expressly to disinherit an adopted son, and this, because there is no natural link between them; not even if, in accordance with the Sabinian senatorial decree, the adopted be one of three brothers; for, in a case of this sort, he shall neither obtain the fourth, nor have an action which will avail him to pursue a claim to it. Those, however, are excepted by our Constitution, who are adopted by an ascendant; for inasmuch as both rights, the natural and the civil, unite in their favour, we have preserved the old regulations, with reference to adoptions of this kind; as we have, also, in the case where the father of a family has given himself in arrogation. But all these matters, in their fulness of detail, may be gleaned from the tenor of the aforesaid Constitution.

Section XV.—The ancient law which showed special favour to descendants from males, called only those grand-children who were so descended, to the succession as proper heirs, and placed them before the *agnati;* but grand-children born of daughters, and great-grand-children born of grand-daughters, the same ancient law reckoned as *cognati* only, and called them to succeed to their grand-father and great-grand-father, to their grand-mother and great-grand-mother, maternal or paternal, only after the whole line of *agnati* had been exhausted. But the Emperors would not permit a wrong so unnatural to subsist, without some adequate reform; and, seeing that the name of grand-child and great-grand-child is common as well to those descended from females, as to those from males, they granted the same rank and order of succession to them all. But, that some especial privilege should be accorded to those, who are supported by the dictates of nature, as well as of the ancient law, the same Emperors thought it but just that the portions of grand-children, great-grand-children, and other lineal descendants of a female, should be somewhat lessened; they decided, therefore, that such should receive less by a third, than their mother or grand-mother would have received, or than their father, or grand-father, paternal or maternal, at the decease of a woman, when her inheritance was under discussion; and although there were no other descendants, provided these entered upon the inheritance, the Emperors did not call the *agnati* to the succession. And as, upon the death of a son, the law of the Twelve Tables calls the grand-children and great-grand-children, male and female, to represent their father in the succession to their grand-father, so the Imperial Ordinance calls them to the succession in the place of their mother or grand-mother, subject only to the aforesaid abatement of the third.

Section XVI.—But as there still remained some ground of dispute between the agnates and the above-mentioned grand-children, the agnates claiming the fourth of the estate of the deceased, under a certain Constitution; we have abrogated the said Constitution, and have not allowed it to be extracted from the code of Theodosius, and inserted in our own. Also, in our own published Constitution, we have abandoned absolutely the spirit of the old regulations, and have enacted that, so long as there are grand-children of a daughter, or great-grand-children of a grand-daughter, the agnates shall not be entitled to claim any interest in the succession of the deceased; and the reason of this is, that collateral may not have the preference over lineal descendants. And we also, hereby, again decree, that this our Constitution shall prevail in to its full force, and that from the date of its publication. And further, as the law ordained that, as between sons and grand-sons by sons, the inheritance should be divided *per stirpes*—*i. e.*, by stocks,—and not *per capita*—*i. e.*, by polls,—so, also, we ordain that a like mode of distribution shall obtain between sons and grand-sons by a daughter; or indeed between all grand-sons and grand-daughters, great-grand-sons and great-grand-daughters, and all other descendants in the right line; so that the issue of either branch may receive the share of their mother or father, their grand-mother, or grand-father, without any abatement. And if one branch chance to have only one child, or two, while the other may have three or four, then shall the one or two be entitled to their half, while the three or four shall be entitled only to their half.

TITLE 2.

OF THE SUCCESSION, BY LAW, OF AGNATES.

If there be no proper heir, nor any of those persons whom the Prætor, or the Constitutions call upon, to act with proper heirs, to take the succession in any way, then the inheritance belongs, by the law of the Twelve Tables, to the nearest agnate relative.

Section I.—*Agnates*, as we explained in the First Book, are those who are related through males, that is, who are of kin by the father; brothers, therefore, sons of the same father, are *agnate* to each other; they are, also, said to be *consanguineous*, as of the same paternal blood; and it is not necessary that they should have the same mother. An uncle, also, is agnate to his brother's son, and contrariwise the nephew to his father's brother. Cousins, the children of brothers, are also agnates. We may thus enumerate many degrees of agnation: children also, born after the death of their parents, acquire the rights of consanguinity. The law, however, does not grant the inheritance to all the agnate relatives at once, but to those only who are nearest in degree, at that period when it is an ascertained fact that the deceased has died intestate.

Section II.—The right of agnation accrues also through adoption; thus the natural, and the adopted sons of one father are agnates; it is, however, doubtless improper to say that such are consanguineous. Also, if one of your agnate relatives, say a brother or a paternal uncle, or, in short, any agnate, how remote soever in degree, adopt any one; he who so adopted is undoubtedly to be reckoned in the number of your agnates.

Section III.—Among males, agnation gives to all, how distant soever in degree, reciprocal rights of succession to an inheritance. But, with reference to females, the rule was that they should take by title of consanguinity, if sisters, but not at all, if connected more remotely; and this, though their male relatives, if agnate, even in the most distant degree, were admitted to succeed to them. Wherefore, the inheritance of the daughter of your brother, or of your paternal uncle or aunt, will be yours; but yours will not belong to them. And this rule was laid down because it appeared expedient that the law should be so settled, that inheritances should, for the most part, fall into the possession of males. But, as it was clearly opposed to all justice, that women should thus be almost wholly excluded, as if they were strangers, the Prætor does admit them to the possession of goods, under that portion of his edict, which gives the promise of possession on account of proximity; by virtue of this, then, women are admitted, but still only in default of any agnate, or nearer cognate relative. The law of the Twelve Tables, however, did not introduce any of these distinctions; but that simple plainness which is the best quality of legislation, called to a reciprocal succession the agnates, of what sex or degree soever, precisely as though they were proper heirs. It was that intermediate system of jurisprudence, after the Twelve Tables and before the Imperial Constitutions, which, in a spirit of subtle nicety, introduced the aforesaid distinction, and absolutely barred females from succeeding to agnates; absolutely—because then no other mode of obtaining the succession was known, until the Prætors, gradually smoothing down the rough justice of the Civil Law, or supplying its defects, were, from kind and equitable motives, led to annex to their edicts, a fresh order of succession. For after the line of cognate relatives are admitted, according to their degrees of proximity, relief was given to females, as the Prætor then gave them that possession of goods which, from the first words of the edict, was known as "*unde cognati*". We, however, while we revert to the law of the Twelve Tables, and follow in its track as to this matter, do still praise the kindly feeling of the Prætors, and think only that they have not discovered any complete remedy for the evil. For, if one and the same degree of natural relationship appertain as well to females as to males, and if all have equally the same title of agnation, why should males have the right of succession to all their agnates, while females, sisters only excepted, have no such right at all? We, therefore, by a thorough reform, and a return to the regulations laid down in the Twelve Tables, have, by our Constitution, enacted, that all persons recognized by the law, to wit, descendants from males, whether themselves male or female, shall be equally entitled to the rights of succession, in cases of intestacy according to the prerogative of their degree; and that no females be excluded because they have not the rights of consanguinity in so near a degree as sisters.

Section IV.—We have also deemed it expedient to add to our Constitution a clause, whereby one whole degree, but one only, is transferred from the line of cognates, to that of the agnates, or legal successors. Thus, not only the son and daughter of a brother, as we have before said of agnates, shall be called to the succession of their paternal uncle, but also the son or daughter of a sister, though only by the same father, or only by the same mother, may, with agnates, be admitted to the succession of their maternal uncle; but this privilege shall apply to none more remote in degree than the son or daughter of such sister. Thus, when a person dies who is both a paternal and maternal uncle, that is, who has children living both by a brother and a sister, then the children of either branch succeed, exactly as if, by a descent from males, they had a legal title to the succession. This, however, is only if the deceased leave neither brother nor sister him surviving; for if such do survive, and accept the inheritance, all others of more remote degree are absolutely excluded; for the division of the inheritance will go *per capita,*—*i. e.* by polls, and not *per stirpes*—*i. e.* by stocks.

Section V.—When there are several degrees of agnates, the law of the Twelve Tables expressly calls the nearest. Thus, to give an instance, if there be a brother, a son of another brother, or a paternal uncle, the brother will have the preference. And, although the law of the Twelve Tables speaks, in the singular number, of the call of " the nearest agnate"; still there is no doubt, but that if there be several in the same degree, all should be admitted. For though, strictly speaking, the expression " nearest degree", must be understood to mean that degree of several which is nearest, yet if all the agnates be in one degree, the inheritance belongs, beyond all doubt, to all.

Section VI.—When a man dies, and leaves no testament, his nearest agnate is considered to be that one who was nearest at the time of the decease of the intestate. But if the deceased have left a testament, he then is nearest who is so at the time when it is certain that there will be no heir to act under the testament; for then only, can a man, who has made a testament, be said to have died intestate. Now this may remain uncertain for a length of time; and during such time, it not unfrequently happens, that, by the death of the actually nearest agnate, one becomes nearest who was not so at the testator's death.

Section VII.—The former rule of law was, that in this mode of acquiring inheritances there should be no succession; so that, if the nearest agnate, called, as we have mentioned, to the inheritance, either refused to enter upon it, or died before he did so, his own legal heir could not be admitted to succeed him. And here too, the Prætors, by a somewhat imperfect measure of reform, did not leave the agnates quite without relief, but ordered that, as they were barred from the benefits of agnation, they should be called to inherit as cognates. We, however, being minded to make our law as complete as possible, have enacted by that Constitution, which, in our clemency, we published concerning the right of patronage, that to agnates shall not be denied the right of legal succession in the inheritance of agnates. For it was absurd enough to refuse to agnates a privilege which the Prætor granted to cognates; and it was especially absurd, as in the case of tutelage, the second degree of agnates succeeded on failure of the first; thus the principle of succession was admitted where there was a burthen to sustain, but rejected where there was an advantage to be gained.

Section VIII.—A parent, also, who has emancipated a son or a daughter, a grand-son or a grand-daughter, is admitted to their legal succession, as agnate; but this formerly, provided only he had entered into a fiduciary agreement. Now, by our Constitution, it is always to be presumed that every emancipation has been made under such an agreement; but among those of former days, the parent was never called to the legal succession unless he had actually made a contract at the time of the emancipation.

TITLE 3.

OF THE TERTULLIAN DECREE.

The law of the Twelve Tables was so full of rigour, showed so decided a preference for males, and excluded so strictly those who were related by the female line, that not even between a mother and her children, was the privilege of reciprocal succession granted. The Prætors, nevertheless, admitted such persons, but only by virtue of their position as cognates, to the succession; and gave them the possession of goods, called, from the first words of the edict, *unde cognati*.

Section I.—But these cramping limitations were, in course of time, enlarged. The Emperor Claudius was the first who gave to a mother the legal inheritance of her children dead; and this, to console her for their loss.

Section II.—Afterwards, however, by the Tertullian senatorial decree, passed in the reign of the Emperor Hadrian, it was established as an universal rule, that mothers, but not grand-mothers, should have the melancholy privilege of so succeeding; so that a mother, born of free parents, who has three children, or a freed-woman who has four, may be admitted to the goods of her children, who have died intestate;

and this, though she herself be under paternal power. When, indeed, a mother is under power, she can only be admitted at the command of him to whose power she is subject.

Section III.—But, children of the deceased son, if proper heirs, or taking rank as proper heirs, whether in the first or any inferior degree, are preferred to the mother. Also, if it be a daughter, not under power, who is dead; that daughter's son or daughter, will be preferred, in the succession to her mother; that is, to their grand-mother. The father of a child, of either sex, is preferred, to the mother; not so the grand-father and great-grand-father; that is, when they and the mother are the only claimants. A brother, by the same father, either of a son or a daughter, excluded the mother; a sister, by the same father, took equally with the mother. Again, if a deceased left a brother and a sister by the same father, then the brother excluded the mother, even though capable by the number of her children, but the whole inheritance was shared equally, between the brothers and sisters.

Section IV.—We, however, by a Constitution, inserted in the Code which bears our name, have deemed it, herein right to relieve the mothers; and this, from a consideration of their natural constitution, their pangs in child-birth, the great danger, and even death itself, to which, from this cause, they are liable. We, therefore, have deemed it actually immoral that what is, in its very nature, but the work of chance, should be turned, by the law too, to their detriment. For if a married woman, free-born, does not bear three children, or a freed-woman bear four, they do not, therefore, deserve to be deprived of the succession to their children. For how can failure of this kind, be brought against them as a crime? So then, we have granted full, legal right to every mother, whether free-born or freed, to be called to the legal succession of her children, and this, though she may not have borne three children, or four, nay may have had that one alone whese inheritance is in question.

Section V.—But, on a close examination of the Constitutions of former Emperors, with reference to the right of succession, we observed that they were partly favorable to mothers, and partly grievous. They did not always call the mother to the full inheritance, but, in certain cases, deducted a third, which was given to certain agnates; while, in other cases, they did just the reverse, and gave a third. To us, however, it seems just the mother should take the succession of her children without abatement, and should have the absolute and exclusive preference over all agnates, or legal heirs, save only the brothers and sisters of the deceased, whether by the same father or not. But as we have so preferred the mother to the whole line of legal heirs, we also call together with her to the inheritance, all brothers and sisters, whether legal heirs or not. But this subject to the rules following: if there survive sisters only, whether by one father or not, and the mother, of the deceased, then shall the mother take half, and sisters the other half of the goods: but if there survive, the mother, and either a brother or brothers only, or brothers and sisters also, whether legal heirs, or inheriting only as cognates, then the inheritance of the deceased son or daughter must be divided *per capita*—by polls—that is, shared equally among them all.

Section VI.—As, however, we have thus cared for the interests of mothers, it behoves them also in return to look to the well-being of their children. Be it, therefore, known, that if a mother neglect, for the space of a whole year, to demand a tutor for her children, or to ask for a fresh one, in the room of one who has been removed or excused, she will be refused the privilege of succeeding to such of her children as die within years of puberty.

Section VII.—Even though there be a doubt as to the

father of a son or daughter, the mother may still, by the Tertullian decree, be admitted to the succession of their goods.

TITLE 4.

OF THE ORPHITIAN DECREE.

CHILDREN, on the other hand, were admitted to the goods of their intestate mothers by the Orphitian Decree, which was passed in the consulship of Orphitius and Rufus, in the reign of the Emperor Marcus Antoninus. By this decree the legal inheritance is given as well to sons as daughters, even though they be under power; and they are preferred to the own brothers, and to the agnates of their deceased mother.

Section I.—But since, by the terms of this decree, grand-sons and grand-daughters were not called to the legal succession of their grand-mother, the omission was afterwards supplied by the Imperial Constitutions; so that grand-sons and grand-daughters were called to inherit, precisely as sons and daughters had been.

Section II.—It may here be remarked, that the successions just spoken of, as derived from the Tertullian and Orphitian decrees, are not destroyed by diminution; for the rule is that the legal inheritances, given by the late law, are not destroyed by diminution, but that it affects those only which arise from the law of the Twelve Tables.

Section III.—Finally, it must be observed, that even

children, as to whose father there is a doubt, are admitted by the Orphitian Decree to the inheritance of their mother.

Section IV.—If, out of several legal heirs, some refuse the inheritance, or have been prevented from entering upon it, either by death or any other cause, their portions accrue to those who have accepted the inheritance; and, even if such acceptors should die, the portions which accrue to them will go to their heirs.

TITLE 5.

OF THE SUCCESSION OF COGNATES.

NEXT in order to the proper heirs, and to those whom the Prætor and the Constitutions call to inherit as among the proper heirs; and to the legal heirs, in whose number are the agnates and those whom the above-named decrees, and our Imperial Constitutions have ranked among the agnates, the Prætor calls the cognates, according to their proximity of degree.

Section I.—Now here, in the succession of cognates, it is the natural relationship which is looked to. For instance, agnates who have suffered diminution, and their descendants, are included, by the law of the Twelve Tables, as among legal heirs; but, by the Prætor, they are called in this third order of succession. We must, however, in this except a brother or sister who have been emancipated, but not their children: for the Constitution of Anastasius calls an emancipated brother or sister, together with those brothers who, not having been emancipated, are still in possession of unaltered rights, to the legal succession of their brother or sister; it does not, indeed, call them to an equal share, but makes a certain abatement, as may be learned from the expressions of the Constitution itself. It prefers them, however, to all agnates of inferior degree, even though such agnates have not suffered, by emancipation, any diminution; and naturally it far prefers them to all cognates.

Section II.—Those, also, who are collaterally related by the female line, are called by the Prætor in the third order of succession, according to proximity.

Section III.—Children, also, who are in an adoptive family, are also called in the same third order of succession to the inheritance of their natural parents.

Section IV.—It is quite clear, that illegitimate children have no agnates; inasmuch as agnation proceeds from the father, and cognation from the mother; but children of this kind are considered as though they had no father. For the like reason, consanguinity cannot be said to subsist between the illegitimate children of one woman; for consanguinity is itself a species of agnation. They are, therefore, allied to each other only as they are related by their mother, that is, by cognation. Hence it is that all such children are called to the possession of goods, by that part of the Prætorian edict, which calls cognates according to the degree of their proximity.

Section V.—Here it is essential that we observe, that by right of agnation any one may be admitted to inherit, even though he be in the tenth degree; and this is so, whether we refer to the law of the Twelve Tables, or to the edict whereby the Prætor promises, that he will give the possession of goods to the legal heirs. But the Prætor promises the possession of goods to cognates, according to their proximity, only so far as the sixth degree of cognation; and in the seventh degree to those cognates only who are the children of a second cousin.

TITLE 6.

OF THE DEGREES OF RELATIONSHIP.

It is, here, essential to explain how the degrees of cognation are calculated. First, then, we must observe, that one species of cognation is reckoned by ascending, another by descending, and a third by going transversely, or as it is called, collaterally. The first, or ascending cognation, is that which a man bears to his ascendants; the second, or descending, is that which he bears to his descendants; and the third, or transverse or collateral, is that which he bears to his brothers and sisters and their issue, and consequently to his uncles and aunts, whether paternal or maternal. The cognation by ascent, and that by descent begin at the first degree; the transverse, or collateral, at the second.

Section I.—In the first degree ascending, are a father or a mother; descending, a son or a daughter.

Section II.—In the second degree ascending, are a grand-father or a grand-mother; descending, a grand-son or grand-daughter; in the collateral line, a brother or a sister.

Section III.—In the third degree ascending, are a great-grand-father or a great-grand-mother; descending, a great-grand-son or great-grand-daughter; in the collateral line, the son or daughter of a brother or sister, and, by parity of reasoning, an uncle or aunt, whether paternal or maternal. A father's brother is in Latin *patruus*, and in Greek πατρῳος; a mother's brother, in Latin *avunculus*, in Greek μητρῳος the word θεῖος is used of both indifferently. A father's sister is in Latin *amita;* a mother's sister, in Latin *matertera;* each is called promiscuously in Greek, θεία, or τηθὶς.

Section IV.—In the fourth degree ascending, are a great-great-grand-father or great-great-grand-mother; descending, a great-great-grand-son or great-great-grand-daughter; in the collateral line, the grand-children of a brother or a sister; as also a great uncle or great aunt, paternal, that is the brother or sister of a grand-father; also first cousins, that is the children of brothers or sisters, such are called *consobrini;* many, however, think, and rightly, that cousins, the children of sisters only, should be called *consobrini;* while those of brothers are called, in strictness, *fratres patrueles,* if males; and *sorores patrueles,* if females: also, the children of a brother, or of a sister are properly called *amitini;* but the sons of your aunt, by the father's side, call you *consobrinus,* and you call them *amitini.*

Section V.—In the fifth line ascending, are a great-grand-father's grand-father, or a great-grand-mother's grand-mother; descending, a great-grand-son, or a great-grand-daughter of a grand-son or a grand-daughter; in the collateral line, a great-grand-son or a great-grand-daughter of a brother or sister; and also, a brother or sister of a great-grand-father or great-grand-mother; also the son or daughter of a first cousin; and the son or daughter of a great uncle or great aunt, paternal or maternal.

Section VI.—In the sixth line ascending, are a great-grand-father's great-grand-father, or a great-grand-mother's great-grand-mother; descending, the great-grand-son or great-grand-daughter of a great-grand-son or great-grand-daughter; in the collateral line a great-great-grand-son, or a great-great-grand-daughter of a brother or sister; also a great-great-grand-father's brother or sister, and a great-great-grand-mother's brother or sister: also second cousins, that is the sons and daughters of first cousins in general, whether such first cousins are related by two brothers, by two sisters, or by a brother and a sister.

Section VII.—Thus far will suffice to show how the degrees of cognation are calculated; and, from the examples given, it is easy to see in what manner we ought to reckon the more remote degrees; for every person born adds one degree; so that it becomes infinitely more easy to answer as to the degree of relationship in which one person stands to another, than to distinguish such a person by his proper title of cognation.

Section VIII.—The degrees of agnation are computed in the like manner.

Section IX.—But, as truth is more firmly implanted in the mind by sight than by hearing, we have deemed it expedient to add a table of the degrees of cognation, as a supplement to the account given of them; that students may, by the exercise as well of eyes as ears, attain the most perfect knowledge of them.

Section X.— It is quite clear, that the portion of the Prætorian Edict in which possession of goods is promised, according to the degree of proximity, does not refer to the cognation subsisting between slaves; for such cognation was never recognized by any ancient law. But, in that one of our Constitutions which we have published as to the right of patronage (a right heretofore obscure, and misty, and confused), we have, at the promptings of kindly feeling, enacted that, if a male slave have a child or children, whether by a free-woman or a slave, or if a female slave have a child or children, whether by a free-man or a slave; then if such father and such mother be afterwards enfranchised, the children who had a slave as mother, become also free; or, if the mother were free, and the father a slave, who afterwards attains his freedom, these children shall all succeed to their father, or to their mother, the right of the patron, in this case, being suffered to remain unexercised. And we have called such children not only to the succession of their parents, but also to their own reciprocal succession; calling them specially by this our law, whether there be but the one succession, all having been born in servitude and afterward enfranchised; or whether they take in the succession with others, born after the enfranchisement of their parents; and also whether they are all by the same father, or by the same mother, or by a different father, or different mother; treating them, in short, exactly in the same manner in which we do those who are the issue of parents legally married.

Section XI.—To repeat the whole purport of what we have said on this subject: it appears that those who are in the same degree of cognation, are not always equally called to the succession; nay more, that not even he who is nearest in cognation is always to be preferred. For, as the first place is accorded to proper heirs, and to those who are reckoned among proper heirs, it is clear that the great-grand-son, or great-great-grand-son is preferred to the brother, and even to the father or mother of the deceased; and this, although, as we have above said, a father or a mother are in the first degree of cognation, and a brother in the second, while the great-grandson is only in the third, and the great-great-grand-son in the fourth; nor is it material whether such grand-children, as aforesaid, were under the power of the deceased, at his death, or out of his power, either as being themselves emancipated, or as being the children of those who were so; nor whether they were descended by the female line.

Section XII.—If, however, there be no proper, or family heirs, nor any whom we have mentioned as called together with them, then an agnate, who has still the full rights of agnation remaining in him, is usually preferred, though he be in the most distant degree, to a cognate in a degree much nearer? thus the grand-son, or great-grand-son or of a paternal uncle, is preferred to a maternal uncle or aunt. Whenever, then, we say that the nearest in degree of cognation is called to the succession, or that, if there be several in the same degree, they are called equally; we say so, only in the event of there being neither proper heirs, nor such as rank as proper heirs, nor any agnate, who, in accordance with the rules which we have laid down, ought to be preferred before them. The great exception being in the case of an emancipated brother or sister, who are called to succeed to their brothers or sisters; for though they have, by being emancipated, suffered diminution, they are still preferred before all agnates of a more remote degree.

TITLE 7.

OF THE SUCCESSION OF FREEDMEN.

LET us now treat of the succession of freedmen. In former days, a freedman might, without being subject to any penalty, wholly omit all mention of his patron, in his testament; for the law of the Twelve Tables called the patron to succeed to the inheritance of the freedman, only when the latter died without a testament, and without a proper heir. Though, therefore, the freedman died intestate, yet if he had left a proper heir, the patron could have had no claim to his estate; when, indeed, such proper heir was the natural son of the deceased, the patron did not appear to have any just cause of complaint; when, however, his proper heir, was merely an adopted son, it was clearly unjust that no claim should accrue to the patron.

Section I.—This unfairness of the law, therefore, was afterwards set right by the edict of the Prætor. For, every freedman who made his testament, was commanded so to dispose of his property as to leave one-half to his patron; and if such testator left either nothing, or a share less than half, still possession of the full moiety was granted to the patron, in opposition to the actual letter of the testament. Also, if a freedman died intestate, and left an adopted son as proper heir, still, as against such heir, possession of a half was granted to the patron. A freedman's natural children, however, prevailed to the exclusion of the patron; and not those children only who were under his power at the time of his death, but those also who had been emancipated, or given in adoption, provided they were instituted heirs for any part; or, even if they were omitted, and had sued for possession in opposition to the testament, by virtue of the Prætorian edict. Disinherited children, however, never served to exclude the patron.

Section II.—Afterwards, however, by the Papian law, the rights of patrons, who had freedmen of the richer sort, were enlarged; for it is, by that law, provided, that the patron shall take an equal share with the freedman's own children, in the distribution of the effects of a freedman who has died with a testament, or without one, and has left a patrimony of a hundred thousand *sesterces*, and fewer than three children. When, therefore, a freedman possessed of such a fortune has left one son or daughter only as his heir, one moiety of his effects is due to the patron, precisely as if the deceased had made his testament, and had died leaving neither son or daughter him surviving. But when there are two heirs, male or female, one-third is only due to the patron; and when three, the patron is absolutely excluded.

Section III.—But our Constitution, which, for the benefit of all, we composed in compendious form, and in the Greek tongue, has laid down the following rules in this matter. If a freed-man, or freed-woman die possessed of less than an hundred golden pieces (*aurei*),—for so we interpret the amount named in the Papian law, calculating one *aureus* as worth a thousand *sesterces*,—the patron shall, if there be a testament, be entitled to no share in the succession. If, however, such freed-man or freed-woman die intestate, and no children survive, then the privileges of the patron are maintained entire, exactly as was formerly the case, under the law of the Twelve Tables. But, if a freed-person die possessed of more than an hundred golden pieces, and leave one child or many, of either sex or any degree, as either his heirs, or the possessors of his goods, we have granted that such child or children shall succeed to the effects of their parent, to the exclusion of every patron and his issue. But, if a freed-person, so possessed, die without children and intestate, we have called the patrons, male or female, to the whole inheritance. Again, if such have made a testament, and have omitted all mention of his patron, having, at the same time, no children, or having disinherited them if he have; or if a mother or maternal grand-father, have omitted them, but still, having so done it that the testament cannot be set aside on the ground of being unnatural, then, under our Constitution, the patron shall succeed by a possession contrary to the letter of the testament, and take, not as formerly, a half, but a third part of the estate of the deceased freed-man; or if the freed-person have bequeathed to the patron, a share of the estate, less than a third, the deficiency shall be supplied to him. This third, however, is to be free of all charge or burthen whatsoever, and shall not be subject to the furnishing of any portion, whether of legacies or trusts, even though given for the benefit of the children of the deceased;

such burthen shall fall wholly on the co-heirs of the patron. We have also, in the before-named Constitution, collected a variety of cases and decisions, which we deemed necessary in the settlement of the law on this subject. Thus patrons of either sex, their children, and collaterals to the fifth degree, are called to the succession of their freed-men and freed-women; as may be clearly seen by a reference to the Constitution itself. Also, if there be several children, and several patrons, one, two, or more, the nearest in degree is called to the succession of the freed-man or freed-woman; and, if many are equal in degree, the estate is divided *per capita* —by polls, and not *per stirpes*—by stocks. The like also is observed with collaterals: for we have rendered the laws of succession as to freed-men almost the same as those which relate to persons free-born.

Section IV.—What has been here said refers to the freed-men of the present time; and they are all now citizens of Rome, as the old orders of *Dedititii* and *Latini* have been abolished. Of these, the *Latini* never enjoyed any legal right of succession; for though in life they had the semblance of liberty, yet when the death-hour came, they lost as well their liberty as life; for their possessions, like those of slaves, were claimed as a kind of *peculium*, or perquisite, by their manumittor, under the law *Junia Norbana*. Afterwards, by the Largian Decree, it was provided, that the children of a manumittor, who were not disinherited by name, should be preferred, in the succession to the estate of a Latin freed-man, to any strangers whom the manumittor might institute his heirs. Next came the Edict of the Emperor Trajan, which enacted that the slave who, thanks to the Imperial favour, but contrary to the will, or without the knowledge of his patron, obtained the freedom of Rome, should in his life-time be looked upon as free, but at his death be regarded merely as a Latin freed-man. But we, by reason of the manifold difficulties consequent on these constant charges of condition, have resolved that, by virtue of our Constitution, the order of Latin freed-men be abolished; and with them the *Lex Junia Norbana*, the Largian decree, and the edict of the Emperor Trajan; to the end, that all freed-men whatsoever, may become free citizens of Rome. And we have cleverly contrived, by aid of some few additional regulations, that the mode whereby the gift of Latin freedom was conferred, should be available also for the gift of Roman citizenship.

TITLE 8.

OF THE ASSIGNMENT OF FREED-MEN.

LASTLY, so far as regards the property of freed-men, we must bear in mind, that the Senate has decreed, that although the goods of freed-men belong equally to all the children of the patron who are in the same degree; it is, nevertheless, competent to a parent to assign a freed-man to any one of his children, so that, after the death of the parent, that child shall be deemed sole patron, to whom the assignment was made; to the absolute exclusion of the other children who would have been equally admitted to a share in the same property, provided no such assignment had been made. But if the assignee should die, and leave no children him surviving, the other children will regain their former right.

Section I.—Not a freed-man only, but a freed-woman also may be the subject of an assignment; and may be assigned not only to a son or grand-son, but to a daughter or grand-daughter.

Section II.—The privilege of making an assignment of this sort is given to him only who has two or more children under his power; and to the children only who are under his power, may a father assign a freed-person, male or female. Whence arose a question, as to whether if a father were so to assign, and afterwards emancipate the assignee, the assignment itself would become null and void. The decision was that it is annulled; and in this both Julian, and most other jurists coincide.

Section III.—Nor is it material whether such assignment be made by testament, or not by testament. Nay, patrons may make it verbally, and in such terms as best they like; this permission was granted by a decree of the Senate, passed when Claudian was Emperor, and Suillus Rufus and Osterius Scapula, Consuls.

TITLE 9.

OF SUCCESSION BY THE PRÆTOR'S GRANT.

The right of succession by what was known as " Possession of Goods," was introduced by the Prætors as a reform in the ancient Civil Law. And this reform the Prætor effected not only with regard to the inheritances of intestates, as we have before explained, but of those also who die after having made a testament. Thus, if a posthumous stranger were instituted heir, although he could not, by the strict letter of the Civil Law, enter upon the inheritance, inasmuch as his institution would be invalid, yet by the Prætorian, or honorary law, he might obtain the possession of the goods, so soon as he had the assent and assistance of the Prætor. In the present day, by virtue of our Imperial Constitution, such an heir may, however, be legally instituted: for he is no longer looked upon as a person unknown to the Civil Law.

Section I.—At times, however, the Prætor makes his grant of possession of goods, with no desire to amend the old law, nor to impugn it, but rather to give it force and sanction; thus even to those who are instituted heirs by a regular testament, he grants possession *secundum tabulas* —*i. e.*, in accordance with the will. He, also, it is who calls the proper heirs, and the agnates, to the possession of the goods of intestates; and this, though even without the Prætorian grant, the inheritance, by Civil Law, would be their own.

Section II.—Those whom the Prætor, by virtue solely of his office, calls to an inheritance, do not thereby become heirs in law; inasmuch as the Prætor cannot make an heir; for heirs are made by law alone, or by that which has the force of law, as a decree of the Senate, or an Imperial Constitution. But when the Prætor grants possession of goods, the grantees, though not heirs, are in the place of heirs, and are called Possessors of the Goods. The Prætor, also, has established several other orders of persons, to whom possession of goods may be granted, to the intent that none may die without a successor. Finally, the Prætor, in the exercise of a wise and equitable jurisdiction, has widened that right of succession to inheritances, which was, by the law of the Twelve Tables, cramped within the very narrowest limits.

Section III.—Grants by the Prætor of possession of goods, when there is a testament, are the two following: (1), the one called *contra tabulas* — *i. e.*, possession contrary to the testament,—which is granted to children whose names are omitted in the testament; (2), that called *secundum tabulas,*—*i. e.,* in accordance with the testament—is promised by the Prætor to all who are legally instituted heirs.

And now, having dealt with cases where there was a will, the Prætor proceeds to settle the possession of the goods of intestates; (3) by the grant called *unde liberi*, he gives possession of goods to proper heirs, or to those who, by the Prætorian edict, are reckoned as proper heirs; (4) by that called *unde legitimi*, he grants possession to the legal heirs; (5) by that called *unde decem personæ*, he grants to ten persons, who were preferred to a manumittor who was a stranger; these ten were—a father; a mother; a grand-father or grand-mother, paternal or maternal; a son; a daughter; a brother or sister, whether by the same father, or same mother; (6) by that called *unde cognati*, he grants to the nearest cognates; (7) by *tum quem ex familiâ*, to the nearest relations of the patron; (8) *unde patronus patronæve*, to the patron or patroness, and to their children and parents; (9) *unde vir et uxor*, to a husband and his wife; (10) *unde cognati manumissoris*, to the cognates of the patron.

Section IV.—Such then are the grants of succession introduced by the Prætorian jurisdiction. And we, also, have omitted nothing through negligence, but being anxious to amend all failings have, by our Constitutions, admitted and retained as of absolute necessity, the grants of *contra tabulas* and *secundum tabulas;* as likewise those two grants in cases of intestacy, called *unde liberi* and *unde legitimi:* but as to the Prætorian grant, which stands fifth in the general edict, namely that called *unde decem personæ*, we have, with kindly feelings, and in but few words, shown it to be superfluous; for whereas, that grant preferred ten kinds of persons to a stranger, who was patron, our Constitution as to the emancipation of children, hath granted permission to all parents to manumit their children, a fiduciary contract being presumed; as therefore, their manumission must of necessity involve this privilege, the above-named grant of *unde decem* is now superfluous.

Therefore suppressing it entirely, we transfer into its place that which was sixth, and have made to stand fifth, the one called *unde cognati*, by which the Prætor gives the succession to the nearest cognates.

Section V.—And as regards the possession called *tum quem ex familiâ*, formerly in the seventh place, and that called *unde patronus* in the eighth, we have now annulled them both, by our Constitution as to the right of patronage. And as we have assimilated the succession of freed-men to those of persons free-born, save that we have limited the former to the fifth degree, that there may still remain some distinction between them, we think that the possessions *contra tabulas, unde legitimi* and *unde cognati* may suffice for all persons to vindicate their rights; especially now, that the over-nice and intricate difficulties of those kinds of possession, the *tum quem ex familiâ* and the *unde patroni* have been abolished.

Section VI.—The other grant of possession of goods, called *unde vir et uxor*, which in the old list of grants held the ninth place, we have preserved in full force, and have promoted it to a higher place, to wit, the sixth. The tenth of the ancient grants, called *unde cognati manumissoris*, having been deservedly abolished, for reasons already given, there now remain in force six only kinds of ordinary grants of possession of goods.

Section VII.—To these, however, a seventh has been added, which the Prætors have, for very wisest reasons, introduced. For by the final clause of the edict, possession of goods is promised to all to whom it is due under the provisions of any law, decree of the Senate, or Constitution. Now this grant, the Prætor has not numbered specifically, with the possessions of either testates or intestates; but has accorded it as a boon, when emergency demands, as the last and extraordinary remedy of those who, by virtue of any special Law, Decree, or Constitution, are called to the succession, whether of testates or intestates.

Section VIII.—The Prætor, then, having thus arranged and placed in proper order, several kinds of successions, thought proper, inasmuch as several persons in different degrees of relationship are often in the same rank with reference to the succession, to fix within a certain limit the time, when alone a claim could be put in for a grant of possession of goods; to the end that the actions of creditors might not be delayed for lack of a proper person against whom to bring them, and also that creditors should not be able to get too easy a possession of the goods of the deceased, and so consult only for their own advantage. To parents, then, and children, whether natural or adopted, the Prætor has granted one year, within which they must either put in their claim, or forego it entirely; but to all other persons, agnates or cognates, he allows but a hundred days.

Section IX.—Also if a person entitled, neglect to claim possession of goods, within the time prescribed, his right accrues first to those in the same degree with himself: and in default of such, the Prætor, by the " *successory edict,*" grants the possession to the next degree; just as though he who preceded had no right at all. If, again, a man actually refuse possession of goods, when offered to him, there is no occasion to wait until the time prescribed is ended, but the next in succession may forthwith be admitted, under the same edict. It must be observed, that in the computation of time prescribed for demanding possession of goods, we reckon those days only which are called *utiles* " useful," *i. e.,* those on which the party might make his application to the Magistrate.

Section X.—The Emperors, our predecessors, have in this case well and wisely provided, that no man need be over-anxious to make any solemn or formal demand for the possession of goods; for if he have, within the time prescribed, shown, in any way, a desire to avail himself of the Prætorian succession, he shall have the full benefit of it.

TITLE 10.

OF THE ACQUISITION OF PROPERTY BY ARROGATION.

There is, also, another kind of universal succession, which had its origin neither in the law of the Twelve Tables, nor in the Prætorian Edict, but in that law which rests on common consent.

Section I.—For example, if the father of a family gave himself in arrogation, all his property, whether corporeal or incorporeal, together with all debts due to him, were formerly the absolute property of the arrogator; excepting always such things as were lost by the diminution, or change of state; as, for example, the obligation of services from freed-men to their patron, and the rights of agnation. As to Use and Usufruct, although they formerly were reckoned as among the rights which were entirely lost by this change of state, yet our Constitution has declared that they shall not be extinguished by the least kind of diminution.

Section II.—But we, in the present day, have narrowed acquisitions by arrogation, within the same limits as acquisitions by natural parents. For now, neither by natural nor adoptive parents, is any thing acquired save the bare usufruct of those things, which come to their children, as it were extrinsically, and of their own right; but the actual property still remains in the children. When, however, an arrogated son has died a member of his adoptive family, then even the actual property in his effects, will pass to the arrogator; provided there be a default of those persons who, according to our Constitution, have the preference over the father, in the succession of those things, which cannot be acquired for him.

Section III.— On the contrary, however, an arrogator is not strictly bound in law, to satisfy the debts of his adopted son; still he may be sued in his son's name; and if he refuse to appear on behalf of his son, the creditors may, on the warrant of the proper Magistrate, seize and sell, by legal means, those goods, of which the property, as well as the usufruct, would have been in the debtor, if he himself had not been in the power of another.

TITLE 11.

OF THE ASSIGNMENT FOR SUSTAINING ENFRANCHISEMENTS.

A NEW method of acquiring by succession arose from a Constitution of the Emperor Marcus Aurelius. For, if slaves have received the gift of freedom by the testament of their master, and no one, under the testament, will enter upon the inheritance; then, if such slaves be desirous that the property be awarded them, in order thus to carry into effect the gift of their enfranchisement, their suit shall be granted.

Section I.—To like purport, is the Rescript of the said Emperor Marcus to Pompilius Rufus; the terms of which are as follows:

"If it be necessary that, in the matter of the estate of Virginius Valens, who has left by testament the gift of freedom to certain slaves, a sale forthwith be held, because there is no successor now that the testament has been set aside, the Magistrate who has jurisdiction in matters of this sort will, upon application, take into consideration the prayer which you have preferred; namely, that for the sake of sustaining the enfranchisement of those to whom it has been granted, whether directly or in trust, the estate of the deceased may be decreed to you, on condition, that you give satisfactory security to the creditors for the payment of their several and respective claims. Then shall all those, to whom their freedom was left as a direct gift, become free, precisely as if the inheritance had been duly entered upon; but those whom the heir was called upon to enfranchise, shall get their liberty at your hands. Also, if you be not minded to accept the assignment of the goods of the deceased on any other condition, than that they even who receive their freedom as a direct gift, shall become your freed-men, then will we lend the weight of our authority to support your wishes in this respect; provided always, they who are to get their freedom will consent. And, to the end that the gracious boon, contained in this our Rescript, be not voided in another way, namely, by a seizure of the property on behalf of the public treasury, be it known to the officers of our revenue, that we will have the gift of liberty held in preference to any pecuniary advantage of our own; and if a levy be made, it must be so conducted as to maintain the freedom of those persons who would have obtained it, if the inheritance had been entered upon according to the terms of the testament."

Section II.—By this Rescript, favour is shown not only to gifts of freedom, but also to the deceased themselves, whose effects are thus prevented from being seized and sold by creditors. For, if there be such an assignment as we have spoken of, in order to maintain enfranchisements, there can be no sale by creditors; for in such case, there is an assignee, who represents the deceased, and he, also, must be solvent and must give ample security to the creditors for the satisfaction of their claims.

Section III.—In the first place, this Rescript holds, whenever the gift of freedom is conferred by testament. But it may now become a question, as to what the consequence will be, if a man have bequeathed freedom to his slaves by codicils, but die intestate, and his inheritance be not entered upon. To this case, we decree, the favour of the Rescript shall extend; and beyond all doubt, the master who dies testate, and leaves the gift of freedom in codicils alone, has the full benefit of the Rescript.

Section IV.—The wording of the Rescript shows, that it is in force only when there is absolutely no successor in case of intestacy. So long, therefore, as it continues a matter of doubt, as to whether a successor do exist or not, the Rescript will not apply. So soon, however, as it is certain that no successor will appear, the ordinance shall take effect.

Section V.—If one, who has a right to demand the restoration of his original position, should decline to enter upon the inheritance, it may be asked, whether, notwithstanding this right of restoration, the Constitution will apply, and an assignment of the goods ought to be granted? And further, how will it be, if, after such assignment to sustain enfranchisements have been effected, the heir should actually be restored? In any case, we declare that the gift of freedom, once acquired, shall never be revoked.

Section VI.—This Constitution was framed to give effect to gifts of liberty; where, therefore, no gifts of liberty are made, the Constitution does not apply. Suppose now, a master to have given freedom to his slaves, even when in health, or in anticipation of death; and suppose, further, that the slaves, in order to prevent the creditors from complaining that such gift was made in fraud of them, should petition for an assignment to them of the effects of the deceased; ought this this petition to be listened to?

We, on the whole, are inclined to say that it should, although the actual letter of the Constitution says nothing on the point.

Section X.—But, perceiving that very many matters were left wholly untouched by this Rescript, we have introduced a very complete Constitution, which contains a number of special cases, serving to complete the exposition of the law as to this kind of succession: and which every one may learn, by a perusal of the Constitution itself.

TITLE 12.

OF ACQUISITIONS BY SALE OF GOODS TAKEN IN EXECUTION.

THERE were many other kinds of universal succession, in use before that treated of in the last Title. Such was that called *bonorum emptio,*—*i. e.*, " sale of goods,"—whereby the property of debtors was disposed of, but with many and tedious formalities. It held its ground, however, during the prevalence of the old system of " ordinary judgments" [where the Magistrate and Judge were both employed, the one to inquire into matters of law, and the other into matters of fact]: but it ceased with the introduction of " extraordinary judgments," [when the Magistrate and Judge were the same person]. Now, it is only under a Judge's order that creditors may take possession of the goods of their debtors, and dispose of them as they think best. This subject, however, will be seen more clearly in the more expanded collection, which we call, the Digest.

Section I.—There was, also, by the Claudian Decree another, and most revolting kind of universal acquisition. When, namely, a woman free-born had degraded herself by cherishing a passion for her slave, she lost her freedom by the decree aforesaid, and with her freedom, her estate. But as this, to our thinking, was unworthy of our age, we have abolished the practice in our Empire, and have not permitted the mention of it to find place in the Digest.

TITLE 13.

OF OBLIGATIONS.

LET us now go on to treat of Obligations. An obligation is a bond of law, by which we are laid under a necessity to render something, according to the laws of our country.

Section I.—The principal division of obligations, is into two kinds, the Civil and the Prætorian. Civil obligations are those constituted by the laws, or, at least, sanctioned by the Civil Law. Prætorian Obligations are those constituted by the equitable jurisdiction of the Prætor; such are also called Honorary.

Section II.—A further division of Obligations, is into four classes; for they arise—(1) from Contract; (2) from Quasi-contract; (3) from Wrong; (4) from Quasi-wrong.

Let us treat first of those which arise from Contract.

These also are divisible into four species—Obligations, then, arising from contract, are produced by possession of the thing; or by a verbal formula; or by writing; or by consent. Let us consider each species separately.

TITLE 14.

OF OBLIGATIONS CONTRACTED BY THE THING.

An Obligation may be contracted by the transfer of the thing itself; as in the case of that species of loan called *Mutuum*. *Mutuum* is the loan of those things which may be reckoned by weight, number or measure, as wine, oil, corn, coin, brass, silver, gold. Now these things we give by number, weight and measure, that they may become absolutely the property of the receiver. And as the identical things lent cannot be given to us in return, but only others of the same nature and quality, this species of loan is called *Mutuum* (*i. e., ex meo tuum*—" from mine thine"), for in this case I so give that what is mine, may become thine. From this contract springs the personal action called a Condiction.

Section I.—A person to whom another has, in error, paid or delivered over something which was not due, is bound by the thing which he has received, and a condiction, or personal action lies against him at the suit of him who has, in error, made the payment. And this action may be brought in the same form, as if the receiver had taken the thing as a *Mutuum*. Hence it is that a pupil, to whom an erroneous payment of this kind has been made, without the authority of his tutor, is not subject to that condiction called *indebiti*—*i. e.*, "never indebted",—any more than he would be to an action on account of the delivery of the thing, as a *Mutuum*. But, in truth, this species of obligation does not seem to spring from a contract; inasmuch as he, who pays with intent to acquit himself of something which he is bound to give, wishes rather to dissolve a contract, than to make one.

Section II.—A person, also, to whom the use of a particular thing is granted, receives what is called a *Commodate*, is bound by the delivery of the thing, and subject to an action for restoration, called *Commodati*.

The receiver of a *Commodate* differs widely from the receiver of a *Mutuum*; for, in *Commodate*, the thing lent, is not lent that it may become absolutely the property of the person to whom it is delivered; and, therefore, he is bound to restore to the lender the identical thing which he has received. Also, in the case of *Mutuum*, he who has received, is still bound to restitution, although by fire, house-fall, ship-wreck, thieves, or public foes, he have lost all that he had received. But, in *Commodate*, the borrower is indeed bound to use exact and scrupulous care in the custody of the thing lent; nor is it sufficient that he bestow the same care upon it, which he is wont to bestow upon his own property, if it appear that another, and more careful person might have preserved it. But he is not liable for the effects of irresistible force, or extraordinary accidents, unless such force or accident would not, but for his fault, have affected the thing lent. If, however, you choose to carry with you on a journey, a thing lent simply for your use, and lose it by foemen, thieves, or wreck, you doubtless, are liable for the loss, and bound to make reparation. A *Commodate*, in strictness, is a thing lent, or delivered to your use, without your paying, or agreeing to pay, any price, recompense, or reward for the use of such thing.

For, if such price or recompense be given, the contract becomes a letting and hiring; for, that it be a real *Commodate*, the loan must be gratuitous.

Section III.—If a thing be deposited with any one, he becomes bound by his possession of the thing, to make restitution of the identical thing, and in default, he is compellable by direct action of deposit. But still, he is responsible only in case of his fraud, and not for a simple fault, such as lack of care or energy. He is, therefore, not liable if the thing be stolen from his custody, even though it were so by reason of his lack of proper care; for he who delivered his property into the custody of a negligent friend, must bear the consequences, and impute them to his own imprudence.

Section IV.—A creditor, also, who accepts a pledge, is bound by his acceptance of the thing; and forced by a special action, to restore the identical thing. But, as a pawn or pledge is given for the good of both parties, of the debtor that he may obtain credit more easily, and of the creditor that what is due to him may be better secured, it has been held, that it will suffice if the creditor be scrupulously diligent in the custody and care of the thing pledged. If, however, it appear that he has used such care, and that nevertheless, the pledge has, by some mischance, been lost, the law holds him not liable, and permits him to sue the debtor for the amount due to him.

TITLE 15.

OF OBLIGATIONS CONTRACTED BY WORDS.

A VERBAL Obligation is contracted by means of a question and an answer, when we stipulate that anything shall be given to, or done for us. From it spring two kinds of actions, both being Condictions or personal actions; the one arising where the stipulation was certain, and the other where it was uncertain. The word "stipulation" is used of this obligation because "*stipulum*" was an ancient expression for "firm"; itself probably, derived from *stipes*, the trunk of a tree.

Section I.—In this kind of contract, the formal words in use were:

Spondes? Spondeo;—*i. e.*, Do you bind yourself? I do so.
Promittis? Promitto;—*i. e.*, Do you promise? I do so.
Fide-promittis? Fide-promitto;—*i. e.*, Do you promise on your honour? I do so.
Fide-jubes? Fide-jubeo;—*i. e.*, Do you promise to become surety? I do so.
Dabis? Dabo;—*i. e.*, Will you give? I will give.
Facies? Faciam;—*i. e.*, Will you do? I will do.

Nor does it matter whether the stipulation be in Latin, in Greek, or in any other language; provided only that both parties understand it; nor need both parties make use of the same language, it suffices if a fit and proper answer be given to each question. Two Greeks may, even, contract in Latin. In former days it was essential to make use of the formal words above cited; but, a Constitution of the Emperor Leo, afterwards enacted, renders this solemn form unnecessary, and demands only the apprehension and consent of each party, in whatever terms expressed.

Section II.—Every Stipulation is either absolute, or performable on a certain day, or conditional. It is simple, when one says—" Do you bind yourself to pay five gold pieces?" Here the money may at once be demanded. It is performable on a certain day, when there is specific mention of a day on which the money is to be paid, as, " Do you bind yourself to pay me ten pieces on the first of the calends of March?" That, however, which we stipulate to pay on a certain day becomes due at once, but cannot be demanded before the arrival of the day; nay, it cannot even on that day be sued for; because the whole day is granted to the debtor to make his payment; as it never can be sure that there has been default in payment on the day specified, until such day is fully ended.

Section III.—But, if you were to stipulate thus, " Do you bind yourself to pay me ten pieces every year, so long as I shall live?" the obligation is looked upon as absolute, and is perpetual; because an obligation cannot remain due for a certain time only. Still, if the heir of the obligee demand payment he may be defeated by the exception, or plea in bar, of " agreement."

Section IV.—A stipulation is conditional, if the obligation be made subject to the happening of something undecided, so that it takes effect only when such thing happens, or does not happen; as for instance, " Do you bind yourself to give me five pieces, if Titius be made Consul." If the stipulation were, " Do you bind yourself to give me five pieces, if I do not go up to the Capitol," the effect would be the same as if the stipulation were, that five pieces should be paid to the stipulator at the day of his death. A conditional stipulation involves a hope only that the thing stipulated may become due; but this hope we transmit to our heirs, if we die before the fulfilment of the condition.

Section V.—Places, also, are wont to be introduced in stipulations, as, for example, "Do you bind yourself to pay me at Carthage?" Now this stipulation, although it appear to be absolute, is yet in reality coupled with the idea of the time whereof the promiser must avail himself, in order to pay the money at Carthage. If, therefore, one at Rome should in a stipulation say, "Do you bind yourself to pay me such a sum, this day, at Carthage?" Such stipulation would be void, because the performance of it would be impossible.

Section VI.—Conditions which have reference to time past, or to time present, either instantly annul an obligation, or do not operate to stay its execution; as, for instance, "Do you bind yourself to give me so much if Titius have been Consul, or if Mævius be alive?" If neither of these things be so, the stipulation is void; but if they be, the contract is already in force. For things which, in themselves, are certain, do not stay the formation of an obligation, even though to our minds, and so far as our knowledge goes, they are not certain.

Section VII.—Not things alone, but acts, may be the subjects of stipulations; as when we stipulate, that something shall or shall not be done. In stipulations, however, of this kind, it is best to add a fixed penalty, in case of non-performance, lest the real worth of the stipulation should be uncertain, and the plaintiff should be called upon to prove the actual amount of his interest. If, therefore, any stipulate, for the performance of a thing, the penalty should be thus stated, "If the act stipulated be not performed, do you bind yourself to pay ten pieces, as a penalty?" Also, if, by one and the same sentence, a stipulation be made, that certain things shall be done, and certain left undone, a clause to the effect following should be added, "If anything be done adverse to the agreement; or anything left undone according to the agreement, do you bind youself to pay me ten pieces as a penalty?"

TITLE 16.

OF JOINT VERBAL CONTRACTS.

As well in the stipulation on the one side, as in the promise on the other, two persons, or more, may be parties. The parties to the stipulation are all bound, if, after all have put the question, the promiser, for his part, answer, *spondeo*—" I bind myself"; as, for example, when, in reply to two stipulators, who have each separately asked the question, the promiser answers, " I bind myself to pay to each of you." Because, if he first promise Titius, and then to another who puts the same question, make the same promise, there will exist two separate obligations, instead of two co-stipulators to one obligation. Two or more become joint promisers, if, after the question has been put disjunctively as, " Mævius, do you bind yourself to give five pieces?" " Seius, do you bind yourself to give five pieces?" each separately replies " I do engage."

Section I.—In joint obligations, such as these, the whole thing which is the subject of the stipulation, is due to each stipulator, and from each promiser. But, as one thing alone is the subject of each obligation, if any of the stipulators receive the thing due, or any of the promisers pay it, the obligation is discharged for all parties, and all are freed.

Section II.—Of two joint promisers, one may engage simply and absolutely, and the other may bind himself to performance on a certain day, or conditionally; but neither day fixed, nor condition named, will secure the promiser who is simply bound, from being sued for payment of the whole.

TITLE 17.

OF STIPULATIONS WITH SLAVES.

A SLAVE obtains, from the legal personality of his master, the right to make a stipulation; but, in many respects, the inheritance represents the legal personality of the deceased; whatever stipulation, therefore, is made by a slave, the property of the inheritance, before the inheritance is entered upon, he acquires for the inheritance, and so for him who afterwards becomes the heir.

Section I.—A slave who stipulates, whether for his master, for himself, for a fellow slave, or for some person un-named, always acquires for his master. The like holds with children who are under the power of their father, in all cases where they can acquire for him.

Section II.—But when the stipulation contains a thing to be done, the person of the stipulator is solely regarded; so that, if a slave stipulate for a right of passage for himself, or beasts, or carriages, it is the slave, and not the master, who is to have no hindrance in his passage.

Section III.—If a slave, the joint property of several masters, enter into a stipulation, he acquires for each of his masters a share in proportion to their interest in him; unless, indeed, he stipulate at the bidding, or in the name of any one master; for, in such case, the thing stipulated for will be acquired solely for that master. Also, whatever a slave held in common by two masters, stipulates for, is all acquired by one of his masters, if it be impossible that part be acquired for the other; as, for instance, if the thing already be the property of one of the two.

TITLE 18.

OF THE SEVERAL KINDS OF STIPULATIONS.

Some Stipulations are Judicial; some Prætorian; some Conventional; some Common, that is Prætorian and Judicial.

Section I.—Judicial Stipulations are those which spring simply from the office of the judge; as of the giving security against fraud, or the engagement to pursue a runaway slave, or to pay the worth of him.

Section II.—Prætorian Stipulations are those which spring solely from the office of the Prætor; as where security is given when danger is imminent, or for the payment of legacies. Also under Prætorian Stipulations must be reckoned those of the Ædiles; for these, too, come from a proper legal authority.

Section III.—Conventional Stipulations are those, which are made by agreement of both parties; that is, by order, neither of Judge, nor Prætor, but by consent of the contracting persons. And of such stipulations there are, so to say, as many kinds, as there are of things contracted for.

Section IV.—Common Stipulations are those, which provide for the security of the property of a pupil; for the Prætor ordains a certain guarantee to be given for this end, and sometimes the judge, if need be, in court decrees it; or, they are for the ratification of things done in another's name.

TITLE 19.

OF VOID STIPULATIONS.

ALL THINGS, which may be submitted to our dominion, may be the object of a stipulation, whether be they moveable or immoveable.

Section I.—But, if a man stipulate for that which neither does, nor can exist, as for Stichus, who is dead, although he thought him living; or for a Centaur, which can have no existence, the stipulation is void and ineffectual.

Section II.—The rule holds equally in case of a stipulation for a thing sacred or religious, which was thought not to be so; or for a thing of public property, given for ever to the uses of the people, as a forum, or a theatre; or for a free-man, thought to be a slave; or for a thing which he, who wishes to make the stipulation, cannot acquire; or for something which already is his own. Every such stipulation shall at once be void; and not remain open and unsettled, because, perchance, the public thing may become private; the free man may become a slave; the stipulator may become able to acquire; or that which now is his may cease to be so. So, on the other hand, although a thing may originally be the subject of a valid stipulation, yet, if afterwards it fall into the list of such things as those before-mentioned, without the fault of the promiser, the stipulation becomes invalid. A stipulation, again, such as the following, is void from the very first, " Do you engage to give me Lucius Titius when he shall become a slave?" for those things, which, by their nature, are exempt from our dominion, can by no means be made the objects of an obligation.

Section III.—If one promise that another shall do, or give something, he is not bound; as, if a man were to promise that Titius shall pay five pieces. But, if he promise that he will cause Titius to pay five pieces, he is bound by that agreement.

Section IV.—If a man stipulate for the benefit of any other, than of him in whose power he is, such stipulation is void. Payment, however, may be made to a third party, as if a man, in his stipulation, were to say, "Do you bind yourself to make payment to me, or to Seius?" Here, the stipulator alone acquires the obligation; but still the debtor may legally make the payment to Seius, even against the wish of the stipulator; the debtor will thus be freed from his obligation, but the stipulator can sue Seius in an action of mandate. Again, if one stipulate that ten pieces shall be paid to him and to a third person, under whose power he is not, such stipulation is effectual; but it has been a question, as to whether the whole amount be due to the stipulator, or a half only; and it has been held that half accrues to him. If, however, you stipulate on behalf of another, who is under your power, you acquire for yourself; for your expressions are as those of your son, and your son's expressions are as your own, in regard to all those things which can possibly be acquired for you.

Section V.—A stipulation is, moreover, void, if the person to whom the question is put does not give a pertinent answer; as if one were to stipulate that you should give him ten pieces, while you promise only five; or if the reverse were the case. A stipulation is also void, if one make his stipulation absolute, while you promise conditionally; or the reverse; provided only, you distinctly disagree, as when a person stipulates conditionally, or for performance at a certain time, and your reply is definite, "I promise for to-day only." Because, if your answer simply be, "I promise," you virtually seem, in few words, to assent to his time, or his conditions. For, in the answer of the promiser, it is not essential that there be an actual repetition of each word which the stipulator has made use of.

Section VI.—A stipulation, also, is void if made with one under your power; and this whether you, or he be the stipulator. A slave, however, is incapable not only of entering into an obligation with his master, but even of binding himself to any one besides. The son of a family, however, can enter into obligations with any, save his father.

Section VII.—It is clear, that a person deaf and dumb, can neither stipulate nor promise. The like is held to apply, also, to the deaf; for he who stipulates, ought to hear the words of the promiser; and he who promises, the words of the stipulator. It is, hence, evident that we are not speaking now of one who hears, though with difficulty, but of one who cannot hear at all.

Section VIII.—A madman can do no sort of legal act; for he understands not the tendency of his actions.

Section IX.—A pupil may do every sort of legal act; provided only the tutor give his assent, where his authority is needed; and this it certainly is, where the pupil would be himself the bounden party; but he can, without the authority of his tutor, bind others to him.

Section X.—What we have just said of pupils, must be understood only as of those who have, already, a certain amount of understanding; for an infant, or a child just out of infancy, differs not greatly from a madman, as pupils of such age can have no understanding. But, to advance their interests, a more favourable construction of the law is permitted to pupils not far removed from infancy; so that they are allowed the same privileges as those close to the age of puberty. A son, however, under power and within puberty, cannot bind himself, even though his father authorize the transaction.

Section XI.—A stipulation, also, is void, if an impossible condition be annexed to the obligation. Now a condition is said to be impossible when nature herself hinders the accomplishment; as if one should say, "Do you promise to do so and so, if I touch the sky with my finger?" But if the stipulation ran in this form, "Do you promise if I do not touch the sky with my finger?" such a stipulation would be interpreted as absolute and unconditional, and performance might, straightway, be demanded.

Section XII.—A verbal obligation is, also, void, if made between absent persons. But, inasmuch as this rule gave ground of strife to the contentious, who alleged, after some time had elapsed, that either they were absent, or their opponents, we put forth our Constitution, addressed to the advocates of Cæsarea, and provided for the speedy settlement of such suits. Wherein, we did enact, that implicit belief shall be placed in such written acts or instruments as declare that the contracting parties were present; unless, indeed, the party who has availed himself of the shameless allegation of absence, shall be able to show, on the clearest evidence, either in writing, or by credible witnesses, that he, or his opponent, was in some other place during the whole day whereon the record of the contract purports to have been made.

Section XIII.—Formerly, a man could no more stipulate that a thing should be given him after his own death, than he could that it should be given after the death of the promiser. Nor could any person under the power of another, stipulate for a thing to be given him after the death of that other; inasmuch it was that other, whether father or master, who seemed to speak through him. Again, if a man were to have stipulated thus, " Do you promise to give me so much on the day before I die? or on the day before you die?" such stipulation would have been void. But, since, as has been said before, all stipulations gain their force from the consent of the contracting parties, we have deemed it advisable to introduce an essential alteration in this respect; so that now, a stipulation is good and effectual, whether it be stipulated that a thing be given after, or the day before, the death, whether of stipulator or of promiser.

Section XIV.—Again, if one in stipulation were to say, " If such a ship arrive to-morrow from Asia, do you engage to give me such a sum to-day?" such stipulation would be void, because preposterous. But, as the Emperor Leo, of illustrious memory, deemed that in the case of marriage portions, no stipulation should be set aside as preposterous; it has pleased us to give a wider effect to this doctrine; and to ordain, that, henceforth, every preposterous stipulation shall be good, not only in the case of marriage portions, but of all other contracts whatsoever.

Section XV.—A stipulation in these words, " Do you promise to give me when I die?" or " when you die?" was good by the ancient law; and it is so still.

Section XVI.—We may also make a valid stipulation, that a thing shall be given after the death of a third person.

Section XVII.—If it appear in writing, on the face of the instrument, or record of the contract, that a person has promised; it is always taken for granted that the promise was duly given in answer to a foregone interrogation.

Section XVIII.—When several things are included in one stipulation, and the promiser answers simply " I promise to give", he thereby binds himself to all. If, however, he promise to give one, or certain, of the things stipulated for, he is bound with respect to those things only, which, in his answer, he promised to give. For, where there are several stipulations, it may chance that some only have been perfected by receiving their separate answers; as for every object of a contract, a separate question, and a separate answer is, in strictness, needed.

Section XIX.—No man, as has already been laid down, can stipulate for the sole benefit of a third party; for obligations of this kind are designed to enable every person to obtain what he has an interest in obtaining; and the stipulator has no interest that something should be given to another. Still, if a person wish to do this, he should stipulate for a penalty to be paid to him, so that if the promiser omit to fulfil his promise, the stipulation for the penalty shall be valid even for one who has no interest in the fulfilment of the promise. Because, when a stipulation includes a penal clause, regard is had, not to the interest of the stipulator, but to the amount of the penalty. If, therefore, a man stipulate that a certain thing shall be given to Titius, his stipulation is void; but if he subjoin a penalty, and say, " Do you engage to give me so many pieces if you do not give this to Titius?" this stipulation will be binding on the promiser.

Section XX.—If, however, a man stipulate for the benefit of another, but is himself interested in the performance of the promise, the stipulation is effectual. Thus, if he who has begun to act as tutor, afterwards cedes the administration to his co-tutor, and stipulates for the careful management of the estate of the pupil; then will such obligation be binding, because, the stipulator has an interest in the performance of the promise, since he is answerable to the pupil in case of mal-administration. So, if a man stipulate for a thing to be given to his procurator, or attorney, the stipulation shall prevail. A valid stipulation, also, is that which a debtor makes for something to be paid over to his creditor; and this, because it is to the interest of the stipulator; either to the end, that he may not become liable to the exaction of any penalty due to his creditor, or that his goods, given in pledge, should not be sold.

Section XXI.—On the other hand, he who promises that another shall perform a certain act, does not appear to be bound, unless he subject himself to a penalty in the event of such act being not performed by the other.

Section XXII.—No man can validly stipulate that a thing which will hereafter belong to him, shall be given him, when it becomes his own.

Section XXIII.—If the stipulator refer to one thing, and the promiser to another, an obligation is no more contracted, than if no answer had been made to the interrogation. As, if one were to stipulate that you should give him Stichus, while you believed him to refer to Pamphilus, under the impression that Pamphilus was named Stichus.

Section XXIV.—A promise made for an immoral purpose, as to commit murder, or sacrilege, is not valid.

Section XXV.—If a conditional stipulation have been entered into, even though the stipulator die pending the accomplishment of the condition, his heir will be entitled, when the accomplishment does take place, to bring his action for execution of the promise. In like manner, the heir of the promiser is liable to be sued.

Section XXVI.—He who stipulates for a thing to be given him in a certain year or month, can have no legal claim upon the promiser until the whole year, or whole month, shall have expired.

Section XXVII.—Also, if you stipulate for a piece of land, or for a slave, you are not entitled to demand immediate delivery, but must wait until a reasonable time for delivery shall have elapsed.

TITLE 20.

OF SURETIES.

In support of him who passes his promise, other persons are wont to bind themselves. There are called Sureties, or Cautioners, or *Fide-jussors,* and creditors generally require them, in order to increase their own security.

Section I.—Sureties may be added in obligations of all kinds; that is whether contracted by delivery of the thing, by word, by writing, or by consent of the parties. Nor is it necessary, that the obligation to which the surety is made a party, be civil or natural; thus, a man may bind himself as surety for a slave, and may do so either to a stranger or to the master of the slave, when the thing due is so by a natural obligation.

Section II.—A surety is not only bound himself, but at his death transmits the obligation to his heir.

Section III.—The obligation of a surety may either precede, or follow that of the principal promiser.

Section IV.—When there are several sureties, however large their number, each one is liable for the whole debt; thus it is in the option of the creditor to demand the whole amount from any surety he will. Nevertheless, by virtue of a Rescript of the Emperor Hadrian, the creditor is compelled to demand separately from every surety, who is solvent at the time of the suit, his own proportional share of the debt; if, therefore, any of the sureties be insolvent at that time, the burthen falls the heavier on the rest. But, if a creditor should obtain the whole amount of his demand from one of the sureties, then if the principal debtor, for whom he became bound, be unable to pay, the entire loss shall fall upon that one surety. And such an one must blame himself alone, as he might have obtained relief by virtue of the Rescript of the Emperor Hadrian, and might have prayed to have been held liable, as surety, for no more than his own share of the debt.

Section V.—Sureties cannot legally be so bound as to owe more than does the principal debtor for whom they are bound; for their obligation is an accessory of the principal obligation, and the accessory cannot contain more than the principal. They may, on the other hand, be bound so as to owe less. If, therefore, the principal debtor owe ten pieces of gold, the surety may be bound for five; but he cannot be bound for ten, if the principal owe but five. If, again, the principal promise absolutely, the surety may promise conditionally; but not the reverse. Also, the words more or less, are used as well of time as of quantity; the obligation is greater, if one give a thing at once, but less if it be given only after a time.

Section VI.—If a surety have made payment for the principal debtor; he can bring an action of mandate against him for the recovery of the sum paid.

Section VII.—A surety may bind himself in Greek by saying Τῇ ἐμῇ πίστει κελεύω, λέγω, θέλω, or βούλομαι,—i. e., upon my faith I order—I say—I wish—I desire. The word φημὶ may be used as equivalent to λέγω.

Section VIII.—It must be observed, that in all stipulations of sureties, whatsoever is, in writing, stated to have been done, is presumed to have been actually done. If, therefore, a man, in writing, confess that he has bound himself as surety, it is presumed that all the usual forms were gone through.

TITLE 21.

OF OBLIGATIONS CONTRACTED BY WRITING.

FORMERLY a species of written obligation was in use, which was effected by registering the names of the contractors; these contracts were thence called *nomina*, but are now no longer in use. But, if a man state in writing, that he is indebted in a sum, which has never been paid over to him, he cannot, after any material lapse of time avail himself of an exception that the money had never been paid over to him; and the limitation of this time has very frequently been set forth by Imperial Constitutions. Hence it is, that in the present day, a man must be bound by his written act, if he can bring no legal exception; and from this written contract arises a condiction; in the absence, that is, of any verbal obligation. In former days, the Imperial Constitutions gave a space of time, of not less than five years, wherein any one might bring his exception, that the money had not been paid. But in the present day, that creditors may not be open for too long a time to the risk of being defrauded of their money, we have, by our Constitution, contracted this allowance of time, and have ordained, that no exception of this kind, shall be brought after the expiration of two years.

TITLE 22.

OF OBLIGATIONS CONTRACTED BY CONSENT.

Obligations are contracted by Consent, in the cases of bargain and sale, of letting and hiring, of partnership, and of mandate or commission. Now, in all these cases, an obligation is said to be contracted by consent, because neither writing, nor the presence of the parties is essential. Neither is it requisite that anything should be given, or delivered in order to make the obligation binding; it suffices that there be the consent of those between whom the business is conducted. Hence it is, that contracts of this sort may be entered into even between parties at a distance from each other, by means either of letters, or of messengers. Further, in obligations by consent, each party is bound to render to the other every thing that equity and good conscience doth demand; while in verbal obligations, the one party makes a stipulation, and the other a specific promise.

TITLE 23.

OF BARGAINS AND SALES.

The Contract of Sale is complete so soon as the price is agreed upon; although nothing has yet been paid, nor even any earnest given; for the earnest is nothing but an evidence that the sale has been contracted. This is, however, to be understood only of bargains and sales made without writing; for, with respect to sales of this kind, we have made no alteration in the rule. But, where there is a written contract, we have ordained, that a sale is not to be deemed absolute and complete, unless a proper instrument of sale have been drawn by the contracting parties, or at least signed by them, if drawn by others. And, if such instruments have been drawn up by a notary, the contract is to be deemed incomplete, unless they be formal, and finished in all respects; for, so long as there is anything lacking in this respect, there is room for change of purpose, and either buyer or seller may, without penalty, draw back from his agreement; that is, if nothing have been paid down in the way of earnest. But, if an earnest have been paid, then whether the contract be in writing or not in writing, the purchaser who refuses to fulfil it, forfeits the earnest which he has paid; and the seller, if he refuse, is compelled to restore twice the value of the earnest: and this, though no agreement as to earnest was expressly made.

Section I.—It is always essential that a price be fixed upon; for if there be no price, there is no sale. And such price must be certain. Formerly, it was a question much mooted by the ancient jurists, as to whether the sale be valid or not, when the contracting parties agree that the thing shall be sold at the sum " at which Titius shall value it." We, however, have settled the point, by enacting, that whensoever a sale is agreed to be made at a price to be settled by a third party, the contract shall be held binding under the condition that, if such third person do fix the price, then in accordance with his valuation, the said price shall be paid, the thing delivered, and the sale completed: and that if either purchaser or seller shall then draw back, he will be liable to an action at the suit of the other party. If, however, the third party named be either unable, or unwilling, to fix the price, the sale is void, as having been made without of agreement as to price. And, as we have made this regulation with reference to contracts of sale, it seems only reasonable to extend it also to contracts of letting and hiring.

Section II.—In a sale, the price should consist in cash, or money told. It has been much questioned whether, indeed, price can consist in anything besides, as in a slave, a piece of ground, or a toga. Sabinus and Cassius were of opinion, that price might consist of anything; and hence comes the vulgar notion, that a bargain and sale is contracted by exchange; and that exchange is, in truth, the oldest kind of sale. They who so argued, used to quote the lines of Homer, who tells us, in the lines following, how the Greeks procured wine, by giving certain things in exchange for it:

> Wine the rest purchased at their proper cost,
> And well the plenteous freight supplied the host:
> Each in exchange proportioned treasures gave,
> Some brass or iron, some an ox or slave.

But other jurists, of another school, maintained the contrary opinion; affirming that exchange was one thing, and sale another; for otherwise, said they, in a mere exchange, it would be impossible to say which was the thing sold, and which the thing given as a price; for it were unreasonable to look upon each article as, at once, the thing sold, and the price given. The opinion, however, of Proculus, that exchange is a contract wholly distinct from sale, has very properly prevailed; supported as he is by other lines from Homer, and also by the stronger arguments. This, also, is the doctrine admitted by preceding Emperors, and fully set forth in our Digests.

Section III.—So soon as the bargain and sale is contracted (and this, as we have observed, in the case of a sale made without writing, is effected so soon as the price is agreed upon,) all risk as to the thing sold belongs to the purchaser; although it has not yet been delivered to him. If, therefore, after sale, a slave die or receive any bodily hurt; or if a house, or part of it, be destroyed by fire; or if a piece of land, or any portion of it, be washed away by a flood, or injured by an inundation, or by a tempest hurling down the trees; the loss in all these cases, must be borne by the purchaser, who is obliged to pay the price agreed upon, even though he never had possession of the thing. Whatever may happen to the thing sold without the evil design or fault of the vendor, the vendor is not liable. So, on the other hand, if after the sale, any accession be made to the land by alluvion, the advantage accrues solely to the purchaser. For the legal maxim is that;—He who runs the risk, should reap the gain. But if a slave who has been sold, either run away or be stolen before delivery, and no evil design nor fraud can be charged upon the seller, it will become a question, as to whether the seller undertook to keep him in safe custody until delivery. If he did, the risk of such casual occurrences falls upon him; if not, the seller is not liable, and the loss falls solely on the purchaser. The like holds as to all other animals and things. The seller, however, is held (as against third parties) to be the owner until delivery; and, therefore, when such accidents occur, he is bound to transfer to the purchaser his rights of action whether real or personal; and it so, also, with regard to actions of theft and damage.

Section IV.—A contract of sale may be as well conditional as unconditional and absolute; as, thus, "If Stichus suit you within such a time, you shall have him for so much."

Section V.—Whoso, of his knowledge, purchases a sacred or religious spot, or a public place, as a Forum or Basilica, makes a void purchase. If, however, taken in by the seller, he purchased, under the impression that what he was buying was profane, or private, then, as he cannot enjoy what he has purchased, he has his right of action against the seller to recover the damage suffered by the deceit. The same rule holds, in the event of his having purchased a free-man, under the supposition that he was a slave.

TITLE 24.

OF LETTING AND HIRING.

THE Contract of Letting and Hiring is very similar to that of sale, and is governed by the same rules of law. As a bargain and sale is contracted so soon as the price is settled, so a contract of letting and hiring is formed so soon as the hire is agreed to; and both letter and hirer have their peculiar legal remedies, if the contract be broken by the other party.

Section I.—What we have above said of the case of a sale wherein the price is to be determined by a third party, may be understood also of a letting and hiring, where the amount of hire is left to the decision of a third party. If, therefore, a man have sent clothes to a fuller to be scoured, or to a tailor to be mended, and have made no previous stipulation as to the sum to be paid for their work, purposing only to give what afterwards they may determine on, no strict contract of letting and hiring can be said to have been made; still, however, either is at liberty to bring an action on the case.

Section II.—Further, as it was formerly often asked whether a bargain or sale could be contracted by exchange, a like question has been frequently put with reference to the contract of letting and hiring. For instance, if one man were to give you a certain thing to use or enjoy, and were in return to receive from you a certain other thing, of which he also should have the use or enjoyment; it has been held, that is not a letting and hiring, but a special kind of contract.

Thus, suppose that two neighbours have each got an ox, and suppose that they mutually agree, each to lend the other his ox, to share in the field-work for ten days, alternately; now if one of the oxen die, while in the custody of the person who did not own it, the owner of the dead beast cannot bring any of the actions formally permitted in breaches of letting, or hiring; nor can he bring one as for a commodate or loan, because there was consideration given; he has, however, his right to an action on the case.

Section III.—Contracts of bargain and sale, and of letting and hiring are so closely allied, that it has, in certain cases, been a question whether the contract were the one or the other. As, when lands have been delivered to one to enjoy for ever; that is, on condition, that so long as a yearly rent is paid to the proprietor, he shall have no legal power to take such lands away from the hirer or his heir; or from any other person to whom the hirer or his heir shall have sold, or given them, whether gratuitously or as a marriage portion. Now, as a contract such as this, was one concerning the nature of which the ancients had considerable doubts, some looking on it as a letting and hiring, and some as a bargain and sale, the Constitution of Zeno was enacted, which declared that it was a contract of a special nature; and that the contract of *Emphyteusis* (so it was called) was not the same with either of the contracts named above, but was supported by its own distinct covenants. It declared, also, that if any special agreement had been made, it should hold, just as though it were of the nature of a contract; but that, if no agreement were made as to any risk which might accrue to the thing, and a total loss were to ensue, the owner should be the sufferer; but, if a partial loss, the burthen should be borne by the occupier. And this is the law which still prevails.

Section IV.—Again, if Titius were to make a bargain with a goldsmith to make a certain number of rings, of particular size and weight, and to furnish the gold; and for this work and materials, Titius was to give, say ten gold pieces, it has been a question whether this contract would be one of sale, or of letting and hiring. Cassius was of opinion that there is a sale of the materials, and a letting and hiring of the goldsmith's labour; it has, however, been now settled to be a contract of sale only. But, if Titius were to supply his own gold, and a sum were agreed to be given for the work, there is no doubt but the contract is one of letting and hiring.

Section V.—The hirer, or lessee, is bound to do all things in accordance with the lease or contract of hire; and if there be any omission in such lease or contract, he is nevertheless bound by the rules of equity and good conscience. He who has given or promised hire for the use of clothes, silver, oxen, or the like, is bound to such care in the custody thereof, as a careful father of a family bestows on the custody of his own property. But if, notwithstanding such care, he lose the thing by some mischance, he is not bound to restore it.

Section VI.—If the hirer, or lessee, die during the continuance of the term of the letting, his heir succeeds to all the rights given by the contract.

TITLE 25.

OF PARTNERSHIP.

PARTNERSHIPS are of two kinds, one, wherein the partners agree to place in common all their property, and this the Greeks emphatically called " Communion"; the other where they join only to carry on some particular business, as the sale or purchase of slaves, wine, oil, or wheat.

Section I.—If there be no express agreement as to the proportions of loss and gain to be shared between the parties, the loss must be equally borne, and the gain equally divided. If, however, there have been a special agreement as to the shares of profit and loss, it must be observed; and, indeed, it has never been a matter of doubt, but that two persons may validly agree that two-thirds of the profit and loss shall belong to one partner, and that the other shall take the remaining third.

Section II.—A partnership, however, of the kind following has been much questioned: Titius and Seius have mutually bargained that two-thirds of the profit and one-third of the loss shall belong to Titius, and two-thirds of the loss and but one-third of the profit to Seius; ought such an agreement to be upheld? Quintus Mutius held it to be contrary to the nature of partnership, and therefore not to be ratified. Servius Sulpitius, however, whose opinion has prevailed, held the contrary opinion, and declared for its validity, because oftentimes the services of particular partners are so valuable that it is but just to admit them into partnership on terms most advantageous. Nay, one cannot hesitate in saying that a partnership may validly be formed, with equal share of profits, between two persons, of whom the one contributes money while the other contributes none; and this, because frequently a man's work is equivalent to money. Also, contrary to the opinion of Quintus Mutius, it has been held, that, by special agreement, a partner may be entitled to share the profit, and yet be without liability as to any share of the loss; and this was held by Servius, in consistence with his other views as to partnerships. This, however, must be understood to mean, that if profit accrue from one transaction, and loss be suffered in another, a balance must be struck, and the surplus of gain over loss, alone be reckoned as the gain.

Section III.—It is also a settled point, that if the proportions on one side only be agreed on, as those of profit only, or those of loss only, the like proportions are to be considered as held on the side whereof no mention is made.

Section IV.—A partnership endures so long only as the parties continue in the intention of remaining partners: but if any one of them renounce the partnership, the partnership is dissolved. If, however, a partner renounce with fraudulent intent, that he alone may reap the benefit of some expected gain; as, for instance, if a man who is member of an universal partnership, *i. e.* one which embraces the whole property of all the partners, renounce in order to gain the sole benefit of an inheritance, he may be forced to share the source of gain with the other partners. If, however, after renunciation, he reap some gain, of which he had no previous expectation, such gain belongs to him alone. The partners, also, from whom he has severed himself by renunciation, are entitled exclusively to all that they acquire after such renunciation.

Section V.—A partnership is dissolved, also, by the death of a partner; for he who enters into this contract has regard to a person with whom he associates himself. And although more than two persons have entered into partnership, the contract is dissolved by the death of any, although several more survive; unless, indeed, special covenants have been framed on the formation of the contract.

Section VI.—A partnership contracted for a special business, or transaction, is determined by the conclusion of such business or transaction.

Section VII.—It is quite clear, that a partnership is determined by the confiscation of all the effects of a partner; for, as another, to wit the public Treasury, succeeds to his property and in his room, he is reputed to be dead in law.

Section VIII.—Also, if a partner pressed by the burthen of his debts, make a surrender of his goods, and they be sold to satisfy the claims against him, public or private, the partnership is at an end. But here, if the parties (including the bankrupt) consent, to continue in partnership, it seems to be the commencement of a new partnership.

Section IX.—It has been a question, whether one partner can be made liable to the other partners, for fraud only, as in the case of one who has suffered property to be deposited with him; or whether he can be for a fault also, that is to say, for lack of care or energy. It has been now settled that he is liable for fault; but such fault is not to be measured by the most rigid standard of carefulness that can be conceived. It suffices that he have used such care in regard to the goods of the partnership, as he is wont to do in regard to his own private property. For he who associates to himself as partner, a man of careless habits, must lay the blame upon himself alone.

TITLE 26.

OF MANDATE OR PROCURATION.

The Contract of Mandate is entered into in five ways; according as a mandator gives you a mandate for his benefit alone; or for your benefit and his; or solely for the benefit of a third party; or for his benefit and that of a third party; or for your benefit and that of another. If, however, a mandate be given you, for your benefit alone, it is useless, and no obligation or right of action can arise therefrom.

Section I.—A mandate is for the sole benefit of the mandator; if, for example, a man give you a mandate to transact his business, to buy him an estate, or to become his surety.

Section II.—A mandate is for your benefit and also of the mandator; if, for example, a man give you a mandate to lend money at interest to a third party, who is to use such money in the affairs of the mandator. Or if, when you are about to sue a man in his character of surety, he give you a mandate to sue the principal at his risk; or to stipulate, at his hazard, for a debt he owes to you, from some other whom he appoints as his substitute.

Section III.—A mandate is solely for the benefit of a third party; if, for example, a man give you a mandate to transact the business of a third party, to buy lands, or to become surety for him.

Section IV.—A mandate is for the benefit of the mandator and of a third party; if, for example, a man give you a mandate to transact the joint affairs of himself and of a third party, or to buy lands, or become surety for him and a third party.

Section V.—A mandate is made for your benefit, and for that of a third party; if, for example, a man give you a mandate to lend money at interest to a third party. If the mandate were to lend it without interest, it would be for the sole benefit of a third person.

Section VI.—A mandate is made for your benefit alone; if, for example, a man give you a mandate to invest your own money in land rather than at interest, or the contrary. A mandate of this kind is, however, more properly advice than mandate, and therefore, produces no obligation; for no man is bound by the effects of any advice which he may give, even though it be not such as is expedient to be acted upon, because every man is at liberty to judge for himself whether advice given to him, be judicious or the contrary. If, therefore, you had a sum of money lying idle in your house, and some one advised you to make a purchase with it, or to lend it out at interest, your adviser is not thereby liable to an action of mandate, although it may have been a loss to you, to complete such purchase, or to make such loan. And this is so clear, that it has been doubted whether an action of mandate will lie, against one who has given you a mandate to lend your money at interest to Titius. But the opinion of Sabinus has prevailed, which affirms such mandate to be obligatory; for you would never have trusted Titius, if such mandate had not been given.

Section VII.—A mandate, again, which is contrary to good morals is not binding; as, for instance, if Titius were to give you a mandate to commit a theft, or do some wrongful act or injury; although you pay the penalty of your obedience to such a mandate, you have still no right of action against Titius.

Section VIII.—He who executes a mandate must not exceed

the limits of his mandate; if, for example, a man empowered you by mandate to purchase lands, or to be bound for Titius to the amount of a hundred pieces of gold; you must not exceed this sum, either in the purchase, or the suretyship, for otherwise you can have no action against the mandator for recovery of the excess. Cassius and Sabinus have indeed held that, even if you limited your action to the hundred pieces authorized by the mandate, you could not recover. Jurists of the other school say that you may rightly bring an action limited to a hundred pieces; and this, clearly, is the better opinion. If, however, you make the purchase for a smaller sum than that specified, you have certainly your right of action against the mandator; for he who gives a mandate that an estate shall be bought for him at the cost of a hundred pieces, is understood to mean that the purchase should be made for less if possible.

Section IX.—A mandate, lawfully contracted, is dissolved if revoked before any act have been done in execution of it.

Section X.—Also if, before any act have been done in execution of a mandate, the mandator, or the mandatory die, the mandate is annulled. But, for general convenience, it has been established, that if, after the death of one who has given you a mandate, you, in ignorance of his death, should execute such mandate, you will be entitled to bring an action for indemnification. Otherwise you would suffer for, and be prejudiced by, what was justifiable and natural ignorance. Upon like principles, it was decided, that if the debtors of Titius made their payments to the slave who was his steward, not knowing that he had been emancipated, they were freed from their debts by such payment; although, by the strict letter of the law, they ought not to have been freed, as they had paid a person other than him whom they ought to have paid.

Section XI.—Any man is free to refuse to accept a mandate; but if he have once accepted, he must go through with it, or else renounce at the earliest opportunity, in order that the mandator may either do himself the business which is the object of the mandate or find another mandatory. For, if the renunciation be not made so that the mandator is in a position to transact the business properly, an action of mandate will lie against the mandatory, in spite of his renunciation; unless he can show good cause for not having made the renunciation, or for not having made it within a proper time.

Section XII.—A contract of mandate may be qualified by a term, or suspended by a condition.

Section XIII.—Finally, it is to be noted, that if a mandate be not gratuitous, it takes the form of another species of contract; for if a price be fixed on, it becomes a hiring and letting. And, we may lay it down as a general rule, that in all cases where, if the duty were undertaken gratuitously, the contract would be one of mandate or deposit, it will become one of letting and hiring, if pay be given. If, therefore, a man give his clothes to a fuller to be scoured, or to a tailor to be made, without the offer or promise of any pay, the contract is one of mandate, and may be supported by an action as such.

TITLE 27.

OF OBLIGATIONS FROM IMPROPER CONTRACTS.

Having now enumerated the different kinds of direct contracts, let us go on to speak of those obligations which do not, in strictness, spring from a contract; but which, as they do not take their origin from a wrong, seem to arise from an implied, or quasi-contract.

Section I.—If a person have transacted the affairs of another in his absence, there arise mutual rights of action between them, which actions are called *negotiorum gestorum*—i. e. " for business done". The action of the owner against the manager of his affairs is said to be " direct"; and that of the latter against the owner is called " contrary". It is clear that these actions spring from no regular contract; for they obtain only when any one, without mandate or authorization, has, of his own will, taken upon him the management of the affairs of another; and consequently those whose affairs are thus managed are bound by an obligation, even against their knowledge. This law has been admitted from motives of public convenience, that the affairs of persons who are forced to depart in haste, without having committed the management to any one, may not be wholly neglected. And, assuredly, no one would take this care upon himself, unless he had a right of action to enable him to recover what he might have expended. But, just as he who has advantageously managed the affairs of another, binds this other to him by an obligation; so, in his turn, is he himself bound to render an account of his administration. In such a case, he is bound to render an account, with the most careful exactness; and it is not sufficient that he use the same amount of diligence as in his own affairs; provided another person of greater diligence might have conducted the affairs of the absent one with greater carefulness and profit.

Section II.—Tutors, also, who are liable to an action of tutelage, cannot in strictness, be said to be bound by contract; for there is no special agreement between the tutor and the ward. But as they are not bound by a wrong, it appears that they are bound by an implied, or quasi-contract. In this case also, both tutor and ward, have mutual remedies by action against each other. For not only has the ward a direct action against his tutor; but the tutor, in his turn, has a cross-action against his pupil, provided he have incurred any expenses in managing the pupil's property, or have become bound for him, or have mortgaged his own goods as security to the pupil's creditors.

Section III.—Also, when a thing is the common property of several persons, without there being any partnership between them; as, for example, if a thing be jointly bequeathed, or jointly given to them all; each is reciprocally bound to the other by an action of common partition, to restore whatever fruits of the thing one of them has received alone, or to re-pay whatever necessary expenses one of them has incurred touching the common property. But yet none of these persons can be said to be bound by a contract, since they made no agreement between themselves; still, as they are not bound by a wrong, it appears that they are bound by an implied, or quasi-contract.

Section IV.—The same law prevails in regard to him who is bound to his co-heir, and is liable to an action for the distribution and partition of an inheritance among co-heirs.

Section V.—The heir, also, cannot properly be said to be bound by contract to the legatee; for the legatee cannot be said to have entered into any contract, either with the heir, or with the deceased; still as the heir is not bound by a wrong, it appears that he is bound by an implied or quasi-contract.

Section VI.—Also, he to whom any one has paid, through error, money not due to him, is bound, as it were, by a quasi-contract. Nay so far is he from being strictly bound by a contract, that, to reason strictly, he is bound by the breach, rather than by the formation of a contract; for he who makes a payment, with intent to discharge his debts, does it with the intention to dissolve, rather than to contract an agreement. He, nevertheless, who receives it, as aforesaid, by mistake, is bound precisely as if it had been given him as a *Mutuum,* or loan, and is liable to a condiction for its recovery.

Section VII.—In certain cases, however, money paid in error cannot be recovered; for the ancient jurists gave it as their opinion that where an action for double the amount of a debt lies upon the denial of it, as, for instance, in actions brought under the Aquilian Law, and in the case of legacies, the debtor can never recover money which he has paid by mistake. These jurists, however, only applied the rule in the case of fixed and certain legacies, devised by obligation on the heir. But our Imperial Constitution, which has placed all legacies and trusts on one and the same footing, has extended to legacies and trusts in general, this effect of denial in doubling the amount demanded. It has not, however, given to all legatees the privilege of not refunding what has been paid when not due, but has restricted it to legacies to churches and other holy places, which are consecrated for the uses of religion and piety.

TITLE 28.

OF PERSONS THROUGH WHOM OBLIGATIONS ARISE.

Having now explained the various kinds of obligation which arise from contracts, or from implied or quasi-contracts, we may now observe that we acquire an obligation, not by ourselves alone, but by those also who are in our power; as by our slaves or children. That, however, which is acquired by our slaves is absolutely ours: but that which is acquired by the obligation of our children, is divided according to the rule in our Constitution laid down, as to the usufruct, and the property of the things. So that, of the profits of any action, the father has the usufruct, but the ownership will be received for the son; that is, when the father brings the action in conformity with the regulations of our new Constitution.

Section I.—An obligation is also acquired for us by free-men, and by the slaves of others, in whom we have a *bonâ fide* possession. This, however, is but in two cases; namely, if the acquisition arise from their own labour, or from something which belongs to us.

Section II.—In the like cases, also, an obligation is acquired for us by a slave of whom we have only the usufruct, or use.

Section III.—A slave, the common property of several masters, undoubtedly acquires for his masters, in proportion to the property which each has in him; unless he stipulate or receive something for one only, whom he mentions by name, when he acquires for this one alone; as, for instance, if he stipulate thus, " Do you engage to give to Titius, my master?" And though formerly it was doubted whether a slave who had stipulated by order of one only of his masters, could acquire for him alone who had given him the order, yet since the publication of our Constitution there can be no doubt of his ability to do so.

TITLE 29.

OF THE EXTINCTION OF OBLIGATIONS.

EVERY obligation is extinguished by the payment, of that which is due; or by the payment, with consent of the creditor, of some thing instead of that which is actually due. And it is immaterial whether the payment be made by the debtor himself, or by some other person on his behalf; for he is freed from the obligation, if payment be made by a third party, and that whether with or without his consent, or even against his will. Also if the debtor himself pay, all who have become surety for him are thereby set free. The same is the case if the surety make the payment; not only is he set free, but the obligation of the debtor to the creditor is extinguished also.

Section I.—An obligation is also extinguished by acceptilation; which is a feigned payment. For example, if Titius be willing to grant a discharge for what is due to him by a verbal contract, he may do so by allowing the following question to be put to him by the debtor, " Do you acknowledge that you have received that which I promised you?" and by himself saying in reply, " I do." An acceptilation may also be worded in Greek provided it be in form similar to that in Latin, which we have above given. Obligations, then, arising from verbal contracts are so extinguished, but not obligations of any other kind; and it seems, indeed, appropriate that a contract formed by words, should be by words extinguished. But any other kind of obligation may be reduced to the form of a stipulation, and so extinguished by an acceptilation. And as a debt may be paid in part, so also there may be an acceptilation of part.

Section II.—A new kind of stipulation, called the Aquilian, has been framed, by virtue of which an obligation of any kind may be reduced to the form of a stipulation, and so afterwards dissolved by acceptilation. The Aquilian stipulation effects a *novation* of all obligations,—*i. e.* substitutes one liability, or obligation for another,—and was framed by Gallus Aquilius, in the terms following: Aulus Agerius stipulated that Numerius Negidius should give him a certain sum of money in lieu of, " whatever, for any cause, you are, or shall be bound to give to or do for me, either or at any future day, absolutely or upon condition; whatever does or may entitle me to maintain against you any actions, whether personal or real, or any prosecutions; whatever property of mine you have, detain, or possess, or of which you have fraudulently quitted possession; be the value of such property, as it may." Numerius Negidius did so engage, and said " I do." Then after this was done, Numerius asked Aulus, saying, " Do you consider as accepted and received, all that by the Aquilian stipulation I have this day promised?" To which Aulus answered that he did consider that it was by him accepted and received.

Section III.—An obligation is also extinguished by novation; as, for instance, if Seius stipulate from Titius, for that which is due from you to Seius. For, by the intervention of a new person, a new obligation arises, and the first obligation is extinguished by being merged in the second; so much so, that it may happen, that the former stipulation, by the effect of the novation, is extinguished, even though the latter be not valid; as, for example, if Titius were to stipulate from a ward, without the authority of his tutor, for a debt which you owe to Titius; in this case, the whole claim of Titius is extinguished, for the first debtor is discharged, and the second obligation is null. The case, however, is not the same, if the second stipulation have been made with a slave; for then the original debtor remains bound, as much as though the second stipulation had never been made. And if the second stipulation be made with the original debtor, there will be no novation, unless the second obligation be different from the former; as, for example, the addition or suppression of a condition, a term, or a surety. But, the assertion that the addition of a condition causes novation, must be understood to mean that if the fresh condition be accomplished, the novation takes effect; but that if it be not accomplished, the former obligation remains binding. The jurists of old held, that there was novation, when the second obligation was entered into for the purpose and with the intention of making the novation; wherefore it often became a matter of considerable doubt, as to whether this intention of making a novation did exist, and divers authorities delivered divers opinions, according to the different cases they had to settle. For this reason, therefore, our Constitution was published, which expressly laid it down, that novation shall take place only when the contracting parties have expressly declared their intention to make the new as a dissolution of the old contract; and where this is not the case, the first obligation shall continue binding, and the second also, as an accession to the first; so that, both the first contract and the second, will give an obligation still binding, according to the provisions of our Constitution aforesaid, which may be learnt more fully by a perusal of the Constitution itself.

Section IV.—We must in addition remark, that obligations contracted by consent, are dissolved by dissent. For if Titius and Seius have agreed that Tititus shall sell, and Seius buy the Tusculan estate for a hundred pieces; and afterwards, before the contract has been executed, that is, before the money has been paid, or land delivered, they agree to annul the sale, they are reciprocally set free. The like rule holds in cases of letting and hiring, and in all other contracts formed by consent alone.

END OF BOOK III.

BOOK IV.

TITLE 1.

OF OBLIGATIONS WHICH ARISE FROM WRONG.

Now that we have, in the preceding Book, treated of obligations arising from contract, and from implied or quasi-contract, let us turn to the consideration of obligations arising from wrong, and from implied or quasi-wrong. The obligations discussed in the last Book are, as we have said, divided into four species; but those of which we are now about to speak form but one species; for they all spring from the thing, that is, from the wrong itself; as from theft, robbery, injury to property, or wrong.

Section I.—Theft is the fraudulent taking of a thing, or of its use, or of its possession; a thing which is forbidden by the Law of Nature.

Section II.—The word *furtum*—*i. e.*, "theft",—is derived from *furvum*—*i. e.*, "black"—because it is committed secretly, and usually in the night; or from *fraus*—*i. e.*, "fraud"; or from *ferre*—*i. e.*, "to carry away";—or from the Greek φώρ,—*i. e.*, a thief.

Section III.—Of thefts there are two species, the manifest, and the not manifest: for the terms applied to thefts of *conceptum*, and *oblatum*, as will appear below, are rather kinds of actions attaching to theft, than actual kinds of theft. A manifest thief, is one taken in the act of thieving, and in the place where he committed it: as, for example, if a man, who had committed a theft in a house, were to be caught before he had got outside the gate of it; or, having stolen grapes or olives, were to be taken in the olive field, or vineyard. Manifest theft must be extended also to the case of a thief seen or seized, by the owner or any other person, in a place, whether public or private, when actually holding the thing stolen, before he has reached the place where he meant to carry and deposit it. If, however, he have carried the stolen property to its place of destination, he is not a manifest thief, even though the property be found upon his person. From what we have said of a manifest theft may be understood what is meant by a not manifest theft; for every theft which is not a manifest is a not manifest theft.

Section IV.—A theft is said to be *conceptum*—"found,"— when a thing stolen has been searched for and found, before witnesses, in the possession of some person; for though such person be not the actual thief, he is liable to a special action called "*concepti*". A theft is said to be *oblatum*—"offered,"— when a thing stolen has been offered to you, and then seized on your premises; that is, if he who offered it did so to the intent that it might be found in your possession rather than in his. And you, on whose premises the thing was seized, would be entitled to bring against him who offered it, a special action, called *oblati*, even though he were not the actual thief. There is also an action called *prohibiti furti*, which lies against any one who prohibits, or hinders another who wishes to search, in the presence of witnesses, for goods which had been stolen. Besides, by the action *furti non exhibiti*, a penalty is provided by the Prætor's Edict, against any man who has not exhibited things stolen, which, upon search held, have been found upon his premises. But all the four special actions which have been here enumerated have fallen into disuse: for search for things stolen is not now made according to the old formalities, and therefore, as a natural consequence, these actions have ceased to be in use; for now it is a point most clearly settled, that all who willingly have received or hidden stolen goods, are subject to the penalty of " theft not manifest."

Section V.—The penalty for manifest theft is fourfold the worth of the thing stolen; and this whether the thief be a free-man, or a slave. The penalty for theft not manifest is double.

Section VI.—Theft is committed, not only when a man takes away the property of another, for the purpose of appropriating it, but also, in a more general sense, when any one takes the property of another, against the will of its owner. So, if a creditor make use of a pledge, or a depositary of the deposit left with him, or he who has the use of a thing for a special purpose, convert it to other uses than those assigned, it is a theft. It is, for example, theft if a man borrow plate, on the plea of having friends to supper, and then carry it into a foreign land; or if a man borrow a horse for a ride, and take it much beyond the distance which he ought; and the jurists said that he who takes a borrowed horse into battle is guilty of theft.

Section VII.—It has, however, been decided that they who borrow things, and use them for purposes other than those for which they were lent, are guilty of theft, only if they well know that they are acting in opposition to the wishes of the owner, who would have forbidden such application, if he had known of it. If, however, they really believed that the owner would have given his consent, they are guilty of no crime. And this is a right distinction; for there can be no theft, unless there be the intent to commit theft.

Section VIII.—Also, even though a man believe that he is using a thing borrowed contrary to the will and intentions of the owner, while in reality the owner agrees to such an application, it is alleged to be no theft. Whence arose the moot point following:—Titius urged the slave of Mævius to rob his master, and to bring the stolen goods to him; of this the slave gave information to his master; Mævius, being minded to take Titius in the act, permitted his slave to take certain things to Titius;—is Titius liable to an action of theft, or to one for having corrupted a slave, or to neither? Now when this doubtful question was laid before us, and we had gone into the conflicting opinions which the ancient jurists held on the subject, some thinking he was liable to neither action, some that he was to that of theft alone; in order to put an end to quibbling niceties we have decided that in this case both actions shall lie. For although the slave may, in reality, be none the worse for the solicitation, and therefore the rules of the action for corruption of slaves do not apply, still the intention to corrupt the honesty of the slave is beyond all doubt; and he is, therefore, as deserving of punishment, as if the slave had really been corrupted; and this especially, lest impunity in his case might encourage others to perpetrate the like offence in the case of a slave more easy to corrupt.

Section IX.—Free-persons also, may be the subject of a theft; as if one of our children in our power be carried off.

Section X.—A man may, under certain circumstances, commit a theft even upon himself; as, when a debtor takes away any particular thing, which he has left in pledge with his creditor.

Section XI.—An action of theft will at times lie against one who has not himself committed the theft; as, for example, against one by whose aid and advice the theft was committed. Of this kind, also, is the case of him who strikes money from your hand that another may pick it up; or of him who has so obstructed you, that another is able to carry off some property of yours; or of him who has driven away your flocks or herds, to the intent that another may steal them. The ancient jurists included in this class the man who frightened a herd from its pasturage, with a piece of scarlet cloth. But, if these acts be done in wantonness alone, and with no *malice prepense* to the end that a theft should be committed, there will lie, not an action of theft, but one upon the case alone. If, however, Mævius help Titius to commit a theft, both are subject to an action of theft. A man, again, may be considered to aid and abet in theft, who has planted a ladder against a window, or broken through a window or a door, to the intent that another may commit a theft. So, too, may he who has lent crow-bars to break open doors, or ladders to plant under windows, with full knowledge of the evil purpose whereto they are to be applied. It is, however, a settled point, that he who has given no actual assistance in the commission of a theft, but has only advised and urged that it should be committed, is not liable to an action of theft.

Section XII.—If persons under power, whether of parents or masters, steal anything, the property of him in whose power they are, they commit a theft, and the thing taken is looked upon as stolen; and cannot, therefore, be acquired by use and prescription, before it has returned into the hands of the owner. In this case, however, no action of theft can be brought, for between parties so mutually related, no action of any sort or kind can lie. If, however, such a theft have been committed by the assistance and advice of another, such other will be liable to an action of debt; because a theft has clearly been committed, and has, as clearly, been so committed through his agency.

Section XIII.—An action of theft is competent to any one who has an interest in the preservation of the thing, even though he be not the owner. And, similarly, the proprietor cannot bring this action, unless he has an interest in keeping the thing from destruction.

Section XIV.—Hence it follows, that a creditor may bring an action of theft if a thing pledged to him have been stolen; and this, although his debtor is solvent, because it may be more to his advantage to rely upon the value of the pledge, than to proceed against the person of his debtor. And this is so clearly laid down, that even though it be the debtor himself who has stolen the thing pledged, an action of theft will lie against him at the suit of the creditor.

Section XV.—Again, if a fuller receive clothes to scour, or a tailor to mend, for a certain fixed sum; and if afterwards, they be stolen from his custody; the fuller, or the tailor, can bring an action of theft, but the owner cannot. For the owner is not deemed to be interested in their safety, as he may bring his action *locati*—" of the thing let and hired"—to recover the value of the thing stolen. If a thing be stolen from a *bond fide* purchaser, he is entitled, like a creditor, to an action of theft. The fuller or tailor, however, cannot maintain an action of theft unless he be solvent; that is, unless he be able to pay the owner the value of the thing stolen; for if any such tradesman be insolvent, the owner, as he has no power to recover from him, may bring an action of theft; and this, because, under such circumstances, he has a direct interest in the safety of the thing. The same rule holds if the tradesman be but partly solvent.

Section XVI.—Ancient jurists held, that what we have here said of the fuller and the tailor is applicable also to the borrower. For, as the fuller, by accepting a fixed sum for his labour, is answerable for the goods committed to his care, so also is the borrower, who accepts a loan in order to make use of it. But we have provided, by our decisions, an improvement in the law on this point, so that the owner is now free to elect whether he will bring an action for the thing lent as against the borrower, or an action of theft, as against the thief. If, however, he have elected to pursue one course of action, it will not be competent to him afterwards to change his mind and avail himself of the other. Also, if he elect to prosecute the thief, the borrower is freed; and if to bring his suit against the borrower, he cannot bring an action against the thief: the borrower, however, may, provided always that the owner, in electing to sue the borrower, well knew that the thing had been stolen. But, if the owner had no such knowledge, or at least considerable doubts as to the matter, and therefore brought his suit against the borrower, but afterwards on learning further particulars wishes to withdraw his action against the borrower, and to recur to an action of theft, he may then be permitted to sue the thief without any obstacle being thrown in his way; and this, because it was only in ignorance of the real facts, that he brought his suit against the borrower. Such will be the case, unless, indeed, the owner's claim shall have been satisfied by the borrower; for then the thief is free from any action of theft at the suit of the owner, but the borrower takes the owner's room in his power to bring such an action. It is, again, most clear that if at first the owner bring his action against the borrower, for a thing which he does not know to have been stolen; and afterwards, when he does know it, chooses to proceed against the thief, the borrower is absolutely secure, whatever be the issue of the suit against the thief. Also, as in the last case, the thief would be freed whether the borrower were able to satisfy the whole, or a part only of the claim against him.

Section XVII.—A depositary is not liable for the safe custody of the thing deposited with him; but is so only if he be guilty of some wilful wrong. If, therefore, the deposit be stolen from him; as he is not bound by the contract of deposit to make restitution, and has no direct interest in its safety, he cannot bring an action of theft; for, in this case, such can he be maintained by the owner only.

Section XVIII.—It is further to be observed, that a question has arisen, as to whether a person within puberty, who has taken away the property of another, can be guilty of theft. And it has been settled, that as intention constitutes theft, one within years of puberty is bound only by the obligation springing from the wrong, if he be very near to years of puberty, and is, therefore, able to understand that he is doing what is criminal.

Section XIX.—An action of theft seeks but to recover the penalty, whether double or quadruple. For the owner can recover possession of the thing itself, either by a *vindication,*—*i. e.* a real action for restitution; or by a *condiction,*—*i. e.* a personal action for the value. The former may be brought against him who has the thing in his possession, whether the thief, or any other; the latter may be maintained only against the thief himself, or his heir; but against either of them it may be brought, although not in actual possession of the thing.

TITLE 2.

OF ROBBERY.

A PERSON who takes a thing belonging to another by force, is liable to an action of theft; for who can be said to take away the property of another more against his will that he who uses force to take it. Such an one is, therefore, rightly called a thief of the worst kind. The Prætor, however, has instituted a special action, called that " of goods taken with violence"; and this, if brought within one year of the committal of the robbery, involves a penalty of fourfold the value of the thing taken; but after the expiration of that time the single value only can be claimed. This action is available against any one who has taken property, however small in value, and has used violence in the taking. But this fourfold value is not wholly a penalty, and such as gives besides a right to sue for the thing itself, as we have said to be the case in the action of theft; but here the thing is included in the fourfold valuation, so that in reality, the penalty is but triple the value. And it is the same whether the robber was, or was not taken in the actual commission of the fact; for it would be an absurdity that he who takes with violence, should be more favorably considered than he who is guilty of a secret theft.

Section I.—Since, however, this action is maintainable only against one who has used wilful fraud as well as force, the man who has forcibly taken a thing, partly because he thought himself the owner, and partly because he was ignorant of the law, and thought that he who really owned a thing might take it, even forcibly, from those in whose possession it was, ought clearly to be discharged of an action of robbery; nay, if such were his real feelings, he would not be liable even to an action of theft. But that robbers, under this pretext, should not find means to indulge their avarice with impunity, it has, by a fresh alteration of the Imperial Constitutions, been determined, that no man may carry off by force a moveable, or thing that moves itself, even though he believe himself to be the owner. And, if any one act in contravention of these Constitutions he is, if the thing be his, no longer to be considered as its owner; and if it be not his, he is called upon not only to restore the thing, but to pay its value also, as a penalty. The Constitutions have enacted that these rules shall prevail, not only in the case of moveables, which may be carried off with violence, but also to forcible entries made on immoveables, as lands or houses, to the end that men may be kept back from robbery of every sort and kind.

Section II.—In this action it is not a question as to whether the thing taken by force were, or were not the property of the complainant. If, therefore, a thing be let, lent, pledged, or deposited with Titius, so that he is directly interested in its not being taken by force; as, for instance, if he have made himself answerable for its safe custody; or if he were a *bonâ fide* possessor, or were entitled to the usufruct, or had any other interest in its not being taken by force, this action may be brought by him; not, indeed, to give him the ownership in the thing, but to give him back that merely which he has lost by the robbery of the thing from among his own goods; that is, to repair the loss to which his interest extends. And we may lay it down as a general rule, that the same causes which entitle a man to bring an action of theft, when a thing has been taken from him secretly and without violence, will entitle to this action, when force has been made use of.

TITLE 3.

OF INJURY TO PROPERTY.

The action for injury to property is established by the Aquilian Law: of this, the first provision is, that if any one have wrongfully killed the slave, or beast of another, the said beast being such as would be included under the general term

" cattle", such offender shall be condemned to pay the owner a penalty equal to the highest value which such property had borne during the preceding year.

Section I.—As this law speaks not of beasts in general, but of such only as may be called cattle, we may gather that it applies neither to dogs, nor to wild animals, but to those beasts only which can in strictness be said to feed in herds, as horses, mules, asses, oxen, goats. Swine, also, have been included; for, as they feed in herds, they may be considered as cattle; thus Homer says in the Odyssey, as Ælius Marcian quotes him, in his Institutes;

> " You'll find him seated by his swine, which feed
> By Corax-crag, and near spring Arethusa."
>
> Od. 13, 407.

Section II.—A man is understood to kill wrongfully, when he kills without having any right so to do. Whoso, therefore, killeth a thief, is not liable to this action, provided he could in no other way avoid the danger.

Section III.—He, too, who kills by accident is not liable under this law; provided always, there were no wilful negligence on his part; for this law punishes wilful negligence no less than wilful wrong.

Section IV.—So, if a man in hurling the javelin, for his sport or exercise, chance to wound your slave as he passes by, a certain distinction must be made. If the mischance happened by the act of a soldier, while he was exercising in camp, or in the place appointed for the purpose, no fault attaches to the soldier; if, however, any other than a soldier did it, he would be held liable. The soldier, also, would be liable if the mischance happened, in any spot, other than that appointed for military exercises.

Section V.—Also, if a man lopping branches from a tree, kill your slave as he passes by; if the act were done near a public road, or near one belonging to a neighbour, and if the lopper did not shout out, and give warning to the passers-by, he is legally liable. If, however, he did shout out, and the passer-by did not take proper care, the lopper is not in fault. He is also equally exempt from liability, if he were at work far from the public road, or in the middle of a field, even though he gave no warning; because, a stranger had no right of passage through such places.

Section VI.—Again, if a surgeon have performed an operation on your slave, and afterwards neglected to attend to his cure; so that, by reason of his lack of care, the slave dies; he is legally liable.

Section VII.—Lack of skill also causes legal liability; as if a surgeon kill your slave, by an unskilful operation, or by the administration of wrong medicines.

Section VIII.—If a mule-driver, by reason of his lack of skill, be unable to manage his mules, and they run over your slave, the driver is legally liable. And, even if he were unable to manage them, simply by reason of his want of strength, he is responsible for the injury, provided a man of greater power could have held them in. The like rules have been held to apply to the case of a horseman, who through want of skill or strength, is unable to manage his horse.

Section IX.—The words of the law " a penalty equal to the highest value which the property had borne during the preceding year", are to be understood in the sense following: that if any one kill your slave, who when so killed is halt, or maimed, or blind, but had within the twelve months next preceding been sound and valuable, he who so kills him shall be obliged to pay, not his actual value, but the greatest value which he ever bore within the year preceding his death. This, therefore, may properly be called a penal action, because an offender is bound to pay not only the actual amount of the damage done, but oftentimes considerably more;

and, therefore, this action does not lie against the heir of the offender, as it would legally have done if the mulct were never greater than the actual damage.

Section X.—It has been held by construction, though not warranted by the express wording of the law, that not only is the value of the thing injured to be computed, in the manner we have already stated, but in addition thereto any further damage which is occasioned by its destruction. As, for example, if your slave, who has by some one been instituted heir, be killed before, at your command, he has entered upon the inheritance; in this case, the loss of the inheritance must be brought into the calculation. So, if there be killed one of a pair of mules, or of a team of horses, or one slave of a troop of players, the estimation must be made not only of the value of the animal or slave destroyed; but account must be taken, also, of the lessened value of what remains uninjured.

Section XI.—The master of a slave who is killed is at liberty both to bring his private action for damages under the Aquilian Law, and also to prosecute the murderer for the capital offence.

Section XII.—The second provision of the Aquilian Law is not now in use.

Section XIII.—The third provision affords a remedy for injury of every kind; if, therefore, a man wound a slave, or any beast, which is reckoned as of cattle, or if he either wound or kill a beast not ranked among cattle, as a dog, or wild beast, an action will lie by virtue of this third provision. Compensation, also, may be obtained under it for all wrongful injury to things animate or inanimate, and for all injuries by fire, spoilage, breakage;—the word "broken," however, would have sufficed to include all these cases, for a thing in any way injured may be said to be "broken"; so not only things actually fractured may be called " broken", but also those cut, bruised, spilt, or in any way rendered of less value.

Finally, it has been held that he who mixes with the oil or wine of another, anything which injures the quality of such oil or wine, may be sued under this third head of the Aquilian Law.

Section XIV.—It is evident that as, under the first provision of this law, a man is liable who, whether through design or negligence, kills the beast or slave of another; so, under this third provision, there is afforded a remedy for every other injury, if occasioned also by design or negligence. In this latter case, however, the doer of the wrong is bound to pay the highest value which the property had borne, not within the year, but within the thirty days next preceding.

Section XV.—In this third head, indeed, it is not expressly stated that the "highest value" shall be recovered. But Sabinus held, and rightly, that the valuation should be made as if the expression "highest" had really been used; because, the Roman Commons, which passed this law on the motion of Aquilius their tribune, deemed it enough to use the word expressly only in the first of the provisions.

Section XVI.—It has been held that under this law, the "Direct Action" (*i. e.*, springing from the letter of the law) will lie only against the man who, by actual, bodily contact, has done the injury. And, therefore, what are called "Useful Actions" (*i. e.*, springing from the extended interpretation of the law) are given against him who does the injury in any other way; as, for example, against the man who so impounds another man's slave, or cattle, that they perish by hunger; against him who drives a horse so violently as to ruin him; who chases a herd till they leap headlong down a precipice; who persuades another man's slave to climb up a tree, or to go down into a well, and the slave in such ascent, or such descent, is killed or maimed; against one and all of these a useful action may be brought. If, however, any one have hurled a slave from a bridge or bank into a river, and if the slave be drowned; as he actually hurled him, there can be no difficulty in deciding that he caused the injury by actual, bodily contact, and that, therefore, he is liable under the Aquilian law. But, if the injury were effected neither by the body, nor to the body, but in some other way, so that neither the direct action, nor the useful can be brought, by virtue of the Aquilian law, then under such circumstances, an action on the case will lie against the doer of the wrong; as, for instance, if one through pity, have loosed the fetters of a slave, in order to facilitate his escape.

TITLE 4.

OF INJURY TO PERSONS.

INJURY, in a general sense, means every action contrary to law; in a special sense, it is, at one time, the same as outrage; at another, as wilful negligence, and so it is used in the Aquilian law; at another, it means iniquity or injustice, thus one who has been unjustly sentenced by Prætor, or by Judge, is said to have received an injury.

Section I.—An injury may be done not only by blows with the fist, or strokes with clubs, or lashes, but also by abusive and outrageous language; by the seizure of the goods of one who owes nothing, when he who seized was well aware that he had no claim against the owner; by writing, composing, publishing a libel, or scurrilous piece of doggrel in abuse of any one, or by wickedly and maliciously contriving that another should so do; by indecent advances to any woman of unblemished reputation, or to any young person; by attempting the chastity of any one; and, in short, by other acts innumerable.

Section II.—A man may receive an injury not in his own person alone, but in that of the children under his power; and in that also of his wife, for such is the general opinion in the present day. If, therefore, you offer any injury to a daughter in power of her father, and married to Titius, the action for the injury may be brought not only in the name of the daughter, but in that either of her father, or her husband. On the other hand, however, if the husband have sustained a wrong, the wife cannot bring an action for the injury sustained; for the law holds that wives should be protected by husbands, but not husbands by wives. The father-in-law, also, may bring an action of injury in the name of his son's wife, provided her husband be still under his power.

Section III.—An injury is never considered as done to a slave himself, but is considered as done to the master, through the person of the slave; but that which is an injury to a wife, or children, does not necessarily amount to one through a slave; to constitute this latter offence, a more flagrant act of wrong must have been committed, and one which more directly affects the reputation of his master; as, for example, if a man were to flog another man's slave in a cruel manner, an action would, in this case, lie against him. But the master has no right of action against him who has publicly used insulting language to his slave, or has struck him with his fist.

Section IV.—If an injury be done to a slave, the joint property of several masters, justice demands that the computation of it, shall not be in proportion to the share which each has in him; but in proportion to the rank and position of the masters; for to them it is that the injury is done.

Section V.—If the usufruct of a slave be in Titius, and the property in Mævius; an injury done to that slave is considered as done to Mævius rather than to Titius.

Section VI.—If, however, an injury have been done to a freeman, *bonâ fide* in your service, the right of action does not belong to you, but he can bring the action in his own name; unless indeed he was injured merely to insult you, in which case you may bring the action of injury. The like rule holds as to the slave of another, who is *bond fide* in your service; so often as he receives an injury which was done with intent to insult you, you have yourself the right to bring this action.

Section VII.—According to the law of the Twelve Tables, the penalty for injuries was a limb for a limb; but if a bone were broken, money fines were levied, proportioned to the great penury in which the ancients lived. Afterwards the Prætors permitted those who had suffered injury, to assess their own damages, so that the Judge might, at his discretion, decree that the defendants should pay the amount of such assessment, or a smaller sum. The system of penalties for injury introduced by the law of the Twelve Tables has fallen into disuse, but that introduced by the Prætors, and called the honorary, is now in general use in the administration of justice, For the computation is higher or lower, according to the social position, and general character of the person injured; and the like gradation, is most properly observed with regard to slaves, so that one penalty is exacted for an injury done to a slave who is a steward; a smaller, for that done to a slave who fills an intermediate office; and one still less, for that done to a slave of the very lowest class, or such as work in chairs.

Section VIII.—The Cornelian Law, also, deals with injuries, and introduced an action of injuries, which may be brought by any who declares that he has been struck, or beaten, or that his house has been broken into. And by the term "his house" we understand a house either really his own, or one which he hires, or borrows free of cost, or lives in as a guest.

Section IX.—An injury is said to be of a grave and atrocious character, either from the nature of the act, as when any one is wounded, or beaten with clubs by another; or from the nature of the place, as when an injury is done in a theatre, a forum, or in the presence of a Prætor; or from the rank of the person injured, as when it is a Magistrate who has suffered the injury, or a Senator who has sustained it at the hands of one of low degree, or a parent or patron at the hands of child or freed-man. For the penalty of an injury done to a senator, parent, or patron, is very different from one done to a stranger, or to one of low degree. At times, also, the part of the body wounded, gives the character of gravity and atrocity to an injury; if, for instance, one were wounded in the eye. And it makes little matter whether an injury of so grave a character have been done to the father, or the son of a family; for in either case it is looked upon as most atrocious.

Section X.—Lastly, it is to be noted, that he who has suffered any injury may elect to bring a civil, or a criminal action. If he sue in the form of a civil action, a computation must be made in the manner stated above, and a penalty then levied; but if he sue criminally, the Judge, in the exercise of his function, inflicts an extraordinary punishment. It is, however, also worthy of observation, that the Constitution of Zeno permits all those who have a right to the title of "Illustrious", and naturally all of higher rank, to bring or to defend any action of injury by their procurators, or attornies; the which may be more clearly seen by a perusal of the Constitution itself.

Section XI.—An action of injury lies not only against the man who has committed the injury; as, for example, against the man who actually struck the blow; but against him also who has wilfully and maliciously caused the blow to be struck.

Section XII.—All right to bring this action becomes lost by concealment of the fact that an injury has been committed; a person, therefore, who allowed an injury to pass unnoticed, that is, who immediately after he had received it showed no signs of anger, cannot afterwards change his mind, and revive an injury which he has suffered to lie dormant.

TITLE 5.

OF OBLIGATIONS WHICH ARISE FROM QUASI-WRONG.

IF a Judge, by an unjust ruling, make a suit his own, he is not, in strictness, subject to an action of wrong; but, as an action neither of malfeasance, nor of contract will lie against him, and as, still, he has been guilty of a fault, he may be sued in an action or quasi-wrong; and will be fined in such sum as shall seem equitable to the conscience of him who sits as Judge upon the case.

Section I.—He, too, who occupies a room from which anything has been so thrown or spilt as to injure another, is held to be liable to an action of quasi-wrong; and this whether the room were his own property, or hired, or borrowed free of hire. He is held to be liable for quasi, rather than for direct wrong, as he is usually so liable, by reason of the fault of some other, of a slave, it may be, or a freed-man. A like case is that of him who keeps placed aloft, or hanging over a public way, something which, if it were to fall, would do an injury to some one; the penalty is, here, settled at ten pieces of gold. In the case of things thrown out, or spilt, an action is granted for double the amount of actual damage done: and if a free-man has been killed, the penalty is fixed at fifty pieces; if, however, he be not killed, but wounded only, the action is for such sum as the judge in his discretion considers equitable. The Judge, in such case, should include in his computations, fees paid to the physician, and all other expenses attendant on the cure, and also, the time and labour which the patient has lost, and is likely to lose, by being rendered unfit for work.

Section II.—If the son of a family occupy a house separate from that of his father; and if, from a room in the son's house, any thing be thrown or spilt, or be so placed or hung as that its fall would be dangerous, Julian holds that an action would lie not against the father, but against the son alone. The same ruling would apply to the case of the son of a family, who in his capacity of Judge has given an unjust decision, or " made the cause his own".

Section III.—The master of a ship, a tavern, or a shed, is liable to an action of quasi-wrong, for every case of damage, and every loss by theft occurring in his ship, tavern, or shed; that is, provided the wrong were not actually committed by him, but by some engaged in the service of his establishment. For, as no action of direct wrong, nor of contract, can be brought against the master, and as he is clearly in some sort guilty of gross negligence in employing dishonest persons as his servants, he is held to be liable to an action of quasi-wrong. In all the cases above enumerated the action granted is one upon the fact, which may be brought in favour of an heir, but not against one.

TITLE 6.

OF ACTIONS.

It now remains that we treat of Actions. An Action is nothing more than the right of demanding before a court of justice that which is our right.

Section I.—All Actions, whereby questions are submitted to the decision of either Judges or Arbitrators, may primarily be divided into two great classes—Real and Personal. For either the plaintiff sues the defendant, as being answerable to him by reason either of some contract, on some wrong; and in this case the action will be personal, as the plaintiff alleges that the defendant is bound to give something to or do something for him; or some similar allegation as circumstances demand. Or, on the other hand, the plaintiff brings his action against the defendant, who is not bound to him by an obligation, but whose right to the possession of some corporeal thing the plaintiff disputes; and in this case a real action will be granted. As, for example, if some one be in possession of land, which Titius affirms to be his property, while the possessor, for his part, declares that he is the proprietor; the action is real.

Section II.—So too if a man assert his right to the usufruct of a field, or of a house; or to walk, ride, drive, or carry water through his neighbour's land, the action brought to support his claim is a real one. Of the like kind are actions for rights of servitude over urban tenements; as when a man asserts his right to raise his building, his right to an unbroken view, his right to throw out a projection, or to lay the beams of his house into those of his neighbour. There are also actions precisely the reverse of these, but which also refer to usufructs, and to servitudes over urban and rural tenements; as where a man alleges that his neighbour has no right to usufruct, to walk, ride, drive, or carry water, to have an unbroken view, to throw out a projection, or to insert his beams. These actions are no less real, but are negative, and are not, therefore, available in questions as to things corporeal; because in such questions the action is brought by him who is not in possession. Because one who is actually in possession cannot bring an action to negative the claim of the plaintiff. There is indeed one case, and one alone, where a man in possession may act the part of plaintiff: but this may more conveniently be seen by referring to the more copious chapters of the Digest.

Section III.—The actions of which we have just spoken, and all others of a like kind, are established by the ancient regulations and the Civil Law; but others there are, as well real as personal, which the Prætor, by virtue of his jurisdiction, has introduced, and of which it is essential that we give some examples. Thus, for example, he often grants a right of action, to a plaintiff who alleges that he has acquired, by prescription, a something which, in reality, he has not acquired; or, on the other hand, to one who alleges that his adversary has not acquired, by prescription, a something which, in reality, he has acquired.

Section IV.—Thus, if a thing be delivered, for good consideration, as purchase, gift, dowry or legacy, to one who has not yet gained a property in the thing delivered; if, by some chance, he should lose the possession, he has no direct action for its recovery; because the Civil Law grants such actions to him only who is actually proprietor. But, as it was clearly a hardship that there should be no right of action at all in such a case, the Prætor has supplied one, wherein the person who has lost the possession, alleges that he has obtained the thing by prescription, although he has not really done so;

and so he may recover possession. This process is called the Publician action, because the Prætor Publicius was the first to place it on the Prætorian Edict.

Section V.—If, on the contrary, a man abroad in the service of the State, or a prisoner in the hands of the enemy, have gained by prescription a thing the property of one who is not abroad; the proprietor may, within one year of the return home of the possessor, bring an action by rescinding the prescription; that is, he may sue on the allegation that the possessor has not acquired by prescription, and that the thing, therefore, still belongs to him. The Prætor, induced by like equitable motions, has granted this form of action to certain other cases also, as may be seen by reference to the more copious treatise of either Digest or Pandects.

Section VI.—If a debtor, with intent to defraud his creditors, transfer any of his property to a third party, at a period after his estate has passed by course of law to his creditors; the creditors may have the delivery rescinded, and claim the property; by the allegation, namely, that there had been no true delivery, and that it continued, therefore, to form a portion of their debtor's goods.

Section VII.—The Servian action, and that called quasi-Servian or hypothecary, take their force, also, from the Prætor's jurisdiction. By the Servian action, a landlord may sue for possession of such stock and effects of a farmer as have been pledged to secure the rent of the farm. By the quasi-Servian, creditors in general may sue for things pledged or hypothecated to them; and, so far as regards this action, there is no difference between a pledge, and a hypothec or mortgage; for both terms are used of anything which creditor and debtor have mutually agreed shall be bound as security for the debt. They differ indeed in other respects; for by the term pledge, is meant property actually delivered to a creditor especially if the thing delivered were a moveable; by hypothec, or mortgage, is meant what is bound by agreement only, and without livery.

Section VIII.—Personal actions, also, have been introduced by the Prætor, as, for instance, the action called *de pecunia constituta*, which was very similar to that called *receptitia*. By virtue, however, of one of our Constitutions, the latter has lost its authority, and no longer appears in our legislation, and whatever was good in it has been added to the other action *de pecunia constituta*. The Prætor, also, has introduced an action concerning the *peculium*,—*i. e.*, private perquisites—of slaves, and of sons under power; another, wherein the question tried is whether the plaintiff has made oath of his debt; and many others also.

Section IX.—The action *de constituta pecunia* may be brought against all who, without the form of a stipulation, have bound themselves to pay money, either on their own account or in the name of another. If, however, their contract be by stipulation, it may be enforced by the Civil Law.

Section X.—The Prætor has established actions concerning *peculium*, against fathers and masters, because, although they are not, according to the Civil Law, bound by the contracts of their children and slaves; yet in equity they should be so, to the extent at least of the *peculium*, which is, as it were, the patrimony, and private possession of sons, of daughters, and of slaves.

Section XI.—Also if a man, at the prayer of the adverse party, make oath, that the debt for which he sues is due and unpaid, the Prætor most equitably gives him the privilege of an action, wherein the question is whether the oath have been duly taken, and not whether the sum claimed be really due?

Section XII.—The Prætors also, by virtue of their authority, have established several penal actions. Thus, a Prætorian action lies against any who has wilfully defaced an Edict; against any who has served a summons on a parent or a patron, without leave first obtained from the due authorities; and also, against any person, who, by force, has abducted one summoned to appear before the Prætor, or who has wickedly incited another to abduct him; with several other actions of like kind.

Section XIII.—Among real actions are to be classed those which are called prejudicial (*i. e.*, preliminary to the principal inquiry, or action). Prejudicial actions are brought to decide a man's social standing; whether he have been born free, or made free; whether he be a slave; and, whether really the son of his reputed father. Of these three, however, that only which decides whether a man be free-born, is instituted by the Civil Law; the rest all take their rise from the Prætor's jurisdiction.

Section XIV.—Actions being thus divided into real and personal, it is clear that a plaintiff cannot sue for that which is his own, by a condiction or personal action, in a form such as this: " If it appear that the defendant ought to *give*." It can never be said that what is already the plaintiff's own ought to be given him, for to give a thing is to confer the property in it, on the person to whom it is given; and a thing which does already belong to the plaintiff cannot become more absolutely his, than now it is. Nevertheless, to evince a thorough abhorrence of thieves, and to render them liable to more numerous actions, it has been decided, that besides the penalty of double, or quadruple the amount taken, to which they are already subject, they may be sued, by a condiction or personal action, for the recovery of the thing stolen, in the form " If it appear that they ought to give." And this, although the party wronged may bring against them a real action, whereby he may demand restitution of the thing as his own.

Section XV.—Real actions are called Vindications; and Personal actions, in which it is alleged that something should be done or given, are called Condictions; to *condict*, in ancient usage, was the same as to denounce; but the term condiction is now used improperly to denote a personal action, wherein the plaintiff contends that something should be given to him, because denunciations are no longer in use.

Section XVI.—Actions, again, are divided into those brought for recovery of the thing itself; into those brought for recovery of a penalty; and into mixed actions.

Section XVII.—For recovery of the thing itself are given all real actions; and so also, of personal actions, all those which spring from contract; as, for instance, the action for money lent, or stipulated for, for commodate, for deposit, for commission, for partnership, for bargain and sale, and for letting and hiring. If, however, an action be commenced for deposit, when the thing has been deposited by reason of riot, fire, house-fall, shipwreck, the Prætor grants an action for double the value of the thing deposited; that is, if the suit be brought against him with whom the thing actually was deposited, or against his heir, on account of fraud; in which case the action becomes a mixed one.

Section XVIII.—Of actions arising from malfeasance, some are for the penalty alone, and some both for the thing itself and the penalty; such therefore are called mixed actions. In an action of theft, however, nothing save the penalty is sued for; and whether, as in theft manifest the quadruple be sued for, or as in theft not manifest, the double, still it is as penalty only. Because the owner may recover the thing stolen by a distinct action, if he allege that it is his; and this, whether it be in the possession of the thief, or any other person soever. The owner has also his right of condiction, or personal action, against the thief, for recovery of the thing.

Section XIX.—An action for goods forcibly taken, is a mixed action, because the value of the thing taken is included in the quadruple value, recoverable by this action; the penalty therefore, is only triple. The action also, under the *Lex Aquilia*, for wrongful damage, is a mixed action; not only when brought for double value against him who denied the fact, but at times when the action is only for the single value; as, if a man have killed a slave, who at his death was halt, or wanting an eye, but who, within the previous year, was sound and of great value; the defendant will be condemned in such sum as the slave was worth in such previous year, and this, in accordance with what we have already observed (*tit.* 3). A mixed action, also, lies against those who have delayed to pay monies left, whether by way of legacy, or gift in trust, to consecrated churches, or other sacred spots, until they have been cited before the Magistrate: for they are then obliged to give the thing, or pay the money bequeathed, and further something more of equal value, as a penalty; thus they are mulcted in double the amount of what was due.

Section XX.—Some actions, also, are mixed, by being as well real as personal; such is the action called *familiæ erciscundæ,*—brought by co-heirs for partition of an inheritance; such, also, is that *de communi dividundo,*—for the division of things held in common by persons not actually partners; and, that called *finium regundorum,*—brought to settle the bounds of contiguous rural estates. Now, in these three actions, the judge has power, in accordance with equity and good conscience, to decree the thing, or matter in dispute, to any of the parties to the suit; and, afterwards, if he seem to have received over much in the adjudication, oblige him to hand over to the other party, a certain stated sum.

Section XXI.—All actions are, further, divided into those involving single, double, triple, or quadruple penalties; and beyond this last no action can extend.

Section XXII.—An action for the single penalty, is brought in cases of stipulation; of loan; of bargain and sale;

of letting and hiring; of mandate; and of other like instances out of number.

Section XXIII.—An action for the double penalty, is brought in cases of theft not manifest; of wilful injury, under the Aquilian Law; and, under certain circumstances, of breach of bailment. It is, also, brought in the case of the corruption of a slave; and lies against him, by whose advice and instigation a slave has run away, has become insolent to his master, dissolute in his habits, or been rendered, in any way, the worse; also, in an action of this kind, a valuation is made of those articles which the slave carried off with him, when he ran away. An action for double value may, as we have before said, be brought in cases of detention of that which has been bequeathed to churches, or to consecrated spots.

Section XXIV.—An action for the triple penalty is brought in cases where suitors, in their particulars of demand, set down more than the amount actually due, in order that the bedels and other officers of the Court, may exact larger fees from the defendant. When this occurs, the defendant who has suffered the wrong, may recover from the plaintiff the triple value of the fee which he has paid; but, in such triple value, the fee itself is included. A Constitution as to the regulation of such fees, adorns our Code; and from it, beyond all doubt, a legal personal action, or condiction may arise.

Section XXV.—An action for the quadruple penalty is brought in cases of manifest theft; of personal threats and intimidation; of money given to instigate any one to commence a vexatious suit; or of money given to stay proceedings. Also, by virtue of our Constitution, a legal personal action, or condiction, lies against those officers of the Court, who demand any fees from defendants, in contravention of the rules set forth in such our Constitution.

Section XXVI.—The action for theft not manifest, and that for the corruption of a slave, differ from the other actions which we have enumerated in the same Section, in that, they are always brought to recover a double penalty. The rest, however, to wit, that under the Aquilian Law for wilful injury, and sometimes that for breach of bailment, are brought for the double penalty if the defendant plead not guilty; but, if he plead guilty, the single penalty only is decreed. In cases of actions brought to get possession of goods, bequeathed to churches or to consecrated spots, the double penalty is given, not only when the defendant denies his liability, but also when he has put off the payment, until he has been cited before a Magistrate. If, however, he confess the liability, and pay the legacy before the summons of the Magistrate has been issued, the single value can alone be given.

Section XXVII.—The action for personal threats and intimidation, also, differs from the others included in the same Section, in that, by the very nature of the action, it is tacitly inferred, that the defendant who, in obedience to the Judge's order, makes restitution of the goods taken, should be discharged. In the other actions for a quadruple penalty, the defendant must invariably be mulcted in the full amount; as in the action of theft manifest.

Section XXVIII.—Some actions, again, are *bonæ fidei*—i. e., "of good faith,"—and some *stricti juris*—i. e., "of strict law".—To the class of actions of good faith, belong the following;—actions of purchase and sale, of letting and hiring, or business done, of mandate, of deposit, of partnership, of tutelage, of loan, of mortgage, of partition of an inheritance, of the division of a joint property; also actions *præscriptis verbis*—i. e., "in prescribed words,"—whether that arising from an estimation or assessment, or that from an exchange; and, lastly, the claim to an inheritance. For, though it was, till quite recently, a matter of doubt as to whether this last action should be reckoned as among those of good faith, our Constitution has clearly declared that it shall be so.

Section XXIX.—The action for recovery of a marriage portion was, formerly, reckoned among actions of good faith; but, when we observed that the action of stipulation, was more comprehensive and advantageous, after laying down several distinctions, we did away with the former action, and transferred to the action of stipulation, when brought to recover marriage portions, all the effects which belonged to the former action. The former, then, being very properly abolished, the action of stipulation assumed the character of one of good faith; but did so only when brought for recovery of a marriage portion. We, also, further gave it the implied authority of a mortgage; and have deemed it right that women, for whose sake alone we put forth this our Constitution, should be preferred to all other mortgagees; provided the woman sue in person for her marriage portion.

Section XXX.—In every action of good faith, free power is given to the Judge to settle, in accordance with the rules of equity and good conscience, the amount which ought to be awarded to the plaintiff; and in this power the following, also, is implied, namely, that if the plaintiff be found to be indebted to the defendant, the amount of such debt shall be allowed by way of set-off, and the defendant be condemned only to pay the balance actually due. In the actions even of strict right, a set-off was permitted, if the defendant pleaded fraud as an exception or bar; and this, by virtue of a Rescript of the Emperor Marcus. A Constitution of our own, however, has given still greater facility to claims of set-off, in cases where the counter-claim on the part of the defendant has been clearly proved. Now, therefore, actions, whether real, personal, or what kind soever, are at once reduced by the amount of the set-off. The only exception is, in the case of the action of deposit, and against it, we have deemed it somewhat worse than inexpedient to allow the claim of set-off, lest under this pretence any should be fraudulently hindered from regaining possession of that which he had deposited in the custody of another.

Section XXXI—Other actions, again, we call *arbitrary*; because they depend upon the " arbitration," or discretion of the Judge. In actions of this kind, if the defendant fail to obey the order of the Judge, whether it be to make restitution, exhibition, payment, or surrender of a slave who has done a wrong, the Judge should proceed to pass his sentence. Now these actions are as well real and personal; real, as the Publician, the Servian, for recovery of goods hypothecated by a farmer as security for his rent, and the quasi-Servian, called also that of pledge, or hypothecation; personal, as those where proceedings are instituted on account of something done under influence of force, fear, or fraud; and that brought for something promised to be given up at a certain place. The action, also, for the exhibition and production of moveables depends upon the arbitration, or discretion of the Judge in these actions, and in others of like kind, the Judge is privileged to fix, in accordance with the principles of equity and good conscience, and in accordance, also, with the merits of the particular case, the nature and the measure of the satisfaction which the plaintiff should receive.

Section XXXII.—A Judge should always, so far as may be, frame his sentence so, that the award be definite, whether for a certain thing, or fixed sum of money; and this, even though the claim which forms the basis of his decree, have been for an indefinite quantity, or sum.

Section XXXIII.—Formerly, if a plaintiff, in his statement of demand, claimed more than was his due, he was unsuccessful in his action, and lost even what was really due to him. And it was no easy matter for him to be re-placed, by the Prætor, in his former position; unless, indeed, he were under the age of twenty-five years; for in this, as in other cases, the usage was to give relief to those under full age, if they had committed any blunder, by reason of their youth. If, too, the reasons of the blunder were so strong, that even the most prudent might have been misled by them, relief was given to persons even of full age. As, for instance, when a legatee brought a suit for recovery of his entire legacy, and afterwards there were produced codicils, whereby part of such legacy was revoked, or whereby fresh bequests were left to others, the legacies in the testament would thus be subject to reduction under the Falcidian Law, and the plaintiff would seem to have laid his claim for more than the three-fourths actually due to him.

A man may, in four ways, sue for more than is his due; with regard, namely, (1) to Amount, (2) to Time, (3) to Place, or (4) to Cause of Action.

(1). In regard to Amount: as when a plaintiff brings his suit for twenty golden pieces, instead of for ten, which are actually due to him; or when he, who is part-owner of a certain thing, demands the whole, or a share larger than he has a title to.

(2). In regard to Time; as when a plaintiff brings his suit before the arrival of the day fixed, or before the time of the fulfilment of a condition; for, on the same principle, that he who pays less soon than he ought to pay, is held to pay less in amount than he ought to pay, he who makes his demand before the time, demands more than is actually due to him.

(3). In regard to Place; as when one who has stipulated that a thing should be delivered to him at a certain place, brings his claim to have it delivered to him at some other place, without making mention, in his formal statement of demand, of the place in which he originally stipulated that delivery should be made. As, for instance, if he who, in his stipulation had said,—Do you bind yourself to give such a thing at Ephesus?—were afterwards to bring his action at Rome, stating simply that the defendant ought to give. Here, the plaintiff would be held to make his demand for more than his due, because, by the unqualified nature of his formal claim, he would deprive the other party of any gain which might accrue to him by making the payment at Ephesus. Hence it is that an arbitrary action is granted to a plaintiff, who makes his demand for payment in a place other than that agreed on; and, in an action of this kind, regard is had to the gain which might accrue to the debtor, if he were to have paid the debt in the place agreed on. And this gain is usually found to be greatest in the several sorts of merchandise; as, for example, in the case of wine, oil, corn, things which bear different prices in different countries. Money, also, is not in all countries, lent or invested at the like rate of interest. If, however, a man bring his action at Ephesus, or at the place where it was stipulated that payment should be made, he is legally entitled to make his statement of demand, simply, *i. e.*, without any actual mention of the place; and this the Prætor will permit, because any advantage which might thence accrue to the debtor, is preserved intact.

(4). In regard to Cause; he who claims more than his due comes very near to him who does the like in regard to place. As, for example, if any were to stipulate with you as follows, "Do you bind yourself to give either your slave Stichus, or ten pieces of gold?" and were, then, to bring his claim specially for one of the two, either for the slave expressly, or for the money expressly, he would be held to have made his claim for more than was due; for, in a stipulation of this sort, the right of choice is in the promiser, as to whether he will give the money, or the slave: he, therefore, who demands expressly either slave, or money, takes from the other party his power of choice, and thus betters his own condition, but renders that of his opponent worse. In such case, therefore, an action has been given, whereby the plaintiff demands that either the slave Stichus, or the ten pieces, shall be given up to him; and thus he frames his claim in conformity with the terms of the stipulation. Further, if one stipulate for a slave generally, and then claim Stichus; or for wine generally, and claim that of Campania; or for dye, and claim Tyrian Purple, he is held to demand more than is due. For he deprives of the power of choice, the other party, who, by virtue of the stipulation, was free to pay another thing, than that expressly claimed.

And, even if the thing expressly claimed be of the very smallest value, still the plaintiff is held to have laid his claim for more than his due; because, oftentimes it happens that it is easier for the debtor to pay a thing of higher value. This was the law which formerly prevailed; but its severity has been restrained by a Constitution of the Emperor Zeno; and also, by one of our own. If the claim be for more than is due in regard to time, the judge will be directed in his proceedings by the Constitution of Zeno, of illustrious memory.

If, however, it be so made in regard to quantity, or in any other way, all loss suffered by him upon whom the claim is made, must be recompensed, as we have before said, by the condemnation of the plaintiff in triple damages.

Section XXXIV.—If, in his statement of demand, the plaintiff include less than is his due; as, for instance, five gold pieces, when ten are due, or, half of an estate, the whole of which belongs to him, he is free from any risk; because, the judge may, under the said Constitution of Zeno, of illustrious memory, condemn the other party, under the same process, to pay the balance, which may be due to the plaintiff.

Section XXXV.—If a man lay his claim for one thing, instead of another, he is free from any · risk; for when the real fact is known, he may correct his mistake, and that too, under the same process; as if he should have demanded Stichus, but had demanded Eros; or had claimed as due under a testament, what was so really by virtue of a stipulation.

Section XXXVI.—Some actions also, there are, wherein we do not sue for the whole of what is due to us, but, sometimes for the whole, sometimes for less. If, for example, an action be brought by way of claim upon the *peculium, i. e.,* " private property," of a son or a slave; if the *peculium* be rich enough to satisfy the claim, the father or master is condemned to pay the full amount; but if it be too small, the father or master is condemned to the extent of the value of the *peculium.* We shall, hereafter, in its proper place, explain how the *peculium* is to be computed.

Section XXXVII.—Also, if a wife prefer a claim for restitution of her marriage portion, the husband must be condemned to pay so far as he is able; that is, so far as his income will allow. If, therefore, his property be sufficient to pay the whole amount of the portion, he must be condemned to pay the whole; but, if it be insufficient, " he must still pay as much as it is in his power to do." This claim for restitution of her portion by a wife, may be lessened by a right on the part of the husband, to retain something; for the husband is allowed to retain a sum equal to that which he may have expended upon the estate given as a marriage portion; and the portion is legally diminished by all necessary expenses, but this will be clearly seen in the more extended treatises of the Digest.

Section XXXVIII.—If, again, a person bring an action against his parent or patron, or if one partner sue another in an action of partnership, he can obtain no higher damages than the defendant is able to pay. The like is the case, when a donor is sued for his donation.

Section XXXIX.—When a set-off is pleaded by the defendant, the general result is that the plaintiff recovers less than his demand; because the judge, proceeding upon principles of equity and good conscience, may deduct from the claim of the plaintiff whatever he owes to the defendant, under the same head; and may, as has already been said, condemn the defendant to the payment of the balance only.

Section XL.—If a debtor have made surrender of his goods to his creditors, and have afterwards acquired a fortune large enough to make it worth their while, the creditors may sue him afresh, and force him to pay as much as he is able; but not more, for it would be a most inhuman thing to condemn in the full amount, a man who has already been stripped of all his fortune.

TITLE 7.

OF ACTIONS ON CONTRACTS ENTERED INTO WITH PERSONS UNDER POWER.

As we have already made mention of the action, which may be brought as to the *peculium* of sons under power, or of slaves, we must now treat more fully of it, and also of all other actions which can be brought against parents or masters, as the representatives of children and of slaves. And as the same rules are, with few exceptions, observed whether the transaction be with slaves, or with those under power of parents, we will, to avoid the charge of being tedious, direct our observations only to slaves and their masters; and what we say, of them, may be taken to apply to parents also, and to children under power. And if, with reference to these latter, there be any special observation to be made, we will make separate allusion to it.

Section I.—If, then, any transaction be entered into with a slave, who acts by command of his master, the Prætor will grant an action against the master for the whole amount due under the contract. Because, he who in such case, contracts with a slave, does so as relying on the credit of his master.

Section II.—On the like principle, the Prætor grants two actions for recovery of the whole amount, whereof the one is called *Exercitoria,* and the other *Institoria.*

The action *Exercitoria* is brought, when any one has placed his slave as master of his ship, and transactions have been entered into with such slave, touching the business wherewith he is entrusted. The action gets its name of *Exercitoria* from this, that he who gets his constant profits from the employment of the ship, is said to be an *Exercitor.*

The action *Institoria* is brought, when any one has placed his slave at the head of a shop, or any other trade or commercial business, and transactions have been entered into with such slave, touching the business wherewith he is entrusted. The action gets its name of *Institoria* from this, that a person to whom the management of a business is given in charge, is said to be an *Institor.*

The Prætor, also, permits both these actions to be brought against the master who has employed either a free person, or another man's slave, in the management of a ship, a warehouse, or any business whatsoever; and this, because the same principle of equity is applicable as well to the one case, as to the other.

Section III.—The Prætor introduced, also, another action called *Tributoria.* For, when a slave invested his *peculium,* or private gains, in trade, and did so with the knowledge of his master; if people had been thus induced to enter into contracts with him, the Prætor will decree, that all the stock, and all the money springing from such traffic, shall be distributed between the master, if he have any legal claim, and the other creditors in rateable proportions. And since the actual distribution is entrusted to the master himself, if any of the creditors complain that he has obtained too small a share, the Prætor will grant him permission to bring the before-named action, which is thence called *Tributoria*, or " Distributory."

Section IV.—The Prætor has, also, introduced an action relative both to the *peculium* and to those things, acquired by a slave, which a master has converted to his own advantage; for, although the traffic of the slave may have been without the consent of his master, still the master, if he have converted to his own uses any profit thence arising, should be liable for the full amount of such profit; and, even though he should have reaped no profit, he ought to be held liable to the full extent of the *peculium* of the slave. Now, by conversion to the advantage of the master, we understand every thing laid out by a slave, in the necessary expenditure of his master; as, for example, if the slave were to borrow money, and therewith, pay his master's debts, or repair his buildings when in evil case, or buy wheat for the household, or land for his master, or any other necessary thing. So, if your slave, out of ten pieces, which he had borrowed of Titius, were to pay five to one of your creditors, and to spend the other five upon himself, you would be condemned to make full payment of the first five, expended for your use; and, as to the other five, you would have to make such payment as the slave's *peculium* would allow. Now, from this instance, it is clear that if the whole ten pieces had been converted to your use, Titius could have recovered all the ten from you; for, although it be one and the same action, whereby it is sought to recover as well the *peculium*, as such sum as has been converted to the master's use, still it carries with it two separate condemnations. The Judge, therefore, before whom an action of this sort is heard, is wont first to inquire whether there have been a conversion to the master's use; and he does not proceed to make any valuation of the *peculium*, until he have first satisfied himself that no portion, or at any rate not all the money due from the slave, has been so expended in the service of his master. Also, when he does proceed to make his valuation of the *peculium*, he first deducts whatever the slave may owe to his master, or to any other under the power of his master, and the balance only is looked upon as the *peculium*. Sometimes, indeed, it happens, that the debt of a slave to another, under the power of his master, is not deducted; as, for example, when such creditor forms part of the debtor's own *peculium*. Thus, when a slave is indebted to the vicarial slave, his attendant, such debt cannot be deducted from the *peculium*.

Section V.—There can, however, be no doubt but that he who has entered into a contract with a slave, acting by his master's orders, and who is entitled to bring either the action *institoria*, or *exercitoria*, is entitled also to bring that relative to the *peculium*, or that *de in rem verso*—*i. e.*, where there has been conversion to the master's benefit. It would, however, be unwise in the extreme for a man to abandon an action whereby he might readily recover his whole claim, and, by the adoption of another form of process, reduce himself to the difficult task of proving that the sum which he had lent to the slave, had been converted to the use of his master; or that the slave was in possession of a *peculium*, and that, too, sufficient to satisfy the whole claim. He, again, who may bring the action *tributoria*, may also bring that relative to the *peculium*, or that where there has been conversion to the master's gain; expedience, however, directs at times the use of the former, and at times of the two latter. The *tributoria* is, on the one hand, to be preferred, because the position of the master is not mainly looked to; that is, monies due to him are not previously deducted, but he is regarded in precisely the same light as are the other creditors. In the action regarding the *peculium*, however, debts due to the master are first deducted, and he is compelled to share the balance among the creditors. In some cases, again, it may be more expedient to bring the action regarding the *peculium*; and this, because it goes to the whole *peculium*, while the action *tributoria* affects that portion only of it which has been employed in traffic; and a slave may possibly have used in traffic but a fraction, a third, a fourth, or any part, however small, and the remainder may have been invested in lands, slaves, or monies lent at interest. Generally, therefore, each person ought to choose the line of remedy which seems, in his case, likely to be most to his advantage. Assuredly, however, the creditor who can prove conversion to the uses of the master of a slave, his debtor, should bring his action in the form which in such cases is provided.

Section VI.—The rules which we have laid down as applying to a slave and his master, must be taken also, to apply to children under power, and to the parents, in whose power they are.

Section VII.—Peculiar regard, however, is had to children by the Macedonian decree of the Senate, whereby loans to children, under the power of their parents, are forbidden. Persons who have made such loans, are refused all right of action against the children, whether still under power, or having obtained their independence by the death of their parent, or by emancipation; and also, against the parents, whether the children remain still under their power, or whether they have emancipated them. This decree was passed by the Senate, because young heirs, burthened with a load of debt contracted for purposes most vile and most debauched, have not unfrequently endeavoured by private treachery to take away the lives of their parents.

Section VIII.—Finally, we may remark that every contract entered into at the bidding of a parent or a master, and every conversion to that parent's or that master's use, may be recovered by a direct action " or condiction," against the parent or master, precisely as though the contract had originally be made with them. He, also, who is liable to an action *institoria* or *exercitoria*, is liable also to be proceeded against by a direct action, or condiction; and this, because the contract is presumed to have been entered into, by his order.

TITLE 8.

OF NOXAL ACTIONS.

Noxal actions are those which arise from the wrong deeds of slaves; as when a slave has committed a theft, or robbery, or done any injury or damage. And, in these actions, if the master of the slave be condemned, it is in his option either to pay the value of the damage done, or to surrender the wrong-doer, as a recompence.

Section I.—By the term *Noxa* is meant the doer of the wrong, to wit, the slave; and by *Noxia*, the wrong deed itself, to wit, the theft, the damage, the robbery, or the injury.

Section II.—And most reasonable it is, that the master should be permitted to surrender his offending slave; for it were most unjust, that the ill conduct of slaves should cause their masters to suffer an amount of damage, beyond the value of the slaves themselves.

Section III.—A master prosecuted in a noxal action, by reason of his slave, is cleared by making a surrender of the slave to the defendant; and the property in such slave is then transferred in perpetuity. If, however, the slave can collect the money, and can give to the master, to whom he has been surrendered, the full pecuniary value of the damage done, he may, by the Prætor's aid, obtain his freedom; and this, though his new master be unwilling.

Section IV.—Noxal actions are constituted either by the Laws, or by the Prætor's Edict. By the Laws, as for theft, by the Law of the Twelve Tables; and for wilful damage, by the Aquilian Law. By the Prætor's Edict, as for injuries and robberies.

Section V.—Every noxal action follows the person of the slave, by whom the wrong was done. If your slave be guilty of a wrong, the action will lie against you, so long as he continues in your power; if he become subject to another, the action lies against that other; but if he be enfranchised, the action lies directly against him, and the option of making a surrender of the slave is, of course, at an end. On the other hand, an action which was at first direct, may afterwards become noxal; for, if a freeman be guilty of a wrongful act, and afterwards become your slave (and how this may happen we have fully set forth in our First Book), the action which was before direct against the slave, becomes a noxal action against you.

Section VI.—Even though a slave commit an act of wrong against his master, no action will lie; because no obligation can be contracted between a master and one under his power; and, if such slave should pass under the power of another master, or should be enfranchised, no action for the wrong done to his former master, can be brought either against the slave himself, or against his new proprietor. Wherefore, if the slave of another had committed any wrong against you, and afterwards become your property, your right of action falls to the ground; because it has been brought into such a state, as to render it impossible. Also, if such slave cease to be under your power, you have still no right of action. In like manner, if a master committed any wrong against his slave, such slave, whether aliened or enfranchised, has no right of action against his former master.

Section VII.—In former days, men admitted this law of personal surrender, in the case of all children, male or female, who were under power. But the kindlier feeling of later times has very rightly thought that such a rigorous procedure should absolutely be exploded; and it has, in consequence, fallen into absolute disuse. For what man could endure to give up, as a penalty, a son; or worse still a daughter? For, if it were a son, the father would suffer greater agony than would the son himself; while, if it were a daughter, the simple rules of decency forbid such a practice. It has, therefore, grown into a custom that noxal actions shall be applicable to slaves alone; and, in the works of the older writers on the law, we find it frequently laid down that, as against sons under power, an action may be brought to recover damages for their misdeeds.

TITLE 9.

OF NOXAL ACTIONS, IN THE CASE OF BEASTS.

By the law of the Twelve Tables, a noxal action is granted where brute beasts, through wantonness, hot passion, or ferocity have done any damage. And if such animals be surrendered as a penalty, they serve to clear the owner from all further risk; and thus it is set forth in the law of the Twelve Tables; as, if a horse, given to kicking, should lash out, or an ox, wont to gore, should wound any one with its horns. This noxal action, however, can be brought in regard to those animals only which are acting contrary to their natural habits; for if the wild fury of the brute be natural to him, no action will lie. If, therefore, a bear break loose from his master, and thus some injury is done, the master is not liable; and this, because he ceased to be the master, so soon as the brute had made its escape. Damage done with no bad intent, is called *pauperies*; and, an inferior animal, void of reason, cannot be held to have had any bad intent. Thus much with reference to noxal actions.

Section I.—It is, however, further to be remarked that the Ædile's Edict forbids a man to keep a dog, boar, wild boar, bear, or lion, where there is a highway; and, if this rule were violated, and any damage done to a freeman, the owner of the beast that did the injury, might be condemned in such sum as the judge should think warranted by the rules of equity and good conscience. In addition, however, to these actions under the Ædile's Edict, an action for the damage—*pauperies*—might be also brought; for when diverse actions, especially those which are penal, may all be brought on account of the selfsame thing, the use of one does not destroy the efficacy of another.

TITLE 10.

OF REPRESENTATIVES IN ACTIONS.

We have now to notice, that a man may carry on an action either in his own name, or in that of another; as, in the name of a procurator or attorney, a tutor, or a curator. In former days, the usage was, that one man could not carry on a suit on behalf of another, unless he did so, as a kind of representative of the State, in a " popular" action, or in the cause of liberty, or for a pupil. Afterwards by the Hostilian Law, permission was given to bring an action of theft in the name of those who were prisoners in the hands of an enemy; of those who were absent on affairs of State; and of those who were under tutelage. And, as there proved to be no little inconvenience in forbidding one man to bring an action, or to defend it in another's name, it gradually became the practice to sue by means of procurators, or attornies. For sickness, old age, unavoidable journeyings and other causes out of number oftentimes hinder men from personally looking to their own affairs.

Section I.—A procurator, or attorney, is appointed without any fixed form of words, and the presence of the adverse party is not needed; nay, the appointment is, in most cases made without his knowledge. Any one, also, whom you entrust with the commencement, or carrying of any suit, is held to be your procurator.

Section II.—The method whereby tutors and curators are appointed, has already been fully set forth in the first Book.

TITLE 11.

OF SECURITIES.

The system of taking securities under the old law, was different from that which custom has in modern days, made general. Because, formerly, if a real action were brought, the defendant or party in possession was compelled to give security; so that if the action went against him, and he neither made restitution of the thing, nor paid the amount at which it was assessed, the plaintiff might sue either him, or those bound for him. This species of security was called *judicatum solvi,—i. e.*, " that the verdict shall be carried out"; and it is not difficult to see why it was so called, for every plaintiff used to stipulate that the requirements of the verdict should be carried out. As defendants, when principals, were called upon to give security, much more were they compelled so to do, who in a real action, defended on behalf of another. The plaintiff who, in a real action, sued in his own name, was not compelled to give security; the procurator, however, who in such actions appeared as plaintiff, was called upon to give security for the ratification of his acts by him, on whose behalf he acted; because, there was a risk of the plaintiff himself afterwards bringing another action for recovery of the same thing. According to the letter of the Edict, tutors and curators, as well as procurators or attornies, were compelled to give security; the rule, however, was at times relaxed, in cases where they were plaintiffs. Such, then, was the usage in the case of real actions.

Section I.—In the case of personal actions, on the plaintiff's side the same rules held, which we have mentioned as obtaining in real actions. On the defendant's side, he who proceeded in the name of another, was always called upon to give security; for, no one was thought to be a competent agent in the defence of another, who did not give security. If, however, in a personal action any one was defendant in his own name, he was not obliged to furnish the security which we before called *judicatum solvi*—" for carrying out the verdict."

Section II.—But, in the present day, rules very different are observed. He who, in his own name, is called upon to act as defendant in any action, real or personal, is not obliged to give security for payment of the value at which the thing sued for is assessed; he does so, only for his own personal appearance in court, until the termination of the suit. This security is given, either by the promise on oath of the defendant himself, which was called a juratory security; or by his bare unsupported promise; or by other security, according to the position of the defendant.

Section III.—If, however, a suit be begun or defended by a procurator, and the procurator who acts on behalf of the plaintiff, have not registered his commission of appointment; or, if the plaintiff in person have not appeared in court to ratify the appointment of his procurator, then must the procurator himself, be forced to give security for the ratification of his acts, by him on whose behalf he appears. The like rule holds, where a tutor, a curator, or such like person, who has undertaken the management of the affairs of others, brings an action by a procurator.

Section IV.—In the case of the defendant, however, if he be present, and prepared to sanction the appointment of a procurator, he can either appear personally in court, and ratify the nomination by giving the aforesaid security of *judicatum solvi* with the usual stipulation; or he may give security without any personal appearance in court, and become himself surety for the due performance by his procurator of all the covenants in the instrument of security for carrying out the verdict; also, whether this security be given in court, or out of court, he is compelled to hypothecate his whole estate and make it chargeable, so that his heirs, no less than himself, are bound by the obligation. Additional security must, also, be given for his personal appearance in court, at the time when judgment is given; or, in the event of his failure to appear, his surety will be obliged to pay whatever sum the sentence may exact, unless there be an appeal against the decision.

Section V.—If, however, from any cause, a defendant do not appear, and another be minded to take up the defence for him, he is at liberty to do so; and this, both in real and in personal actions. It is only required that he give the ordinary security for carrying out the verdict, and payment of the assessed value of the thing at stake. Because, in accordance with the ancient rule above alluded to, no one was thought to be a competent agent in the defence of another who did not give security.

Section VI.—But all these formal matters will be learned, more clearly and more perfectly, by constant attendance in the courts themselves, and by the study of deeds and legal documents.

Section VII.—We deem it fit that these our regulations shall obtain not in this our Royal City only, but also in all our provinces, albeit there, through lack of knowledge, other usages may have hitherto prevailed. For, it is essential, that all the provinces should imitate and be guided by the practice of our Royal City, the capital of all our wide dominions.

TITLE 12.

OF ACTIONS PERPETUAL AND TEMPORARY.

We must here remark, that in former times all actions which took their rise from the Law, from a Senatorial Decree, or from the Imperial Constitutions, might be brought without any limitation of time; until, at length, the latter Constitutions assigned certain limits to actions, as well personal as real. Actions which arise from the peculiar jurisdiction of the Prætor, last in most instances only for a year; for such was the duration of the Prætor's power. In certain cases, however, even Prætorian actions are what the law calls perpetual, that is, are extended to the limits introduced by the Constitutions; actions of this kind, are those which the Prætor grants to the possessors of goods, and to others who stand in the place of heirs. The action also of theft manifest, although it has its rise in the jurisdiction of the Prætor, is nevertheless perpetual; for it was deemed ridiculous that an action of such kind should be limited to a single year.

Section I.—Not every action which can be brought against a man, whether by virtue of the Civil Law or of Prætorian Edict, can be brought, also, against the heir. For, it is a settled rule of law, that actions which involve damages and spring from malfeasance, are not competent against the heir of the defendant; such, for example, is the case in actions of theft, of robbery, of injury to persons, and of wilful damage. Heirs are, however, competent to bring such actions; and such competency is never denied save in actions of injury to persons, and in some others of like nature. In some cases, however, an action on contract, even, is not competent against the heir; as, for instance, when the testator had been guilty of wilful fraud, and the heir, under the testament, derived no profit from such fraud.

Those actions for damages, however, whereof we have above spoken, are competent both to and against the heirs of the parties, provided the principals had come to *litis-contestatio*— *i. e.*, had actually joined issue on them.

S*ection II.*—It remains for us to observe, that if, before sentence given, the defendant give full satisfaction to the plaintiff, the judge is bound to discharge such defendant; and this, although, from the first commencement of the suit, it was clear that the defendant would be cast. This is the meaning of the old and common saying, that there could be no action wherein a defendant might not be discharged.

TITLE 13.

OF EXCEPTIONS.

It next follows, that we treat of Exceptions. These have been called into existence, for the protection of those who are defendants in actions. For, oftentimes, it happens that the suit of the plaintiff, although right and equitable in itself, may yet be wrong and unjust with respect to the party against whom it has been made.

Section I.—If, for example, forced by fear, deceived by dole, or led astray by misconception, you had promised Titius on a stipulation, that which you were not called upon to promise; clearly you are bound by the rules of Civil Law, and an action, alleging that you are bound to fulfil the engagement, will validly lie against you. It would, however, be contrary to equity that you should be cast in such an action; and therefore, to impugn it, there is granted you the exception of fear and intimidation, of force and fear, or of error as to facts.

Section II.—The same is the rule, if one were to stipulate with you, for the payment of a certain sum to him in consideration of a loan to you, and were then to fail to make the loan. He can, most certainly, sue you for the money; and you are called upon to pay him, inasmuch as you are bound by the contract. But, as it would be contrary to equity, that you should be cast in a suit like this, it has been held that you may defend yourself by the exception *non numeratæ pecuniæ*—i. e. "of money not paid," or "no consideration." We have, by our Imperial Constitution, introduced a limitation of the time within which this exception may be brought; but of this we have already treated in a former Book.

Section III.—The debtor, also, who has made an agreement with his creditor, that no proceedings shall be taken for recovery of the debt, does still continue bound. Because obligations are not wholly extinguished by agreement only. An action, therefore, in which the statement of demand begins with the formal words, "if it seem that he ought to give," would be good against the debtor. But, as it would be contrary to the rules of equity, that he should be cast in spite of the agreement, he may avail himself, in his defence, of the exception *pacti conventi*—i. e. "of compact and agreement."

Section IV.—In like manner, if an oath be administered to a debtor, at the instance of the creditor, and such debtor swear that he is not indebted, yet is he still held liable. But, as it were contrary to the rules of equity, that the question of perjury should be gone into, the defendant is permitted to avail himself of the exception *juris jurandi*—i. e. " of oath administered." In real actions, also, exceptions of this sort are no less necessary; as, when one in possession, having had an oath administered to him at the instance of the plaintiff, swears that the property is his, while the plaintiff still persists in the assertion of his claim. Because, although the plaintiff's claim may be a true one, it would be contrary to the rules of equity, that a verdict should be given against him who has the possession.

Section V.—Further, if an action, whether real or personal, have been brought against you, the obligation nevertheless subsists; wherefore, according to the letter of the law, you may be sued, in a second action, for recovery of the same thing. You may, however, obtain relief by the exception *rei judicati*—i. e. " case tried."

Section VI.—It may be enough to have given these specimens of exceptions. But, as to the number and variety of cases wherein exceptions are of avail, information may be had in the more extensive treatises of the Digest, or the Pandects.

Section VII.—Now, of exceptions, some obtain their influence from the laws, and from enactments which are equivalent to laws; others, again, obtain it from the jurisdiction of the Prætor.

Section VIII.—Some exceptions are called Perpetual and Peremptory; others, Temporary and Dilatory.

Section IX.—Perpetual and Peremptory Exceptions are those which are at all times competent against the plaintiff, and which always absolutely bar and defeat the action.

Of this kind are, the exception of fraud, that of fear and intimidation, and that of compact and agreement, where the plaintiff has agreed not to sue the defendant.

Section X.—Temporary and Dilatory Exceptions are those which are for a certain time only competent against the plaintiff, and which only cause delay. Of this kind is the exception of compact and agreement, where the plaintiff had agreed not to make the demand during a certain stated time, as, for example, five years; for after that time, the plaintiff is no longer hindered from bringing his action. They, therefore, who being anxious to advance their claim before the expiration of the stated time, have been repelled by the exception of compact and agreement, must put off and postpone their suit, and renew when the time agreed on has expired; and from this "putting off" these exceptions get their name of *dilatory*. Formerly, if plaintiffs brought their action within the time agreed on, and an exception were used to repel their claim, it not only stayed them from obtaining in that cause; but, even when the time had expired, they were not allowed to proceed again, because they had rashly brought the matter into court, and lost their privilege of claim. We however, in the present day, are minded to proceed less harshly; and decree, that he who presumes to bring his action, before the time stated in the obligation or agreement has expired, shall be liable to the provisions of the Constitution of the Emperor Zeno, set forth by that most pious ruler with reference to those who, in respect of time, ask more than is their due. So that, if a plaintiff set at nought the time allowed, that time which either he himself of his free-will has allowed, or which is implied in the very nature of the action, the defendant who has suffered such ill-treatment shall become entitled to twice the time before allowed. And, even when such double time has sped, defendants cannot be forced to enter an appearance, unless they have been reimbursed for all their costs in the former action; and this, that plaintiffs, in fear of so heavy a penalty, may learn to observe the proper season for commencement of their suits.

Section XI.—There are, also, dilatory exceptions, arising

from the person of the plaintiff. Such are those where objection is made to the procurator or agent, and this is admitted where a party desires to have his cause conducted by a woman or a soldier. As for soldiers, indeed, they cannot, though they have the sanction of an Imperial Rescript, act on behalf of even father, mother, or wife; they are at liberty, however, without breach of military discipline, to act in their own affairs. As for the exceptions which formerly were set up, against the persons of procurators, by reason of the infamy, whether of the procurator, or of him on whose behalf he was appointed, we found that were absolutely obsolete in the practice of the courts. We have, in consequence, decreed their abolition, and this, because we feared that if matters of this kind were disputed, the discussion of the real point at issue might be retarded.

TITLE 14.

OF REPLICATIONS.

At times it happens that an Exception, which at first seems just, is in reality unjust. In such cases, a fresh allegation is needed to assist the plaintiff, and this is called a Replication —*i. e.* " an unfolding,"—because it unfolds, and resolves the force and right of the exception. If, for example, a man have made an agreement with his debtor not to demand payment; and afterwards the two enter into a contrary agreement, to wit, that he may demand payment. In this case, if the creditor commence his action, and the debtor plead in exception, that judgment should be given against him only if the creditor have not made an agreement not to demand payment; this exception stops the creditor. For it is a fact that such an agreement was made, although one contrary was afterwards concluded. As, however, it would be contrary to the rules of equity, to put the plaintiff out of court by the exception, he is allowed to plead the second agreement as a *Replication*.

Section I.—The Replication, again, may at first seem just, but be in reality unjust. When this occurs, another allegation is necessary, to assist the defendant, and this is called a *Duplication*.

Section II.—And, if the Duplication, in its turn, at first seem just but be in reality unjust, there is need of another allegation to assist the plaintiff, and this is called a *Triplication*.

Section III.—The great diversity of practice carries, at times, the use of all these exceptions far beyond what we have mentioned; but all these matters may more clearly and readily be seen by a reference to the more extensive treatise of the Digest.

Section IV.—Exceptions which are competent to a debtor, are usually, and with justice, competent to his sureties; because what is sued for from them is, in reality, sued for from the debtor, for, by an action of Mandate, he will be obliged to restore what they have paid on his account. If, therefore, a creditor have agreed with his debtor not to sue for payment, the sureties of such debtor may plead the exception of " compact and agreement," precisely as though the agreement not to sue for payment, had been directly made with them. There are, indeed, certain exceptions, which are not granted them; as, for example, if a debtor have made surrender of his goods, and a creditor sue him; he may defend himself by the exception of "surrender", but this exception is not allowed to his sureties. And for this reason, that the creditor who accepts security for the payment of money advanced by him, looks especially to the recovery of the debt from the sureties, in the event of failure of the principal.

TITLE 15.

OF INTERDICTS.

We have next to treat of Interdicts, or the actions which are brought to supply their place. Interdicts were certain verbal formulæ whereby the Prætor ordered or forbade something to be done; and these formulæ were chiefly resorted to in disputed questions of possession, or quasi-possession.

Section I.—The main division of Interdicts is as follows; the Prohibitory; or Restitutory; or Exhibitory.

Prohibitory Interdicts, are those whereby the Prætor forbids something to be done; as, for example, where he forbids the forcible disturbance of a man in possession without legal vice, or of one who is burying a dead body, where legally he may be buried; or to build on consecrated ground; or to do anything whether in a public river, or on its banks, whereby the navigation may be injured.

Restitutory Edicts, are those whereby the Prætor orders the restitution of something; as, for example, where he orders that the possessor have restored to him possession of those goods of an inheritance which are actually in the possession of one who has assumed the rights of heir or of possessor;

or where he orders restitution of possession to a person, who has been violently dispossessed.

Exhibitory Interdicts, are those whereby the Prætor orders the production of a person, or a thing; as, for example, of a man whose liberty has been called in question; or of a freed-man whose services are needed by his patron; or of children to the father under whose power they are.

Some persons hold that, in strictness, those only are interdicts, which are prohibitory, because the word *interdicere* is " to denounce," or " to prohibit"; and that, what we have called restitutory and exhibitory interdicts should be termed " decrees". Custom, however, has given to all alike the name of interdict, and because they are given between (*inter*) two parties.

Section II.—The next division of Interdicts is, that some are given, to acquire possession; some, to retain possession; and others, to recover possession.

Section III.—An Interdict to acquire possession is given to him to whom the Prætor has granted possession of goods. It is called, from its first words, *Quorum Bonorum;* and its effect is to compel restitution to the possessor of the goods, of those effects which, passing under the Prætorian Grant, are still actually in the possession of some other as heir, or as possessor. A person is considered to possess as heir, who actually believes himself to be heir; but, as possessor, when without right or title, he takes possession of all or part of an inheritance, well knowing that it does not belong to him. This interdict is said to be to obtain possession, because it is of avail to him only who first endeavours to acquire possession. To him, therefore, who having gained possession, has afterwards lost, this interdict is unavailing. Another interdict is granted to acquire possession; this is the Salvian Interdict, and it is had recourse to by proprietors of farms, in order to acquire those chattels of the former which have been pledged as a security for payment of the rent.

Section IV.—Interdicts to retain possession are those which from their first words, are called *uti possidetis* and *utrubi;* they are provided in cases, where there is a dispute as to the ownership of a thing, and there arises a previous inquiry as to which of the litigants is in actual possession, and which, therefore, is plaintiff. For, unless it be first decided which has the possession, no real action can be instituted; for law and reason both demand that one party should have the possession, while the other seeks to gain it. And, as it is far more advantageous to have possession, than to sue for it, there is usually great contention as to this right. Now, the advantage of possession consists in this; that even though the thing in question be not the property of the possessor, still, if the plaintiff cannot prove it to be his, the possessor remains undisturbed in his possession; when, therefore, the claims of both parties are but doubtful, it is usual to decide against the plaintiff or demandant. The interdict *uti possidetis* is intended to apply to disputes as to the possession of immoveables, as lands and buildings; and that *utrubi* to moveables. In former days, these interdicts differed widely in their effects; for, in the interdict *uti possidetis,* he was successful, who had possession at the time of the interdict; provided, he had not gained it from the other party, by either force, or double-dealing, or as a revocable gift. If, however, he had gained it, from any save the other party, it mattered not whether he had done so by force, or double-dealing, or as a revocable gift. But, in the interdict *utrubi,* he was successful, who had held possession during the greater portion of the year immediately preceding the time of action brought; and had not gained it from the other party, by force or double-dealing, or as a revocable gift. Now, however, another custom prevails, for the influence of the two interdicts, so far as regards possession, has been made equal. Whether, therefore, the dispute regard immoveables or moveables, that party is successful, who, at the time of *litis-contestatio*—*i. e.*, " of joining issue",—is in possession, without having gained it from the other party by force, or double-dealing, or as a revocable gift.

Section V.—A man is held to possess, not only where he himself is actually in possession, but also, where another is in possession in his name; and this, even though such actual possessor be not under his power, as the tenant of a farm or house. One who has made a deposit, or a loan, may possess also through the instrumentality of the depository or borrower; and this is what is meant, when it is said, that one may retain possession by means of another who possesses in his name. By mere intention, also, possession may be retained; that is to say, although a person be not himself in possession, and no other is so in his name, still if separated himself from the thing, with the intention not of abandoning the thing, but of again returning to it, he is still held to retain the possession. We have already, in our Second Book, explained by means of what persons possession may be acquired. It is, however, clear beyond all doubt, that possession cannot be acquired by mere intention.

Section VI.—An interdict for recovery of possession is given, when a man has forcibly been ousted from possession of a farm or house. The interdict so given him was called, from its first words, *unde vi;* and by it the person, who so turned him out with violence, is forced to restore to him the possession; and this, although the person, to whom the interdict is granted, has himself by force, or double-dealing, or as a revocable gift, regained possession from him who had so ousted him. By the Imperial Constitutions, however, it is, as we have said before, provided, that if a man place himself forcibly in possession of a thing which is really his own, he shall forfeit his property in it; and, if it be not his own, he shall first make restitution of the thing, and afterwards pay its estimated value, to him who has sustained the wrong. He, also, who has forcibly dispossessed another is liable to the *Lex Julia* for private or for public violence; for private violence, if the violence were committed without the use of arms; for public violence, if the dispossession were effected with force and arms. By arms, we understand not shields alone, swords and helmets, but clubs and stones.

Section VII.—The next division of Interdicts is this; that they are either Simple or Double.

Simple Interdicts, are those wherein one person is plaintiff, and another person defendant. Of this kind are restitutory and exhibitory interdicts; for the plaintiff is he who wishes to have exhibition or restitution, and the defendant, he from whom such exhibition or restitution is required. Of prohibitory interdicts some are simple, and some double. Simple, as when the Prætor forbids something to be done in a consecrated piece of ground, on a public river, or upon its banks; for the plaintiff is he who wishes the thing not to be done, and the defendant he who endeavours to do it. Double, as when the interdicts are those of *uti possidetis*, or *utrubi*.

Double Interdicts are so called, because the position of each of the parties litigant is equal; neither can be held to be in any special manner either plaintiff or defendant, but each in his turn sustains the character of both.

Section VIII.—It would, in the present day, be waste of time to speak of the ancient process and effects of interdicts. For, when the jurisdiction is extraordinary, and now it always is so, interdicts are unnecessary; and judgment is now given in the absence of interdict, just as though an equitable, or " useful" action had been granted by interdict.

TITLE 16.

OF PENALTIES IMPOSED UPON RASH LITIGANTS.

We may here observe, that our Legislators and Magistrates have ever been most anxious to prevent persons from entering upon reckless and vexatious suits; and in this anxiety we do most heartily agree. Now, it seems that such prevention may be best effected, by restraining the recklessness as well of plaintiffs as of defendants; at one time by pecuniary fines, at another, by the obligation of an oath; and at another, by the threat of infamy.

Section I.—By virtue, then, of one of our Constitutions an oath is administered to all against whom any action is brought. Nor can the defendant be permitted to enter upon his defence, until he have first sworn that he resists the claim of the plaintiff from a conviction of the goodness of his own cause. In particular cases, the penalty decreed against such as had denied their liability, was double or treble the value of the thing itself: as in suits on account of wilful damage, or for legacies given to consecrated spots. In certain actions, also, the penalty is, from the very first, above the single value; as in the case of theft manifest, where it is quadruple; and of theft not manifest, where it is double. In these, and certain other actions of like kind, the penalty is above the single value, whether the defendant denies, or acknowledges the charge against him. The vexatious claims (*calumniæ*) of the plaintiff are, also, kept in check; for, by one of our Constitutions, he is compelled to take the " Oath of Calumny." The advocates of both parties are also obliged to take an oath which is set forth in another of our Constitutions. All these several formalities have been introduced in lieu of the ancient action of calumny, now fallen into disuse, whereby the plaintiff was mulcted in the tenth part of the thing in dispute; we, however, never heard of the penalty being enforced. In lieu, therefore, of its provisions, there has been introduced the oath above alluded to; and we have, further, ordained that the reckless and vexatious plaintiff be compelled to reimburse the other party, for all his damage and expenses in the suit.

Section II.—In certain cases, persons if condemned become infamous; it is so in actions of theft, robbery, wilful damage, fraud. The like occurs also in actions of tutelage, mandate, or deposit, when direct, but not when contrary. So, too, in the action of partnership, which is direct by whichever of the parties brought; he therefore, of them who is condemned in such a suit is branded with infamy. Infamy attaches not only to those who have been found guilty in actions of theft, robbery, wilful injury or fraud, but to those who have been connected with them; and rightly, because there is a wide difference between the debtor by a wrong, or by a contract.

Section III.—The first matter to be looked to in bringing any action, arises from that portion of the Prætor's Edict, in which he treats of the *Vocatio in Jus,—i. e.* " citation into court." For, before all other steps, the defendant must be cited to appear in court, before the Magistrate who is to determine the cause. And, in this said portion of his Edict, the Prætor shows so great respect for parents and patrons, and even for the parents and children of patrons, that children and freed-men can cite them into court, only when they have first obtained permission from the Prætor. And if any presume to cite them, without having first obtained this permission, he is mulcted in the sum of fifty golden pieces.

TITLE 17.

OF THE DUTY OF A JUDGE.

We have still to inquire into the duty of a Judge. And, first of all, his care should be, in no case to judge otherwise than in accordance with the Laws, the Constitutions, or with Custom.

Section I.—If, therefore, in the decision of a Noxal action, the master deserve to be condemned, the Judge should word his condemnation thus :—" I condemn Publius Mævius to pay ten pieces to the plaintiff Lucius Titius ; or, if he will, to make surrender of the doer of the wrong."

Section II.—If, in a real action, the Judge decide against the claimant, he ought to dismiss the possessor; and if against the possessor, he ought to decree the restitution of the thing which was in question, together with its fruits. If, however, the possessor allege that he is unable to make immediate restitution, and if he appear to sue for a longer time, from some other than a mere desire to make the decree of no avail, the indulgence should be granted him ; provided, however, that he furnish sufficient surety for payment of the estimated value of the thing in dispute, in the event of his failing to make restitution within the additional time accorded him. And if an inheritance be the matter in dispute, the like rules hold as to the produce which we have mentioned as holding in the case of particular things. If the defendant have been in possession *malâ fide,* the account as to the fruits, whether gathered by the possessor, or, through his carelessness, not gathered, is all but the same in both sorts of action. If, however, the defendant have been in possession *bonâ fide,* no account is demanded of the fruits, whether consumed by him, or left ungathered before the commencement of the suit. But, from the time when proceedings have commenced, the possessor must account for all the fruits, whether they have been consumed by him, or, by his carelessness, left ungathered.

Section III.—In the case of an action *ad exhibendum* it is not enough that the defendant exhibit and produce the thing itself; he must exhibit, also, all that there-from is accruing; that is, the plaintiff must be placed in the same condition in which he would have been, if the matter in dispute had been exhibited when first he demanded it. If, therefore, thanks to his delays, the possessor gain a title by prescription to the thing, he will nevertheless be condemned to make restitution. The Judge ought, further, to take an account of the mesne profits; that is, of the fruits during the time which has intervened between the bringing of action for production, and the termination of the suit. Also, if the defendant allege his inability to make immediate exhibition of the thing in question, and petition for a longer time, with no appearance of doing so only to invalidate the sentence, such time should be accorded him; but only when he has given security for his making restitution. If, however, he neither make immediate exhibition, when the Judge decrees it, nor give security for its production at a future day, he must be condemned in such amount, as shall be equivalent to the loss which the plaintiff has sustained, by the refusal of the defendant to produce the thing at the first commencement of the suit.

Section IV.—In the action *familiæ erciscundæ*—*i. e.*, "for partition of an inheritance," the Judge ought to adjudicate the several things which form the inheritance to each of the heirs separately; and if such adjudication seem to be more favorable to one than to the other, he who is so favored in the distribution must be adjudged to pay a proportionate sum of money to his co-heir. In like manner, also, an heir should be decreed to pay to his co-heirs, the value of such fruits of an inheritance as he has exclusively enjoyed, or of such portions of the inheritance as he has either damaged or consumed. The same rules hold whether the number of co-heirs be two or more.

Section V.—The like is observed in the action *de communi dividundo,* for the division of several things held in common by several persons. Where there is to be division of a single thing, as, for example, of a piece of land, provided it can readily be parcelled out into shares, one of such shares should be adjudicated to each of the parties; and if the share of one preponderate, that one must be adjudged to pay a proportionate sum of money to the other. But, if the property cannot conveniently be divided, as, if it were a slave, or a mule, the whole must be awarded to one of the parties; who, in his turn, must be decreed to make compensation to the other by a payment in money.

Section VI.—In the action *Finium regundorum*—i. e., " for the settlement of the boundaries of contiguous rural estates," —the Judge ought, first, to examine if the adjudication be called for. And this it clearly is in one case, namely, when it is expedient that lands should be marked out by clearer limits than those which formerly existed. In this case, it becomes necessary that some land of one man be awarded to a neighbouring proprietor; and, therefore, it is but just that the latter should be decreed to pay over to the former, a stated sum as an equivalent. He, also, is liable to be mulcted in this action, who has fraudulently meddled with the boundaries; as, for example, by shifting boundary-stones, or felling boundary-trees. In these proceedings, parties may, also, be punished for contumacy; as, for example, may he who refuses to allow a survey of his land, when such has been ordered by the judge.

Section VII.—Whatever, in these proceedings, is adjudicated, becomes at once the property of him to whom it is adjudicated.

TITLE 18.

OF PUBLIC PROSECUTIONS.

PUBLIC Prosecutions do not originate in actions, nor have they any similarity to the other legal remedies, whereof we have just treated. In these prosecutions there is great difference, as well in the mode of commencing, as of carrying them on.

Section I.—They are called Public, because the privilege of conducting them is, in most instances, accorded to any member of the Roman People.

Section II.—Of Public Prosecutions, again, some are Capital, and some not Capital. Capital Prosecutions are those, to which the penalty attached is death; interdiction of fire and water; deportation or banishment; or labour in the mines. Not Capital, though Public, are Prosecutions which involve infamy and pecuniary fines.

Section III.—The following laws relate to Public Prosecutions. The *Lex Julia Majestatis,* which directs the severity of its provisions against those who have engaged in plots against the Sovereign Majesty of Emperor, or State. Its penalty is loss of life, and condemnation of the culprit's memory, even after death.

Section IV.—There is, also, a *Lex Julia* for the suppression of Adultery; and this punishes with death, not only those who violate the marriage bed, but those also who commit unmentionable crimes of lust. The same law punishes the defilement, without force, of a virgin, or widow of good conversation. This latter crime is punished, in the case of offenders of rank and consideration, by the confiscation of half their goods; and in the case of those of low degree, by corporal punishment and relegation, the lesser kind of exile.

Section V.—The *Lex Cornelia de Sicariis* punishes with death those who are guilty of homicide; and those, also, who go about wearing a *telum*—*i. e.*, "weapon," with intent to kill. The expression *telum*, according to the interpretation of Gaius in his commentaries on the Law of the Twelve Tables, usually means anything which is shot from a bow; it may, however, mean anything hurled from the hand. It follows, therefore, that a club, a stone, a piece of iron, may be comprehended in this term. It means, indeed, anything thrown far off, to a distance; the derivation being from the Greek τηλου—" far away". We may trace the same primary meaning in the word, which in Greek corresponds to *telum*; for that which we so call, they know as βέλος, derived from βάλλειν—*i. e.*, " to throw". Xenophon, even, tells us this when he says:—" they carried with them βέλη, in the shape of spears, arrows, slings, and a vast quantity of stones." Assassins get their name of *Sicarii*, from *Sica*, a poniard or short sword. By the same law, the penalty of death was inflicted on such as took away the lives of men, by means of odious practices, of poisons, and of magical incantations; it punished, in like manner, those who publicly sold pernicious drugs.

Section VI.—Another Law, to wit the *Lex Pompeia de Parricidiis*, provides for the most execrable of crimes, the most strange of punishments. By it, the man who has hastened the death of a parent or a child, or of any other included in that tie of close relationship, the breach of which by murder is legally called parricide, shall be condemned to suffer the punishment of parricide; nor does it matter whether the crime were committed openly, or stealthily; he, too, who incites the murderer to the deed, or who is privy to the crime is, even though he be a stranger unconnected with the family, held guilty of the crime of parricide. The criminal is not put to death, by means of sword, or faggot, or any other wonted punishment; but, is sewn into a leathern sack, with a cur, a cock, a viper, and an ape, and when cooped up in this fearful prison, is hurled either into the sea, or into some neighbouring river, according to the situation of the place. Thus, then, the parricide, while yet alive, is doomed to lack the use of the very elements; to be denied the air while still he lives, the earth when he is dead. If a man be guilty of the murder of other persons, of kin to him only by cognation or by marriage, he will be condemned to suffer the penalties set forth in the *Lex Cornelia*, as to stabbers.

Section VII.—The *Lex Cornelia de Falsis*, called also *testamentaria*, punishes him, who of his knowledge and with fraudulent intent, has written, sealed, suppressed, or substituted a false testament, or other instrument; or who, with like knowledge and intent, has fashioned, graven, or impressed a false seal. The penalty provided by this law is, in the case of slaves, death, the same as that decreed by the *Lex Cornelia* against stabbers and poisoners; and, in the case of free persons, it is deportation.

Section VIII.—The *Lex Julia de Vi*—" concerning violence public or private"—is pronounced against such as are guilty of violence, whether with arms or without them. If it be proved that there was violence with arms, the penalty, by this

Law, is deportation; if without arms, the confiscation of the third part of the offender's goods. When, however, a rape has been committed upon a virgin, a widow, a woman who has taken holy vows, or upon any one besides, both the principal offenders and their accomplices are punishable with death; and this, in accordance with the provisions of our Constitution, where fuller information on this matter may be found.

Section IX.—The *Lex Julia de Peculatu* punishes those who have made away with public funds, or with anything consecrated and set apart for holy uses. Judges themselves who, in their official capacity, embezzle and appropriate the public monies, are punishable with death; and not they alone, but all who have aided them in the commission of their theft; and those, also, who wittingly have taken the sums so stolen. All others who transgress the provisions of this Law are subject only to the pains of deportation.

Section X.—Of the Laws as to Public Prosecutions, is to be reckoned the *Lex Fabia de Plagiariis*—i. e., "concerning kidnappers." The penalty which it inflicts is in certain cases, by virtue of the Imperial Constitutions, that of death; in others, however, it imposes one less severe.

Section XI.—Of other Laws relating to Public Prosecutions may be numbered the several Julian Laws following; that *de ambitu*, against unlawful trafficking in public offices; that *repetundarum*, against the bribing of Magistrates; that *de annona*, against forestalling, regrating, engrossing, and monopolizing; and that *de residuis*, against malversation and misappropriation of the public funds. These all have reference only, to the cases comprehended under their several appellations; they do not involve the penalty of death, but threaten with lesser punishments, such as offend against them.

Section XII.—The few matters which we have here set forth, with reference to public prosecutions, are intended only as a sort of Index, or general guide to their more careful study. A fuller knowledge may, with the blessing of God, be gained from a study of the more copious treatises of the Digest and the Pandects.

END OF THE INSTITUTES.

APPENDIX.

NOVEL CXVIII.

OF SUCCESSION TO INTESTATES.

NOVEL CXVIII.

CHAPTER 1.

OF THE SUCCESSION OF DESCENDANTS.

IF one who dies intestate, leave, him surviving, a descendant of either sex, or any degree, such descendant is to be preferred to all ascendants and collaterals; and this, whether he descend through the male line or female, whether he be under power or independent. And, even though the deceased were under power, we will, that his descendants of either sex or any degree, be preferred to those in whose power the deceased so was, so far as it regards those things which, by virtue of our other regulations, children do not acquire for parents; but in respect to the usufruct of all those things which can be acquired, or given to parents, we will that our former regulations be upheld. If, also, it should chance that any such descendant die, leaving sons, daughters, or any other descendants him surviving, such survivors shall take the place of their parent; and this, whether under power or independent; taking that share of the institute's estate, which their father would have taken, if he had survived. This is what the ancient Jurists called the succession *in stirpes*—*i. e.*, "by stocks." For, in the succession of descendants, we recognize no difference of degree: but we admit grand-children, by a son or daughter dead, to take equally with sons and daughters; without making any distinction between males and females, between those descended from the male or the female line, or between those under power and those who are independent. Such are the regulations which we have laid down as to the Succession of Descendants.

CHAPTER 2.

OF THE SUCCESSION OF ASCENDANTS.

IF, however, the deceased intestate leave no descendants him surviving, but if a father, or mother, or other ascendants do survive, we ordain that these be preferred to all collaterals; save only brothers of the whole blood, as will be, afterwards, set forth. Also, if there be many ascendants, we will, that preference be given to those who are nearest in degree, whether male or female, on the father's or the mother's side. If, however, there be several of like degree, the inheritance must be divided into such shares between them, that ascendants on the father's side may take one-half, and ascendants on the mother's side may take the other half; and this without regard to the number of persons on either side. If, however, there survive brothers or sisters of the whole blood, together with ascendants also, such collaterals shall take equally with the ascendants of the next, or *first* degree, even though such should be a father or a mother; and the inheritance must be divided among them in such manner, that each of the ascendants, and each of the brothers shall take equal portions. Nor shall the father, in this case, claim the usufruct of the share of his sons or daughters; because, in lieu thereof, we have, by this our regulation, given him the sole property in one portion. And we admit of no distinction between those who are so called to share, whether they be males or females, connected by males or females, whether under power or independent.

CHAPTER 3.

OF THE SUCCESSION OF COLLATERALS.

BUT, when the intestate dies and leaves neither descendants nor ascendants him surviving, we call first to the inheritance, those brothers and sisters of the whole blood, whom we have, before, called equally with fathers, or ascendants of the *first* degree. If, however, there be none such living, we call the brothers and sisters of the half blood; and this, whether by the same father only, or by the same mother. If, again, the deceased leave brothers, and also children of a deceased brother or sister, such children shall, with their uncles and aunts of the whole blood, be called to succeed to the inheritance. But, how numerous soever they may be, they all shall take such portion only as their father would have taken, if he were alive. Whence it follows, that if a brother of the whole blood die leaving children him surviving, and also brothers of the half blood only, such children, although but in the third degree, are to be preferred, in the succession, to their uncles; because, their father, in whose room they stand, would have been preferred, if he were yet alive. So, on the other hand, if a brother of the whole blood survive, we exclude from the inheritance children of a brother of the half blood; and this because the father would have been excluded, if he were yet alive. We have, however, accorded this privilege of representation among collaterals, to none beyond the children of brothers and sisters ; and to such even, we grant it only, on condition of their concurring with their uncles or aunts, whether on the male or female side. But, if ascendants be, as aforesaid, called with the brothers of the deceased to the inheritance, we by no means permit the children of a deceased brother or sister to share in the succession ; even though their father or mother was of the whole blood with the deceased. When, therefore, we have accorded to the children of a brother or a sister the privilege of representing their own parents, we have only allowed those in the third degree, to inherit with those who are in the second. This is evident, because such children are preferred to the uncles and aunts of the deceased, whether by the male or female line ; and this, although both stand in the third degree. If, however, a deceased leave neither brothers, nor children of brothers him surviving, all the rest of the collaterals are called in, according to their prerogative of degree, the nearer being preferred to the more remote. And, if there should be several in the same degree, the inheritance must be portioned out among them, according to the number of individuals ; a partition which our law describes as *in capita*—*i. e.* " by polls".

INDEX.

A.

	Page.
Abduction of women,	293
——, freemen, or slaves,	293
Acceptilation,	222
Accession,	55
Acquisition,	52
——, by use,	71
Act of the Emperor,	4
Actions, what,	245
——, arbitrary,	255
——, bonæ fidei,	253
——, for business done,	218
——, of calumny,	285
——, of commodate,	186
——, communi dividundo,	251
——, contrary,	218
——, corruption of a slave,	228
——, direct,	218, 238
——, exercitoria,	261
——, for exhibition,	58, 288
——, familiæ erciscundæ,	219, 251, 288
——, finium regundorum,	251, 289
——, institoria,	261
——, intimidation,	253
——, mixed,	250
——, negative,	246
——, noxal,	265

302 INDEX.

	Page.
Actions, as to peculium,	262
———, de pecunia constituta,	248
———, perpetual,	273
———, personal,	245, 248
———, portion, for recovery of,	254
———, Prætorian,	246
———, prejudicial,	249
———, Publician,	247
———, real,	245
———, receptitia,	248
———, Servian,	247
———, stricti juris,	253
———, subsidiary,	42
———, temporary,	273
———, of theft,	218
———, de tigno juncto,	58
———, as to unnatural Testaments,	111
———, useful,	238, 284
———, violence, of goods taken with,	233
Administration of tutor,	41
Adopted children, disinherison of,	97
——— succession in intestacy,	150
Adoption,	20
Advice,	215
Affinity,	18
Agnates,	30
———, legal succession of,	154
Agnation,	30
Alienation, power of,	79
Alluvial increase,	50
Animals, offspring of,	255
———, property in,	52, 4
Answers of the Jurists,	5
Aquilian Law,	234
——— stipulation,	222
Arrogation,	20
———, acquisition by,	179
As, Roman, division of,	101
Ascendants, succession of,	298
Assignment, to sustain enfranchisements,	180

INDEX.

	Page.
Assignment, of Freedmen,	173
Attorney, appointment of,	269
———, security required for ratification of his acts,	270
Authority of tutors,	27, 37
Avoiding of testaments,	108

B.

	Page.
Banks of river,	51
Bargains and sales,	204
Bastards,	19
———, issue of,	163
Beam, right of fixing, in another's wall,	58
Bedels, fees of,	252
Bees,	52
Bequests in trust,	134
Bonâ fide possession, acquisition by,	61
———, necessary to prescription,	72
Bonorum Emptio,	183
Borrower, when guilty of theft,	226
Boundaries, settlement of,	251
Brothers and Sisters, succession of,	163, 299
Building, on land of another,	59
———, with materials of another,	58

C.

	Page.
Calumny, oath of,	285
Capital prosecutions,	290
Captivity, testaments made in,	94
Casual homicide,	235
Cautioners,	201
Channel of a river,	55
Children, acquisitions by,	82
———, loans to,	255
———, posthumous,	29, 95, 127
———, succession of, to the mother,	162
———, unable to make testaments,	92
Choice, legacy of,	125
Citation into Court,	286

		Page.
Civil law,	...	3
—— obligation,	...	184
Cloth, woven with another's purple,	...	57
Codicils,	...	143
Cognates,	...	30
————, succession of,	...	162
Collaterals,	...	165
————, succession of,	...	299
Commodate,	...	186
Common, things in,	...	50
Communion,	...	211
Conceptum,	...	226
Condictions,	...	80, 249
Confusion,	...	57
Conjunction,	...	57
Consanguinity,	...	254
Consent, obligations by,	...	204
Consolidation,	...	69
Constituta Pecunia,	...	248
Constitutions of the Emperors,	...	4
Contract, obligations from,	...	184
Corporeal things,	...	65
Corruption of a slave,	...	228
Cousins, marriage of, lawful,	...	18
Curators,	...	39
————, exemption of,	...	43
————, security required of,	...	41
————, suspected,	...	47
Curials,	...	20, 145
Customs,	...	5

D.

Damage, from unskilfulness,	...	236
Damnationem, legacy *per*,	...	118
Days, useful,	...	178
Decree of the Senate,	...	5
————————, Largian,	...	172
————————, Macedonian,	...	264
————————, Orphitian,	...	162

INDEX.

	Page.
Decrees of the Senate, Pegasian,	136
——————————, Sabinian,	152
——————————, Tertullian,	159
——————————, Trebellian,	135
Decurions,	20, 145
Dedititii,	9, 172
Deliberation, the heir's time for,	116
Delivery, acquisition by,	62
Deposit,	187
Depositary, how far liable.	231
Derelicts,	64
Descendants, disinherison of,	95
Dilatory exceptions,	276
Diminution, social,	31
Disinherison,	95
Dissolution, of partnership,	212
Distribution of effects of Intestates, [and Appendix]	145
Donations,	75
————, ante nuptias,	77
————, mortis causâ,	75
————, inter vivos,	76
Dotal estate, restraints on alienation of,	78
Duplication,	279

E.

Edicts of the Magistrates,	4
———————— Prætors,	5
Emancipated children, succession of,	97
Emancipation of children,	125
Emperor, legislative power vested in,	4
Emphyteusis,	209
Emptor familiæ,	85
Error, recovery of payment made in,	219
——, in legacy,	127
Exceptions,	274
————, of case tried,	276
————, of compact and agreement,	275
————, dilatory,	276

P 2

Exceptions, of error as to facts,	275
———, of fear and intimidation,	275
———, of money not paid,	275
———, of no consideration,	275
———, of oath administered,	276
———, peremptory,	276
Exchange, wherein different from sale,	206
Exemptions of Tutors and Curators,	43
Exercitor,	261
Exercitoria Actio,	261
Exhibitory Interdicts,	280
Extraneous heirs,	115

F.

Falcidian Law,	131
Familiæ erciscundæ,	219, 251, 288
Family heirs,	114
Father, power of,	15
Fide-jussors,	201
Fidei-commissa,	134
Fiduciary inheritance,	134
——— guardianship,	34
Finium Regundorum, *see* Boundaries.	
Found things,	64
Free-born,	7
Freed-men,	8
———, assignment of,	173
———, succession of,	169
Freedom,	6
Fruits,	61
———, in actions how adjudged,	287
Fruits of animals,	61
Furtum,	225

G.

Gift,	75
Goods, Prætorian possession of,	174
Guardians, authority of,	37

INDEX.

	Page.
Guardians, security required from,	41
Guardianship, by affinity,	30
———, expiration of,	38
———, fiduciary,	134
———, by magisterial appointment,	35
———, of parents,	33
———, of patrons,	32

H.

Habitation, servitude of,	70
Heirs, three kinds of,	114
——, institution of,	99
——, what actions competent to, and against,	273
Hiring,	208
Homicide,	235
Honorary Law,	5
Hypothecary action,	247
Husband, need not be Curator to his wife,	46

I.

Illegitimate children,	19
Incorporeal legacies,	125
———— things,	65
Industrial accessions,	56
Ineffectual stipulations,	194
———— testaments,	110
Infamy, attaches in what actions,	286
Infants,	196
Ingenuus,	7
Inheritances, fiduciary,	134
————, intestacy, [and Appendix,]	145
Injury to persons,	239
——— property,	234
Institor,	261
Institoria Actio,	261
Institution of heirs,	99
Intimidation, exception of,	275

		Page.
Intention, power of, to retain but not acquire possession,	...	283
Interdicts, origin of, ...	...	280
———, three main sorts of, ...	...	280
———, possessory, ...	...	281
———, Salvian, ...	...	281
———, simple and double, ...	...	284
———, unde vi, ...	...	283
———, utrubi, ...	...	282
Intestates, ...	...	145
———, succession to, ...	...	145
[and Appendix,]		
Islands, new, ...	...	55

J.

Javelin, care required in hurling,	...	235
Joint contracts, ...	...	191
Joint ownership, ...	...	219
Judge, duties of a, ...	...	287
Judicatum solvi, ...	...	270
Jurisprudence, ...	...	1
Justice, ...	...	1

K.

Kidnapping, ...	...	293

L.

Land, use of, ...	...	69
Latini Juniani, ...	10,	172
Law, a, ...	...	4
———, civil,...	3,	5
———, maxims of, ...	...	2
———, of nations, ...	...	2
———, of nature, ...	2,	6
———, private, ...	...	2
———, public, ...	...	2
———, written, ...	...	4

INDEX.

	Page.
Legacies,	118
———, by way of penalty,	130
———, error in,	127
———, four kinds of,	118
———, of choice,	125
———, revocation and transfer of,	131
Legal guardianship of parents,	33
——————————— patrons,	32
——— succession of agnates,	154
Legitimation,	20
Letting and hiring,	208
Lex Ælia Sentia,	11
——— Atilia,	35
——— Atinia,	72
——— Aquilia,	234
——— Cornelia,	94, 241
——————, *de falsis*,	292
——————, *de sicariis*,	291
——— Fabia de Plagiarus,	293
——— Falcidia,	131
——— Fusia Caninia,	13
——— Hostilia,	269
——— Julia *de Adulteriis*,	291
——————, *de Ambitu*,	293
——————, *de Annona*,	293
——————, *Majestatis*,	290
——————, *de Peculatu*,	293
——————, *de Residuis*,	293
——————, *de vi*,	292
——————— Norbana,	172
——————— Velleia,	96
——— Papia,	171
——— Pompeia *de Parricidiis*,	292
——— Regia,	4
Libripens,	85
Lights, right to restrain obstruction of,	66
Limitation of actions,	273
Litis-contestatio,	274, 283
Livery,	62
Lunatics,	40

M.

	Page.
Macedonian decree,	264
Magistrates, edicts of,	4
Maiming, malicious,	241
Majority, at what age attained,	34
Mandate, contract of,	214
————, extinction of,	216
————, five species of,	214
Manumission,	8
—————, how effected,	9
—————, fraudulent,	10
Manumit, disabilities to,	10
Marriage, see Matrimony.	
Master, power of,	14
Matrimony, defined,	15
—————, how contracted,	16
—————, prohibited degrees of,	17
Military peculium,	82, 87
———— testament,	89
Mixed accessions,	58
———— actions,	250
Mixture of materials,	57
Mother, succession of,	160, 162
Mutuum, contract of,	185

N.

	Page.
Natural accessions,	55
———— children,	19
———— law,	2, 6
Necessary heirs,	114
Neglect and incapacity, damage done by,	236
Nomina, obligations formerly so called,	203
Novation,	223
Novel cxviii, see Appendix.	
Noxa,	265
Noxal action,	265
—————, in case of beasts,	268
Nuncupative testaments,	89

O.

	Page.
Oath of calumny,	285
Oblatum furtum,	226
Obligations, defined	184
———, civil,	184
———, by consent,	204
———, extinction of,	222
———, from improper contracts,	217
———, joint,	191
———, natural,	184
———, Prætorian,	184
———, from quasi-wrong,	243
———, through whom they may arise,	220
———, verbal,	188
———, written,	203
Occupancy,	52

P.

Painting on another's canvas,	60
Parental authority,	15
———, dissolution,	23
Parents, legal guardianship of,	33
Parricide, punishment of,	292
Partnership, contract of,	211
———, dissolution of,	212
———, liability of members of,	213
Patriciate,	24
Patrimony, things in, and out of,	50
Patrons, legal guardianship of,	32
———, right of succession to freed-men,	170
———, power to assign freed-men,	173
Pauperies,	268
Payment, place of,	256
Pawn,	187
Peculium castrense,	82
———, bequest of,	87
———, of slaves, bequest of,	124
———, of slaves in trade,	261
———, action as to,	262

312   INDEX.

	Page.
Pegasian decree,	136
Penalty, legacies by way of,	130
Per æs et libram,	85
Perpetual exceptions,	276
Persons, divided as to rights,	6
———, independent,	14
Plagiary, crime of,	293
Plants, ownership of,	59
Plebiscite,	4
Pledge,	187
Possession, general principles regarding,	283
————, presumption in favor of,	282
————, of goods, by Prætor's grant,	174
Posthumous children,	29, 95, 127
Postliminium,	25
Præceptionem, legacy per,	114
Prætor, Commissary of Trusts,	135
———, edicts of,	5
Prætorian edict, defacement of,	248
————, stipulations,	193
————, succession,	174
————, tutor,	37
Preference, fraudulent,	247
Prescription,	71
Presumption of truth,	197
Price, consists in what,	206
——, essential to a sale,	205
Private law,	2
Procuration, or mandate,	214
Procurator, appointment of,	269
————, security required from, for ratification of his acts,	270
Prohibitory interdicts,	280
Promise, of one for another,	195, 199
Proof, burthen of, on him who claims,	120
Puberty, how determined,	38
Public law,	2
———, things,	50
Pupils, alienation by,	80
Pupillary substitutions,	105

Q.

			Page.
Quasi-contract,	...	...	184, 218
Quasi-wrong,	...	...	... 243
Quirites,	...	...	... 3
Quorum Bonorum, interdict so called,		...	... 281

R.

Rash litigants, penalties imposed on,	...		... 285
Ratification of Procurator's acts,		...	... 270
Replications,	...	...	... 278
Relationship, degrees of,		...	... 165
Representatives in action,		...	... 268
Restitutory interdicts,	...	...	... 280
Revocation of testaments,		...	... 108
Risk of things sold and not delivered,		...	... 207
River, bed of,	...	...	... 55
Robbery,	...	...	... 232

S.

Sacred things,	...	...	... 51
Sale, contract of,	...	...	... 204
——, price in,	...	...	... 205
Sanctions,	...	...	... 51
Securities,	...	...	... 270
Security, required of Tutors,		...	... 41
————, ———— Procurators,		...	... 270
Senatus—Consulta, *see Decrees.*			
Servant, liability of master for acts of,	...		... 243
Servi,	...	...	... 7
Servitudes,	...	...	65, 66
————, real,	...	...	... 67
————, personal, *see Usefruct: Use: Habitation.*			
Ship, things thrown from,		...	... 64
Sinendi Modo legacy,	...	...	... 119
Skill, lack of,	...	...	... 236
Slaves,	...	...	... 7
———, acquisition by,	...	...	... 83

	Page.
Slaves, appointed tutors,	28
———, contracts made by,	261
———, corruption of,	228
———, instituted heir,	99
———, of punishment,	24
———, Orcinus,	142
———, stipulations with,	194
Social diminution,	30
Social standing, actions as to,	249
Spendthrifts,	40
Soldiers, testaments of,	89
———, may not act as procurators,	278
Spurious children,	19
Status, *see* Social standing.	
Stipulations,	188
———, kinds of,	193
———, void,	194
———, preposterous,	198
———, with slaves,	192
Subsidiary action,	42
Substitutions, pupillary,	105
———, vulgar,	104
Successory edict,	178
Sureties,	201
———, liability how limited,	202
Surgeon, liability of unskilful,	235
Survivorship, acquisition by,	78

T.

Tavern-keeper, liability of,	244
Temporary exceptions,	276
Testamentary trusts,	134
Testaments, avoidance of,	108
———, defined,	85
———, ineffectual,	110
———, law of, tripartite,	86
———, nuncupative,	89
———, of those unable to make,	92
———, unnatural,	111
Things, classification of,	50

INDEX. 315

	Page.
Things, corporeal and incorporeal,	65
———, common,	50
———, holy,	52
———, mode of acquiring,	52
———, religious,	52
———, sacred,	51
Tignum,	58
Tradition, acquisition by,	62
Treasure-trove,	62
Trebellian decree,	135
Trees, right of property in,	59
Tributoria Actio,	261
Trusts,	134
Tutelage, defined,	27
————, how determined,	38
Tutors,	27
———, exemption of,	43
———, fiduciary,	34
———, legal,	30
———, Prætorian,	37
———, suspected,	47
———, testamentary,	28

U.

Unde cognati,		156
——— legitimi,		176
——— liberi,		176
——— vi,		283
——— vir et uxor,		176
Unskilfulness,		235
Use, servitude of,		69
——— and habitation,		70
Useful action,	238,	284
——— days,		178
Usucapion, *see* Prescription.		
Usufruct, servitude of,		67
————, of land,		61
————, of fruits,		62
————, how terminated,		68

V.

	Page.
Verbal injury,	239
Vicarial slaves,	124
Vice,	74
Vindication,	80, 250
Vindicta,	9
Vulgar substitutions,	104

W.

Wardships,	27
Way, right of,	66
Wife, portion of,	79
———— ————, action for recovery of,	254
Wild animals,	52
Women, may accuse tutors,	47
————, may not act as procurators,	278
————, when permitted to adopt,	22
Words, obligations by,	188
————, joint contracts by,	191
Writing, obligations by,	203
Writings, on paper of another,	60
Written law,	4

F. CARBERY, BENGAL MILITARY ORPHAN PRESS.

www.ingramcontent.com/pod-product-compliance
Lightning Source LLC
Chambersburg PA
CBHW030135170426
43199CB00008B/67